Wake for a Fat Vicar

Father Juan Felipe Ortiz, Archbishop Lamy, and the New Mexican Catholic Church in the Middle of the Nineteenth Century

Fray Angélico Chávez

&

Thomas E. Chávez

Wake for a Fat Vicar

Father Juan Felipe Ortiz,
Archbishop Lamy,
and the New Mexican Catholic Church
in the Middle of the Nineteenth Century

Fray Angélico Chávez

&

Thomas E. Chávez

LPD Press, Albuquerque

For information: LPD Press
925 Salamanca NW
Albuquerque, NM 87107-5647
Telephone: (505) 344-9382
www.nmsantos.com

Book and cover design by Paul Rhetts & Barbe Awalt

Library of Congress Control Number 2003112870

ISBN 1-890689-06-8

First Edition
10 9 8 7 6 5 4 3 2 1

DEDICATED TO

FABIAN CHÁVEZ, JR.,
A BROTHER AND UNCLE TO THE AUTHORS

AND TO

ANTONIO E. CHÁVEZ,
A BROTHER AND FATHER TO THE AUTHORS

BOTH HAVE MADE HISTORY IN THEIR OWN RIGHT.

Table of Contents

Illustrations

"He is a fat jolly fellow…(and yet) a very grave respectable looking person, of fair complexion…"

Lieutenant William H. Emory, *Notes*, 1846

Foreword

"If you try to introduce European civilization here and change our old ways, to interfere with the secret dances of the Indians, let us say, or abolish the bloody rites of the Penitentes, I foretell an early death for you. ...You are among barbarous people, my Frenchman, between two savage races. The dark things forbidden by your Church are a part of Indian religion. You cannot introduce French fashions here."

The speaker, showing "his long, yellow teeth" and denied the protective cover of even a pseudonym, was Padre Martínez of Taos. "My Frenchman" was "Father Latour," Bishop of the recently established Vicariate of New Mexico. His real name, and the hero of Willa Cather's novel *Death Comes for the Archbishop*, was Jean Baptiste Lamy.[1]

It has taken more than a half century since the 1927 publication of *Death Comes for the Archbishop* to call to account this popular book and the ethnocentric, if not patently racist, attitudes to which it panders. But payment is finally coming due.[2]

---

[1] Willa Cather, *Death Comes for the Archbishop*, (New York: Alfred A. Knopf, 1927), 148.

[2] See Ray John de Aragón, *Padre Martínez and Bishop Lamy*, (Las Vegas: Pan-Am Publications, 1978); Fray Angélico Chávez, *But Time and Chance: The Story of Padre Martínez of Taos, 1793-1867*, (Santa Fe: The Sunstone Press, 1981); and *Très Macho – He Said: Padre Gallegos of Albuquerque, New Mexico's First Congressman*, (Santa Fe: William Gannon, 1985); E. A. Mares and others, *Padre Martínez: New Perspectives from Taos*, (Taos: Millicent Rogers Museum, 1988); and E. A. Mares, *I Returned and Saw Under the Sun: Padre Martínez of Taos*, (Albuquerque: University of New Mexico Press, 1989).

In 1821, lands once a part of Nueva España, New Spain, became those of an independent México. Included within this sizable empire was Nuevo México, a territory begun as a Spanish "kingdom" in 1598 by conquistador Don Juan de Oñate. Among its populace were many native-born *gente de razón*, or "people of reason," who sympathized with the ideals of the executed fomenter of the Mexican Wars for Independence and "Father of the Country," the secular priest from the Diocese of Dolores, Miguel Hidalgo y Costilla. For them, a new government held the prospect for a better life.

Contributory to this "better life" were the easing of restrictive trade barriers and elimination of laws making it illegal to do business with merchants of other countries. Goods, as well as people, began almost at once to flow into Nuevo México from St. Louis over the Santa Fe Trail. Anglo American men married native *Nuevomexicanas* and settled down to become the vanguard in what eventually proved to be an overwhelming rush of United States citizens into a place subsequent promoters proclaimed as the Land of Enchantment.

Throughout pre-Hispanic times, the Native American men, women, and children of what came to be known first as Nuevo México and subsequently as New Mexico had been gradually evolving their particular social, political, religious, as well as economic adaptations to one another. They also had to adapt to an arid environment stingy in its production of life's necessities. With the arrival of the first permanent foreign colonist in 1598, New Mexico's doors were thrown open to additional peoples such as Spaniards, Native Americans of Mexican origin, other Europeans, and "colored" classes, including *mestizos* (or *coyotes*), blacks, mulattos, *tercerones, lobos,* and a welter of racial mixes variously labeled depending on place and time. Nuevomexicanos even generated a new class, *genízaros*, ransomed Indian captives who were incorporated into colonial society. And from Oñate's day forward, there were *peninsulares*, natives of Spain, often derisively referred to as *gachupines* by *criollos*, Spaniards born in the New World.

At its inception, New Mexico was by royal directive a missionary enterprise of the Spanish crown. Its priests and brothers were regular clergy of the Order of Friars Minor, i. e., Franciscans. Although a few secular or "diocesan" clergy were assigned to Nuevo México in the eighteenth century, including native Nuevomexicano Father Santiago Roybal (1730-1774), the dissemination of the tenets of Christianity remained largely the responsibility of the Franciscan Custody of the Conversion of St. Paul and, beyond Nuevo México's boundaries, the Province of the Holy Gospel in Mexico City.

None of these Spanish-period Franciscans was a native New Mexican.

Secularization of the Nuevo México parishes began in the late 18th century with more priests of the Diocese of Durango arriving on the local scene. In 1817, five native Nuevomexicanos, one of whom is the subject of this book, left their homes to study for the priesthood at the Tridentine Seminary of Durango, a trend destined to continue until the Church authorities in Rome severed New Mexico from Durango in 1850.

Natives of Nuevo México who lived there through the initial half of the 19th century felt the impacts of three major changes in their lives, not a one of which was directly fostered by themselves. The first of these was the change from monarchical Spain to, ultimately, republican México. The second, occasioned in 1846 by the Mexican War, was the takeover of their territory by the United States. And third, in 1851, following the creation of the Vicariate Apostolic of Santa Fe, was an invasion of their innermost religious precincts – to say nothing of well-founded social customs – by fundamentalist Catholic French clergy from the province of l'Auvergne. If there was one group of Nuevomexicanos who bore the brunt of these changes, it was the native clergy. We find in their biographies a microcosm of the lives of other Hispanic Nuevomexicanos who lived through these unsettling times. Their stories, moreover, are twice important: once for what they tell us concerning the clash of cultures, and again for what they reveal about acclaimed 20th-century American literature and, by extension, about ourselves.

Negative stereotypes concerning Nuevomexicanos began to appear in English as early as 1844 with the publication of Josiah Gregg's *Commerce of the Prairies* (New York: Langley, 1844). Tennessee-born Gregg made nine trading trips between 1831 and 1840 over the famed Santa Fe Trail connecting Independence, Missouri, and Santa Fe, New Mexico. The book, which resulted from those experiences, was translated into German and appeared in both England and the United States in at least fourteen editions, half of them when Gregg was still living. In more recent times, one historian of the Santa Fe Trail has labeled this work a "neglected classic," and writer and literary critic Frank Dobie called it "bedrock Americana."[3]

Native New Mexican intellectual, poet, fiction writer, folklorist, artist, and historian Fray Angélico Chávez instead called Gregg's book a "bible of bigotry," one to which subsequent writers, W. W. H. Davis among them,

---

[3] Lawrence Clark Powell, *Southwest Classics: The Creative Literature of the Arid Lands. Essays on the Books and Their Writers*, (Los Angeles: The Ward Ritchie Press), 13 & 20.

"kept appending their own scurrilous commentary."[4]

The Black Legend directed at Spain and things Spanish by British and American propagandists whenever it suited them transferred itself easily toward Hispanics in general and Californios, Tejanos, and Nuevo Mexicanos in particular with the collapse of Spain's New World hegemony. The northern half of México, after all, would be wrested by the Americans from Mexicano hands beginning in 1836, and the more justification for its taking the better.

It must also be remembered that during the preceding two-and-a-half centuries the relationship between France and Spain, when not openly hostile, had always been an uneasy one. Hispanics and Gallicans frequently interacted with mutual mistrust. In this atmosphere, it is not surprising that while Bishop Lamy and his intimate friend, Vicar Joseph P. Machebeuf, stopped in Galveston to visit with Bishop Jean-Marie Odin as they headed to their Santa Fe assignment, their fellow French-born priest prepared them to expect the worst from New Mexico's clergymen. Lamy should, said Odin, first go to France to bring reliable priests with him to New Mexico. In France, moreover, "he could procure new vestments and the rest to replace the old rubbish which he would find in all the New Mexican churches, and he would thus instantly correct a great scandal in that country."[5]

Nor was that all. Lamy "would find scandalous native clergy" in New Mexico (where Odin, incidentally, had never been) as well as Anglo-American Catholics waiting for reform in their church. It was even possible, in fact, that Lamy would have to excommunicate some incorrigible priests![6]

When Lamy and Machebeuf arrived in Santa Fe, having been advised as to what they might expect, they – and especially Machebeuf – soon gave ear to "certain ones among the newcomers" to Santa Fe, "like those first

[3] Lawrence Clark Powell, *Southwest Classics: The Creative Literature of the Arid Lands. Essays on the Books and Their Writers*, (Los Angeles: The Ward Ritchie Press), 13 & 20.

[4] A. Chávez, *Três Macho – He Said*, 30. W. W. H. Davis, *El Gringo, or New Mexico and Her People*, (New York: 1857). The scope of Fray Angélico's talents is suggested in Phyliss S. Morales, *Fray Angélico Chávez: A Bibliography of His Published Writings (1925-1978)*, (Santa Fe: The Lightning Tree, 1980); and Ellen McCracken (editor), *Fray Angélico Chávez: Poet, Priest, and Artist*, (Albuquerque: University of New Mexico Press, 2000).

[5] Paul Horgan, *Lamy of Santa Fe: His Life and Times*, (New York: Farrar, Straus, and Giroux, 1975), 92.

[6] Ibid.

newspaper editors who still looked down on their fellow citizens of Hispanic or Mexican descent, and most especially their clergy, as low-down
Catholic Mexicans."[7] They were also entertained privately by the more prominent English-speaking Santa Feans, both Catholic and Protestant, whose
prejudices against native New Mexicans were ill-concealed if at all.

"Even down to our times," wrote worldly, sophisticated, and dignified
Fray Angélico Chávez, "within my memory of thirty-four active ministerial
years, English-language priests coming to labor in New Mexico first gravitated toward the company of people sharing their same origin and background; some of these new friends of theirs filled them with not too favorable opinions, whether seriously or in jest, about the characteristics of their
new Hispanic parishioners; in their turn, some of these same priests eventually relayed such things to me in conversation, curiously forgetting for the
nonce that I myself was one of those Hispanic natives."[8]

His dealing with people with whom he felt more culturally at ease –
including English-speaking and mostly Protestant civilians – caused Lamy
to be charged by New Mexico's 1856 Territorial Legislature with favoring
Protestantism. While that particular charge was preposterous, "Even from
my own recollections and those of others, the alien bishops and priests in
New Mexico seldom if ever let the native folk into their residences beyond
the front office, while they did entertain others, including non-Catholics, in
the privacy of their homes."[9]

The new French priests, even without the prodding of others, found
much in New Mexico to displease them. Among these were the homemade
statues (*bultos*) and paintings (*retablos*) fashioned by native *santeros*. Lamy
and Machebeuf favored French versions of the same holy scenes and person-
ages. Neither did they like the use of musical instruments in church that
were also used to accompany *bailes* and *fandangos*, the Spanish terms for
dances. And while Lamy's condemnation of New Mexico's well-known Pious Fraternity of Our Father Jesus Nazarene, the so-called Penitentes, was
never vehement, he nonetheless condemned the "undirected and rigorous
penance" of its adherents, sometimes resulting in serious injury and even
death, as "blasphemous and unexemplary behavior."[10]

---

[7] A. Chávez, *But Time and Chance*, 90.

[8] A. Chávez, *Très Macho – He Said*, 30.

[9] Ibid., 77.

[10] Marta Weigle, *Brothers of Light, Brothers of Blood: The Penitentes of the Southwest*,
(Albuquerque: University of New Mexico Press, 1976), 57.

Fray Angélico Chávez has written charitably of Bishop Lamy who "never flaunted his French nationality to the playing down of others,"[11] altogether disregarding the bishop's everlasting monument to French ethnocentrism, the out of place Franco-Romanesque Cathedral in Santa Fe which towers in grim, stone-cold mien amid the flat-roofed adobes that have made Santa Fe the "City Different." Although it is too late now, the bishop would never have gotten away with such hometown arrogance in today's overly precious and self-conscious capital city.

The mid-19th century clash of cultures in New Mexico also manifested itself in less obvious ways. In the present biography, we learn that Vicar Ortiz and others "had come to suspect that the American way of life had something to offer." At the same time, "Their [Hispanic] civic leaders, knowing how certain resident *Americanos* showed more vim and know-how in civic and economic enterprise, rightly feared that under the United States rule the newcomers would make themselves masters of their land in every way" [p. 49].

"Vim and know-how" are generally products of cultures whose members value individual achievement, and individual rights, over those of the community. Collective good in such societies gives way to individual good, and while large numbers of individuals may profit and things are produced that come to be desired by everyone, it is not easy to evaluate the trade-off in purely personal terms.

Native New Mexican society, aboriginal American as well as Hispanic, was organized around the ideal of collective good. This explains in part what appears to non-participants in such cultures as an undue preoccupation with genealogies, for example. Communities are not comprised of isolated individuals but of persons tied together historically in webs of real and fictive kinship. Political, economic, social, and religious relationships are mediated through these networks. Such concepts as "friends" and "neighbors" in these communities, to say nothing of *compadres* and *parientes*, carry a great deal of emotional weight. So are such relationships linked to mutual obligations – even though these may be observed in the breach as well as in their doing? Either way, one cannot understand the inner workings of such social structures without knowing their genealogical makeup.

People characterized by "vim and know-how" are more likely to be individualists, whether rugged or lonely. Certainly foreigners who went to

---

[11] A. Chávez, *Très Macho – He Said*, 33.

New Mexico in the mid-19th century fit the characterization and are typically members of small and nuclear families rather than of those that are large and extended. Having fewer obligations imposed upon them by their less-structured societies, they operate with fewer constraints. We Americans and people of other industrialized countries might view it as "license." Either way, this is an area where values collided head on when Native American, Hispanic, Anglo, and French clergymen came together in Santa Fe in the summer of 1851.[12]

Added to the problem of ethnic prejudices and cultural misperceptions, the native New Mexican clergy also had to contend with the neurotic personality of Bishop Lamy's right hand man, Father Machebeuf. In the first two volumes of this trilogy of biographies, Fray Angélico Chávez takes pains to examine – in the context of Machebeuf's priestly calling – the psychological makeup of the French vicar, a person who emerges in these studies as the principal villain, although it was the nature of the relationship between him and Lamy which lay "at the bottom of the many troubles which were to arise in the relationship of both Frenchmen with the native clergy of New Mexico."[13]

Machebeuf was more overtly anti-native Mexican clergy than his bishop, the latter apparently the subordinate in terms of their *amitié particuliere*. After having been in Santa Fe less than a week, Vicar Machebeuf wrote in a letter that the native clergy "were all horrible lechers who dreaded a reform of their sexual morals." And at the Vatican in 1855, when he was defending himself against charges of having broken the confessional seal, he lashed out at his accusers and "all of the people of New Mexico [who] were both dishonest and immoral." His Vatican judge apparently agreed with the assessment; Machebeuf was absolved of any wrongdoing.[14]

Bishop Lamy's closest friend, if Fray Angélico Chávez is correct, was possessed of an "innate morbid 'scrupulosity'...a sick preoccupation with sexual matters which in its headlong blind fanaticism took grim delight in sniffing out immorality everywhere he turned, and most especially with regard to the relationships between male and female."[15]

Overtly masculine priests, as those of New Mexico's native clergy seem

[12] For a different way of saying the same thing see Thomas E. Chávez, "Horatio Alger Meets Paco," *The Public Historian*, Vol. 19, no. 1 (winter 1997), 49-51.
[13] A. Chávez, *But Time and Chance*, 95.
[14] Ibid., p. 94; and *Très Macho – He Said*, 81 & 85.
[15] A. Chávez, *But Time and Chance*, 101.

to have been, priests who danced in public, priests who gambled, priests who occasionally over-indulged in liquor, and priests whose housekeepers may have appeared comely – these, in Machebeuf's tortured French Catholic puritanical mind, were altogether unworthy souls.

Fray Angélico Chávez, who observes that one aspect of the vicar's affliction "poses no mystery at all to anyone who for decades, like myself, had to treat a certain spiritual *malaise* which was called 'scrupulosity' in Catholic religious circles," explains:

> …[O]ne need not trespass into the accepted psychotherapy of our times, which is strictly clinical and materialistic. But one can stillrecur to Freud's original expressions describing the encounter ofPsyche (the *spiritual* soul) with Eros (the body's *carnal* nature) within the ambience of the Christian ethic regarding chastity. Unfortunately, in Machebeuf's day as well as in later times, Catholic children, while trained and counseled to keep their souls pure, were seldom if ever instructed in the mysteries of sex, and particularly as to how natural arousements were of themselves no unchaste sins at all. As a result, that scrupulous malady of deeper confusion and bothersome misgivings had to rear its ugly head in many a precocious child, and this perturbation was too often carried into adulthood.

> …[T]he more immediate cause of scrupulosity ran very deep, to long-suppressed imaginary sins now boiling in the subconscious. By way of illustration, these could consist of such innocent if childhood games like "playing doctor" and the like; or even actual sexual molestation by some degenerate adult. But most often they consisted of very early precocious sexual awakenings, whether heterosexual or homosexual, which likewise had been buried in the subconscious as most shameful sins. Hence the result was that for the victims of such chasms and delusions, the least "bad thought" or natural erotic feeling were actual sins against Holy Chastity capitalized…

> [T]his…spiritual psychosis tended to bring out in more positive characters, like Machebeuf's, a tense fanaticism against any impurity detected or even suspected in others. Only this type of religious scrupulosity can explain Machebeuf's

14

fanatical obsession with matters of the flesh, and the basic cause can then be traced to a latent homosexual inclination which at first had attracted him to the exclusive male companionship in the barracks, but which his innate piety supplanted with that of the seminary. And he would have died from anger or shame had a seraph from on high revealed to him the real cause, especially with regard to his unusual affection for his friend Lamy. On the other hand, Lamy seems to have been a normal self-contained person, except for a tendency to become depressed in moments of indecision.... This could well have been what mainly drew Machebeuf's domineering nature to him, although for Lamy the resulting friendship was a perfectly legitimate one in thus having a sturdy friend to rely on when his spirits were low. And so there had developed an amitié particuliere, or amicitia particularis in Latin, which was much frowned upon in the ascetical manuals.

...Seminary rectors and religious superiors kept a sharp eye for it in order to weed out any cases of overt homosexuality. Obviously, since nothing of this kind existed between these two good pious friends – Machebeuf's proclivity being as much hidden to his superiors as it was to himself – there were no grounds for any such suspicions.

This particular friendship was not only glorified as something most admirable by a spinster like Willa Cather in her novel, but by other celibate biographers as well...[16]

In *Wake for a Fat Vicar* we have the concluding book in a trilogy which carefully, objectively, and without rancor sets the historical record straight concerning many of the tumultuous – as well as routine – events leading up to, during, and immediately following mid-19th century New Mexico. In doing so, these books call into question more literary works on the same subject, most especially Willa Cather's *Death Comes for the Archbishop* and Paul Horgan's *Lamy of Santa Fe* as well as such effusive appraisals of Cather's work as that by Lawrence Clark Powell who called it a "masterpiece," one that "justly ranks in the highest realm of American literature."[17]

---

[16] A. Chávez, *Très Macho – He Said*, 35-37.

[17] Powell, *Southwest Classics*, 122 & 132.

Good literature in insight and imagination set in good prose. Great literature, however, is characterized by something more. And that is transcendent truth. It is here that Cather and Horgan – as we now know – are found wanting.

Wake for a Fat Vicar, unlike the first two volumes of this trilogy of priestly biographies, is obviously a collaboration. This cooperative venture is one between an octogenarian uncle, now deceased, and his much younger historian nephew. The senior author, "steeped for a lifetime in ecclesiastical proceedings," is uniquely qualified to evaluate and to understand church-related documentary and published sources – sources often misinterpreted by less-credentialed writers. The junior author, a professional historian and museum director, is also deeply rooted in New Mexico and writes with the understanding of an insider to its native culture. This happy combination has produced an important book.

Bernard L. Fontana
The University of Arizona

Introduction

El Señor Vicario of Santa Fe, Don Juan Felipe Ortiz, was so obese that he could not escape a welter of first impressions of this score. Several Anglo-Americans of his day remarked on his girth in their letters and journals. He also had a very fair complexion as some of them noted, apparently amazed by such a quality in a so-called Mexican. He was a redhead as well, as these attributes of fatness, fair skin, and red hair were likewise observed in a first cousin of his who was also a priest, Padre Rafael Ortiz. These family traits had to have an origin, and some of these are found in the ancestral Ortiz family that had come to New Mexico from Mexico City in 1694.

When the first draft of this biography was ending with the death of Vicar Ortiz, two word associations were brought to mind. The first was from Oliver Goldsmith's poem, "The Vicar of Wakefield," and the second from Ortiz himself, who stood out among his contemporaries as a congenitally fat man in his later years. No irreverence is intended in this title, as the obesity was regarded with affection among those who knew him. Of far more relevance, it was a quality for which the first bishop of Santa Fe, the famed Jean Baptiste Lamy, debased him as a lazy fellow, which he never was, thus setting the stage for his miserable last years and sad demise.

Juan Felipe Ortiz lived during a crucial and turbulent time in Southwestern history. He spent his youth to adulthood as a Spanish subject in distant New Mexico. Most of his service as a Mexican-educated secular priest occurred during the brief interlude in New Mexico's long history known as the Mexican Period from 1821 until late 1846. For most of that time and the early years of United States occupation when New Mexico became a U. S.

Territory, he fulfilled the role of church leader in his homeland. He was *Vicar Forane*, the Rural Dean or Vicar as appointed by the Bishop of Durango, Mexico, who had the distant northern land as part of his See or Diocese.

As a secular priest, Father Ortiz represented both ancient truths as well as changes in New Mexico's long church history. There had never been enough priests to serve the needs of large and sparsely inhabited areas. Initially settled as a missionary area to convert sedentary Indians whom the Spanish called "Pueblos" for the villages where they lived, New Mexico's spiritual needs remained in the hands of the Franciscans for over two centuries. Just a little before Ortiz's birth the bishops in Mexico started indicating that it was time to replace the missionaries with secular priests. The Franciscans were not happy with this idea. A subsequent visit by one bishop from Durango confirmed his idea that New Mexico was sorely in need of an ecclesiastical change. A few secular priests were indeed sent to the north. One was even New Mexico's first native born priest. Yet, other priorities within the Church and Spanish empire dictated that the poor, mysterious, if not perplexing, province of New Mexico continue as before.

Then came Mexican independence from Spain followed by a Mexican policy not nearly as cooperative to the Church as had been the previous Spanish position. In New Mexico, Franciscans were replaced with secular priests educated and trained in Mexico. Part of their education included tenets of patriotism to the new country of Mexico. That local young New Mexicans could be educated for the priesthood and returned to their homeland to serve was another deviation from the past.

Father Ortiz was one of the Mexican-educated priests returned to his home. He worked, as did all his predecessors, with a group of men that was short in numbers and too distant from the seat of authority to expect any real help. After a little more than two and a half decades he had to lead his flock through another and more pronounced change. In 1846 the United States declared war on Mexico and occupied New Mexico.

The change in secular administration was a shock to New Mexico's undermanned and patriotic priests, but the change did not initially change the ecclesiastical order of things. The Bishop of Durango and his Vicar Ortiz remained in charge of the spiritual needs of New Mexico's Catholics. But the Church was not long in reacting to the new political geographical boundaries resulting from war, for a new vicariate-apostolic was formed from the old rural vicariate and its new political order, heralded a new and sometimes incomprehensible leadership in Spain's old colony. Father Ortiz was the man who had to lead his flock into and through this shock.

Continued references to the man in various books of the time, including the subsequent biographies of Padre Martínez of Taos, *But Time and Chance*, and Padre Gallegos of Albuquerque, *Très Macho – He Said*, have suggested a future book concerning Vicar Ortiz.

The present tome, in fact, is the last of a trilogy that Fray Angélico Chávez had contemplated. In the last years of his life Fray Angélico asked that I, his nephew, finish the book. This honor has become a task the effort of which has extended far beyond anything we contemplated, for the book became not only a mere biography of Ortiz but a story of him and his Church at a crucial time of its history in New Mexico. Nevertheless, Fray Angélico's message, ideas, and words continue.

Along with those two earlier books, this final effort presents a totally different picture about New Mexico's priests during the Mexican period. They were men who were so much denigrated in the writings of Bishop Lamy and his own vicar, Joseph Machebeuf, and no less by subsequent writers who depended heavily on those writings. Of these three native clergymen, Martínez, Gallegos, and Ortiz, the latter was the most innocent and perhaps the most maligned. Because of his peaceful nature, he failed to fight back as did the other two clergymen. Because of his position, too, we have a better view of the Mexican Church in New Mexico and, thus, a fuller context for what would follow with Lamy's arrival in the area.

I would like to thank my good friends and fellow scholars for their insistent encouragement and help. Nasario García, formerly of New Mexico Highlands University, is the ultimate colleague who reviewed the manuscript in detail, oftentimes feeling as if he would strain our friendship. That, of course, is impossible, but this book without him may not have happened. Bernard "Bunny" Fontana of the University of Arizona championed the publication of the manuscript, critically reviewed it, and wrote the foreword. If not for his persistence, Fray Angélico Chávez's last effort could have wasted in an archive never to be published. Jack Clark Robinson, O.F.M., a former colleague of Fray Angélico, and friend who has written and taught both about Fray Angélico and the Church in New Mexico, made some very important suggestions. Thomas J. Steele, S.J., formerly of Regis University in Denver, constantly reminded me that this was not another publication but a responsibility. He never used those words but his periodic inquiries about where I was with the manuscript made the point. His final review of the manuscript is a special honor. That four men such as these pushed and worked to see this done is reason enough to know that something of some value to the history and patrimony of our region and country needed to be completed.

Fray Angélico Chávez was part of a large family, all of whom continue to be very proud of him. His surviving brothers and sister, Francisco Eugenio, Fabian, Antonio (my father) whose anxiety to see this book published is surpassed by none, José, and Consuelo have been anxious in their support for me to finish. I thank them for their love of a brother and patience of a nephew and son.

Nothing encourages a person more than to honor those that a person cares for most. I hope that, along with those mentioned above, my mother Marilyn, my wife Celia López Chávez (herself a historian), my daughter Nicolasa (named for Fray Angélico's mother) will accept this effort with pride. My other daughter, Christel Angélica, passed away before the completion of this project but she knew about it and laughed over my computer problems during the process. She was always proud to receive a book written by her dad. But most of all, the greatest desire is that this final product is what "uncle Pio" envisioned when he asked me to finish it for him.

Part I

The Ricos of Santa Fe

Just before 1800, a large Santa Fe family of the Ortiz surname had become quite wealthy by taking advantage of a fast-growing mercantile trade between Santa Fe and Chihuahua. The original Ortizes had come with the new Spanish colony from Mexico City and its environs in June 1694, following the 1693 reconquest of New Mexico by Diego de Vargas. Hence their designation as Españoles Mexicanos. They were among the first settlers in 1696 of the new Villa of Santa Cruz de la Cañada from where they spread to the Nambé and Pojoaque valleys and finally to Santa Fe during the following century. This clan, as it prospered in mercantile activities, also began acquiring considerable real estate in the capital and its surrounding area.

One outstanding member was Don Antonio José Ortiz who used his own resources to restore the parish church of San Francisco and the much older chapel of San Miguel, as well as building the first Rosario Chapel of La Conquistadora – all within the first decade of 1800.[1] Knowing this family background is important to help understand the serious property disputes that arose many decades later. Besides, three grandsons of Antonio José Ortiz were to become priests as well as two grand-nephews – all of who played a continuous role in New Mexico's history from Spanish settlement through the brief Mexican period and into American times.

---

[1] A. Chávez, *Origins of New Mexico Families* (Albuquerque: University of New Mexico Press, 1973), 247-51, 329-32; and Bruce T. Ellis, *Bishop Lamy's Santa Fe Cathedral* (Albuquerque: University of New Mexico Press/Historical Society of New Mexico, 1985), 62-63.

Foremost among these descendants was Juan Felipe Ortiz, a grand-nephew whose high standing as Vicar for the Bishop of Durango, in addition to his many other activities, made him prominent among his clerical Ortiz first cousins, padres Fernando, Rafael, and Ramón Ortiz – as well as his half-brother José Eulogio Ortiz.

Juan Felipe Ortiz was born in Santa Fe on 15 September 1797, the only child of Juan Rafael Ortiz and María Loreto Ribera. His mother died prior to 1801 when his father took a second wife by whom he had at least four children between 1805 and 1812. When this second mate died, Ortiz took a third wife who bore him no fewer than eight more children between 1816 and 1825. The youngest of these was José Eulogio Ortiz, who would eventually be ordained by Bishop Lamy, thus adding on more priests to the much older list of Ortiz clergymen. From all of this we can also see that the future vicar had a raft of much younger half-brothers and half-sisters.[2]

A young Juan Felipe Ortiz, who was more or less of the same age as his three first cousins, could well have left with them for the seminary in Durango around 1817. He most likely came back home as an ordained priest toward the end of 1824, for his signed entries, from January to November 1825 and to February 1826, first appear sporadically in the books of Santa Fe's military chapel, Our Lady of Light, popularly known as *La Castrense*.[3] During these early years he assisted the Mexican-born pastor Don Tomás Terrazas and on occasion filled in at *La Castrense* where his cousin Fernando Ortiz was the chaplain.[4] The latter, as data on his career indicate, was either ill at this time or else away with the troops on some foray.

In July 1826, Governor Antonio Narbona initiated a subscription campaign for supporting schools in the region, and the Departmental Assembly commissioned Padre Juan Felipe Ortiz, himself a member of the Departmental Assembly, and José Antonio Martínez, to collect the contributions. By an edict issued in October, the magistrates of each town were ordered to assist him in the task. Evidently this is what misled historian Benjamin Read to state that Ortiz, like Padre Martínez in Taos, had established a school in Santa Fe at his own expense. However, he may have contributed generously

---

[2] A. Chávez, *Origins*, 329.

[3] Baptism, B-15, *Castrense*; B-68, Santa Fe, Archives of the Archdiocese of Santa Fe (AASF). For the history of the Castrense see John Kessell, *The Missions of New Mexico Since 1776* (Albuquerque: The University of New Mexico Press, 1980), 44-48.

[4] Ellis, *Lamy's Cathedral*, 83-84.

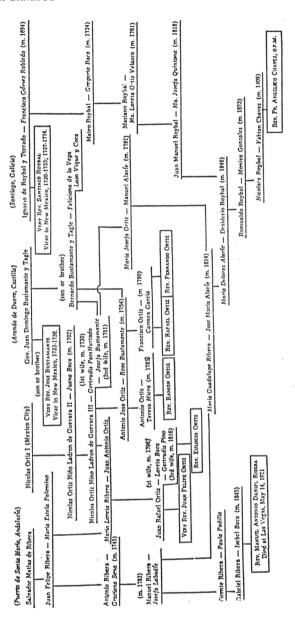

A Clerical Chart — Native clergy in New Mexico were rare in the past. The few shown here, curiously, can be placed in one group formed by the Ribera, Ortiz, Bustamante, and Roybal families. This diagram was originally compiled for an article, "Ramon Ortiz: Priest and Patriot," in New Mexico Historical Review, *October, 1950, and in Angélico Chávez,* Origins of New Mexico Families, *1954.*

from his own resources. By 1831, the assembly had enough money to support a teacher to operate a public primary school in six New Mexican towns.[5]

More of his signed entries appear in Castrense books until July of 1826, when it is specifically mentioned that the chaplain was ill. Then, in the same month, he received his first pastorship with an assignment to San Juan Pueblo, where his entries ran until May 1828. From San Juan he also attended the high mountain parish at Picurís Pueblo from October to December 1826, and again in June 1827. One interesting item notes that he asked Franciscan Fray José de Castro of Santa Clara, one of the last friars left in New Mexico, to take the Fiesta Mass of San Lorenzo at Picurís on 10 August 1826.[6] Also while pastor of San Juan, he traveled to Taos to conduct the funeral of Padre Antonio Martínez's father, Don Severino Martínez, on 29 June 1827.[7]

[5] Lansing Bartlett Bloom, "New Mexico Under Mexican Administration," *Old Santa Fe (OSF)*, Vol. I, 249; Benjamin Read, *Historia Ilustrada de Nuevo México* (Santa Fe: Compañía Impresora del Nuevo Mexicano, 1911), 343; and David J. Weber, *On the Edge of Empire: The Taos Hacienda of Los Martínez* (Santa Fe: Museum of New Mexico Press, 1996), 52.

[6] B-29, Marriages-28, San Juan; B-22, M-21, Picurís, Loose documents, 1826, no. 14, *AASF*.

[7] A. Chávez, *But Time and Chance*, 29; and Weber, *Edge of Empire*, 69.

Pastor of Santa Fe and Vicar

Mexico's independence from Spain in 1821 resulted in problems for the Catholic Church, especially on the northern frontier. With characteristic fervor, the new government dismantled the mission system, which decreased the number of Franciscans and opened the way for secular clergy to replace the padres. Because of complications in Mexico, such was not the complete result. Beset with problems that arouse out of the revolution, the Church found itself weakened in many aspects, not the least of which was leadership. The split from Spain resulted in a diplomatic struggle between Mexico and the Vatican. In New Spain, peninsular born Spaniards made up most of the Church's hierarchy, which was decimated in the 1820s when the Archbishop of Mexico and some of the bishops returned to their Native Spain rather than swear allegiance to the new country. By mid-1829 not a single bishop served Mexico, and the Vatican refused to appoint replacements until 1831.

Through all of this the See of Durango, which served New Mexico, suffered the least interruption. Durango had a hiatus of only six years between the death of Bishop Juan Francisco Castañiza in 1825 and the appointment of José Antonio Laureano de Zubiría in 1831. Although the resumption of appointing Church leaders helped, the Church's problems were beyond the bishops' power to solve. Exacerbated by a decline in the number of secular priests, a shortage of leaders continued. In 1830, Mexico had barely over half as many priests as it had in 1810, and the frontier suffered. Antonio Barreiro, a Mexican attorney who moved to New Mexico, suggested that priests in the far north should receive a reward for frontier duty and those who lasted ten years should be given preference for a deserved cathedral appointment in one of the nation's "civilized communities."[1]

One way to alleviate the frontier shortage was to train native priests. Priesthood for the Ortizes, Martínez, and, later, José Manuel Gallegos, was a result of such an effort in New Mexico that began just before independence.[2] Thus the major portion of Juan Felipe Ortiz's career began at age thirty. On 12 February 1828, he was appointed pastor of his hometown, Santa Fe, the long-time capital of New Mexico. A little over four years later, on 23 June 1832, Bishop Zubiría named him Vicar Forane, or the Bishop's Rural Dean, in charge of New Mexico.[3] The Vicar Forane position usually included the authority, as vested by the bishop, to perform such special functions as granting enumerated dispensations, inspecting church records, and generally supervising the Church in a particular region.

Ortiz had the signal honor of being the first New Mexico native to enjoy this high vicarial office since Don Santiago Roybal, who had become the first vicar slightly over a hundred years before in 1730.[4] Ortiz's initial series of entries in the church registers began in Santa Fe in May, 1828. Included among them is a note on one visit to Pecos. The next series does not occur until May or June 1830. During the interval he had been attending the Pecos mission of San Miguel del Vado, farther down the Pecos River. He also attended a synod in faraway Durango, Mexico, to compete in examinations whereby he could acquire the greatly coveted title and status of *cura propio*, or irremovable pastor. With this end in view, he had taken along an endorsement from New Mexico's Legislative Assembly.[5] Thus at an early age he attained the status of *cura propio*, an accomplishment that the sometimes vain Padre Antonio Martínez of Taos must have resented over and above Ortiz's holding high office as the bishop's vicar for New Mexico.[6]

---

[1] Antonio Barreiro, *Ojeda Sobre Nuevo México...* (Puebla, Mexico: 1832) in H. Bailey Carroll and J. Villasana Haggard, translators and editors (Albuquerque: Quivera Society Publications, 1942), 54; and David J. Weber, *The Mexican Frontier, 1821-1846: The American Southwest Under Mexico* (Albuquerque: University of New Mexico Press, 1982), 69-80.

[2] A. Chávez, *Très Macho – He Said*, 8-9.

[3] B-29, Santa Fe, *AASF*; and Ellis, *Lamy's Cathedral*, 84-85.

[4] For Vicar Roybal's story see, A. Chávez, "El Vicario Don Santiago Roybal," *El Palacio*, Vol. 55 (1948), 231-252.

[5] Patentes LXIX; Loose Documents 1830, number 19, *AASF*.

[6] A. Chávez, *But Time and Chance*, 69, 87-88.

José Antonio Zubiria, Bishop of Durango, Mexico. Photo courtesy Museum of New Mexico, Neg. No. 13140.

During this time, New Mexico was designated a territory in the newly created country of Mexico. The responsibility of devising a plan for New Mexico's internal government rested with the National Congress. Much to the people's dismay, Congress was unable to approve a plan and local government continued to operate under the old Spanish regulations of 1812 and 1813. In the view of New Mexicans, their governmental assembly, called the *diputación territorial*, lacked the authority to be effective. The assemblies were mere advisory bodies.

By the 1830s, New Mexicans had become frustrated enough to act. To this end, the new vicar joined some of his fellow New Mexicans in the assembly and drew up a plan for statehood in which New Mexico would become the State of Hidalgo. The same group further proposed importing a printing press as necessary for governmental operations. Although the plan was widely endorsed in New Mexico, the idea was tabled by the assembly.[7] Here is an instance of Vicar Ortiz's loyalty to New Mexico and of the Mexican patriotism he acquired during his studies in Durango when Mexico won its independence. On one hand, he was frustrated over New Mexico's territorial status; on the other hand, he supported the new move to honor a Mexican hero. Had New Mexico been named after the Mexican revolutionary leader of 1810, it would have lost its historic name that was more than centuries old at the time.

Also around this time, 1831, Vicar Ortiz purchased for himself the old Franciscan *convento* property next to his parish church of San Francisco. The deal was supposedly made with one of the chancellors in Durango sometime before the ascension of Zubiría as the new bishop. It was not the illegal transaction that Bishop Lamy tried to characterize twenty years later, as will be shown. Nonetheless, in obtaining this property as in other instances, the young vicar revealed in himself the real estate acquisitiveness that characterized the Ortiz clan in Santa Fe. Twenty-five years before, his grand uncle had acquired the property of the ancient San Miguel chapel after restoring it at his own expense.

Between April of 1831 and November of 1833, Ortiz spent months at a time at the vacant and fairly distant parishes of Picurís and San Miguel del Vado. The former was north of Santa Fe and the latter southeast. For some unknown reason Ortiz decided to vacate Santa Fe when Juan Rafael Rascón,

---

[7] Bloom, "Mexican Administration," *OSF*, Vol. I, 268-78; and Weber, *The Mexican Frontier*, 27-28.

a visitor sent by the Durango Cathedral Chapter, had arbitrarily made himself the vicar of New Mexico as well as pastor of Santa Fe. By July of 1832, Ortiz was happy to announce that Durango had a new prelate in the person of Zubiría, and that the latter had confirmed him as his vicar with additional authority.[8] His next important announcement came on 15 April 1833 when he shared the news of an impending visit to New Mexico by the new bishop, who was to arrive in May.[9] A visit by the bishop was the kind of event that had not occurred in the memory of the faithful, save perhaps among some of the older folks who remembered having seen a bishop but probably forgot that his name was Pedro Tamarón y Romeral. Tamarón y Romeral visited New Mexico seventy years before when those who remembered were small children.

Juan Felipe Ortiz's early life demonstrates the zealous activities of a young cleric of genteel breeding who, not content with the comforts of hometown and family, voluntarily assisted in the distant and difficult places whose flocks, at the time, were bereft of a shepherd.

---

[8] Loose documents, 1830, no. 20, 1832, no. 1; Patentes, LXXIX, *AASF.*

[9] Loose documents, 1833, no. 1, *AASF.*

A Bishop and His Vicar

The year of 1833 marked the first Pastoral Visitation of New Mexico by any Durango bishop in seven decades. Bishop Tamarón's memorable visitation in 1760 was the last one. The prelate wrote a journal in which he related the hardships of travel through wild country as well as the economic retardation of the area and the serious language problems that kept the Indians in ignorance of the faith.[1] In 1833, Bishop Zubiría, having been appointed to the Durango See for little more than a year, decided to view this most abandoned and mysterious land in the far north. His diocese was a very extensive one in north central Mexico. Its immediate northern section had developed considerably, especially the Chihuahua region, which had grown into a populous mining and commercial center. But this dampened neither his curiosity nor his zeal to proceed farther north to El Paso del Norte and to an area that must have appeared to him as the ultimate frontier. From El Paso he kept going still farther northward to a land that seemed to lie at the very end of the earth, a place whose only claim to fame, both in Spain and in its American colonies, was as the Land of the Franciscan Martyrs.

In preparing for this arduous trip, he might have sought out the 1760 journal of Tamarón and, likewise, the decree of a much later bishop, Don Francisco Gabriel de Olivares. In 1797 the latter bishop secularized the parishes of Santa Cruz and Santa Fe, with no idea of what they were like. In the following year he sent the first two secular pastors from Durango.[2] Secular-

---

[1] Pedro Tamarón, *Bishop Tamarón's Visitation of New Mexico, 1760*, Eleanor B. Adams (editor), (Albuquerque; Historical Society of New Mexico Publications in History 15, 1954).

[2] Loose documents, 1797, no. 7; 1798, no. 2, *AASF*.

ization, the process or replacing missionaries (in this case the Franciscans) with secular or parish (today called diocesan) priests had long been threatened. "Secular" or "diocesan" in the description of priests refers to those who are ordained for the service of a particular diocese or archdiocese, headed by the local bishop or archbishop. Diocesan priests gave more control to such members of the church hierarchy as bishops, whereas the friars answered to the leaders of their order. Gabriel de Olivares's action had caused a stir in New Mexico because he acted without a real knowledge of the area. Now, not quite four decades later, Bishop Zubiría would do what Gabriel de Olivares had neglected to do and inspect what he had inherited in the farthest reaches of his jurisdiction.

By 1833, only five of the old Franciscan padres were left from the exclusive Franciscan ministry which had begun when New Mexico was founded in 1598. Besides these friars, there were ten secular priests, six of them from Durango and four who were natives of the land. Bishop Zubiría must also have noted that his immediate predecessor, Don Juan Francisco de Castañiza, had ordained a certain Martínez from a village called Taos and four Ortiz young men of the capital, Santa Fe, whose names were Juan Felipe (whom he chose as his vicar), Fernando, Rafael, and Ramón. He already knew this last one because he had been stationed closer to his See city of Durango. A few years later Zubiría made him the *cura propio* of El Paso del Norte as well as vicar for that area.

On 15 and 23 April 1833, Juan Felipe Ortiz, the Bishop's newly confirmed and busy vicar in Santa Fe, issued two circulars. One announced the bishop's arrival on May 17th. The other was an episcopal edict banning, for sanitary reasons, future burials inside the churches.[3]

Since Bishop Zubiría brought a secretary with him, Vicar Ortiz did not have to accompany him as he visited different parishes. He was in Santa Fe on 18 October, when the bishop transferred Mexico-born Padre José Vicente Chávez from Socorro to San Miguel del Vado. The bishop charged Chávez to confer with Ortiz along the way because the latter had also been taking care of San Miguel del Vado since August of 1832, the previous year. On this same date, the bishop made other special assignments, to be forwarded through Ortiz for other secular priests and two friars.[4]

But the item of major significance was an announcement by the bishop of an unusual authority that he had received from Pope Gregory XVI whereby

---

[3] Loose documents, 1833, no. 1; Patentes, XI, LXIX, *AASF*.
[4] Loose documents, 1833, no. 14, *AASF*.

he could delegate some of his clergy to administer the Sacrament of Confirmation ordinarily reserved bishops. He granted it, for a term of five years, specifically to Vicar Ortiz in Santa Fe and its environs, and, anonymously, to the current and future pastors of Taos for Río Arriba (upper Rio Grande) and of Tomé for the Río Abajo (lower Rio Grande). Clearly he must have approved of Vicar Ortiz's competence, for on 22 December 1833, two months after his departure, he further augmented Ortiz's faculties as vicar.

During his lengthy visit, Bishop Zubiría asked the faithful to pray for the new country of Mexico, which happened to be in a state of revolutionary turmoil. He also announced that the present regime had done away with the civil obligation of paying church tithes. Hence, Vicar Ortiz began the new year of 1834 with a circular dated 25 January, stating that the new federal law, by abrogating the people's obligations to render their tithes through the civil arm, effectively had reduced other contributions as well.

Here it is necessary to note the problems that Vicar Ortiz faced and what Bishop Zubiría had discovered during his five to six months' visitation. Whether he had actually perused the 1760 Tamarón journal or not, the journal written so many years before was valid. In fact, conditions seemed to be worse due to several factors. The chief one was the Indian menace of every side of the Rio Grande valley from the greatly increased presence of Utes and from raiding activities of Apaches and Navajos. These Indian groups constantly raided both Hispanic and Pueblo Indian settlements in New Mexico. Another factor was the considerable growth of the Hispanic population, which made it that much harder for the few remaining friars and newer secular clergy, since their numbers had neither kept up with the population growth nor with the vast distances over which the population had spread.

Not only had the scattered *estancias* (later called *ranchos*) all over the territory grown in number, but many of the older ones also had evolved into populous villages. The population now included numerous *genízaros*, who generally were descendants of the children of Plains tribes captured by the Comanches or, in some cases, the Navajos. For generations the Spanish settlers had ransomed such captives from the Comanches and Navajos, among others, and reared them as Spanish-speaking Christians.[5]

---

[5] A. Chávez, *But Time and Chance*, 15-16; Ward Allen Minge, "Frontier Problems in New Mexico Preceding the Mexican War, 1840-46," Ph. D. dissertation, University of New Mexico, 1965; and Steven M. Horvath, Jr., "The Social and Political Organization of the Genízaros of Plaza de Nuestra Señora de los Dolores

According to Zubiría, the many outlying adobe churches and chapels were in the saddest possible state of poverty and disrepair, or so it seemed to a person used to the more solid and ornate stone structures of Mexico. While the faith of the people was to be admired, much ignorance prevailed in religious as well as secular instruction. Tabernacles and confessionals did not come up to canonical standards. In Santa Cruz, he condemned what he considered as sheer butchery or carnage a weird society of *Penitentes*, which had fairly recently taken root in that parish. He applauded Padre Martínez's efforts to limit the *Penitentes'* excesses of "body and soul" in Taos.[6]

Just like his remote predecessor of 1760, he mourned the Pueblo Indians' superficial understanding of Christianity, while he romantically considered the once-glorious Franciscan missions. Consequently, he urged the few priests on hand to apply themselves as best they could to remedy the sad situation.[7] But, as said before, those who had to do the work under these most trying circumstances consisted of the five aging Franciscans and ten secular priests, including the vicar himself, who bore the responsibility of being the Church's leader in the area.

---

de Belén, New Mexico, 1740-1812," Ph. D. dissertation, Brown University, 1980. Horvath is the first to amply demonstrate the degree to which Pueblo Indians had become included as *genízaros*.

[6] Martínez to Zubiría, 21 February 1833 and Zubiría to Martínez, 1 April 1833 in William Roth, *Images of Penance, Images of Mercy: Southwestern Santos in the Late Nineteenth Century* (Norman: The University of Oklahoma Press, 1991) 172-73.

[7] Patentes, XI, XII, *AASF*.

The Burdens of Office

Being a vicar in New Mexico was not easy. As suggested by some of the records that have survived, there were the normal problems within Don Juan Felipe's church jurisdiction as well as without. On 15 February 1834, Ortiz had to make a judgement concerning the cemetery at Las Truchas, and in May he was called to settle a dispute in Albuquerque that concerned the lay *mayordomos*, leaders of the parish.[1] On 16 June, upon announcing the burial at Sandía Pueblo of Fray Manuel García del Valle, the last Franciscan *Custodio*, or *custos*, the appointed leader of the Franciscans in New Mexico, Ortiz not only mourned the severe scarcity of priests but also expressed his reluctance to overburden the few who were left.

Hence, Ortiz wrote at this time that he was personally assuming charge of the Pueblo Indian parishes of Cochití and Santo Domingo and their Hispanic villages for the time being. Friar José Mariano Sánchez Vergara, a Franciscan stationed at Sandía, would take charge of the widespread pueblos of San Felipe, Santa Ana, Zia, and Jémez and their respective Spanish settlements. Yet Sánchez Vergara, who was already getting on in age, opposed the redistribution of what he considered inalienable Franciscan places. A long but polite correspondence then ensued between the two in which the vicar eventually prevailed. At the same time, secular Padre José Francisco Rodríguez, a Durango priest who was the short-lived pastor of Albuquerque at the time, likewise complained about the vicar's having removed the Sandía parish from under his care.[2] Both the aging friar and secular pas-

---

[1] Patentes, XIX; Loose documents, 1855, nos. 4 & 5, *AASF.*

[2] Loose documents, 1834, no. 2; Patentes XI, *AASF.*

tor had more than they could handle, but such were the headaches to be endured by one in authority that even after volunteering to take some of the burden upon himself, they resisted.

Then there was the ever-present problem of hostile Indians, which required the vicar's attention both as church superior and as a member of New Mexico's civil assembly. The year 1835 began with his circular of January 4th on a governor's *bando* or proclamation calling for volunteers to go on a campaign against the marauding Apaches and Navajos and requesting prayers for its success. Another unrelated circular of the 24th relayed the bishop's rulings of 2 December 1834, concerning matrimonial dispensation.[3] There are no other official acts of this extant for the remainder of the year. He did spend this period fulfilling a busy schedule attending, as shown by their respective registers, the Pueblo parishes of Cochití and Santo Domingo with their several nearby villages. He continued visiting all the parishes and villages sporadically, whenever the need arose, until as late as August 1845. On 13 November 1836, he took part, as the "first vocal" of the civil assembly, in a meeting convoked by Governor Albino Pérez to consider the levying of taxes for a war against the Navajo Indians. The final decision, as pushed by the clerical members, was that the big landowners (*dueños*) should be taxed and not the poor.[4]

Much of 1836 was also taken up by internal church problems. For some years there had been all kinds of disputes in the parish of Belén. Bishop Zubiría had tried to settle them in his Visitation of 1833, and now on 21 May 1836, Vicar Ortiz found himself obliged to go down to Belén for a meeting with Mexico-born Padre Luis Díaz Luján and the district's civic council. He had ordered this pastor to return to Belén from the mission of Chamisal where he had moved.[5]

In connection with Padre Luján, Ortiz had an encounter in Santa Fe around this time with an American traveler and trader named Josiah Gregg, whose prejudiced book, *Commerce of the Prairies*, is now a favorite source of reference. Gregg brought suit before the vicar concerning a debt owed him by the Belén priest, and Ortiz, unwilling to get involved in such a petty matter, simply told Gregg to see the Belén magistrate as the competent authority.[6] One wonders if this unpleasant but slight encounter caused the

---

[3] Patentes, XI, XII, XIX, *AASF*.

[4] Bloom, "Mexican Administration," *OSF*, Vol. II, 8.

[5] Patentes, XII, *AASF*.

[6] Accounts, LXXVI, *AASF*. Gregg's book *Commerce of the Prairies* was first published in 1844 and was quickly followed by a second edition in 1845. See Josiah

American trader, already most critical of New Mexico's people and their padres, to poke fun at the priest in his book.

With reference to the Belén troubles just cited, it must be noted that, contrary to what Gregg and others like him would later publish, New Mexico's Catholics were not what they called "priest-ridden."[7] Throughout the territory's long colonial history, individuals or groups had been quarreling with their priests over the slightest pretext, especially those individuals who happened to be invested with brief authority. The situation worsened following Mexican independence in 1821 and further deteriorated after the American occupation of 1846. Of all this Vicar Ortiz was to bear the brunt in his own characteristic way.

Gregg, *Commerce of the Prairies*, Max L. Moorhead, editor (Norman: University of Oklahoma Press, 1974).

[7] Gregg, *Commerce of the Prairies*, 172-183.

Deputy in Congress

Mention has been made of Ortiz's having been an elected member of the civil departmental assembly for New Mexico. Some of his other clerical contemporaries also had been elected to office, including Padre Martínez of Taos who stands out in particular because of his bellicose personality. This was a result of Mexican patriotism and civic consciousness acquired by secular priests in Durango when the country came into being. Moreover, a dearth of well-educated lay leaders could well have prompted them to take an active part in the civil government.

As deputy or assemblyman, Vicar Ortiz found himself the recipient of another high honor when, on 1 May 1837, his clerical and lay peers unanimously elected him to the National Congress in Mexico City. At this time, he wrote Governor Albino Pérez and the general junta about this important honor, likewise issuing a circular to his clergy on the subject. On 27 May, he entrusted his Santa Fe parish to Padre José Francisco Leyva y Rosas, an older Mexico-born priest who was his assistant at the time. Leyva took over until Ortiz returned two years later, on 14 July 1839.[1] In the meantime, Padre José Ignacio de Madariaga of Tomé, who was also a Durango priest, had taken his place as interim vicar. Leyva replaced him as well upon his death.

While in Mexico City, Ortiz received a letter dated 7 May 1838 from Governor Manuel Armijo, who told him about his recent victory over local insurgents at El Puertecito de Pojoaque. The revolution alluded to by Armijo was the notorious 1837 Chimayó Rebellion. The locals rose against Governor

---

[1] Loose documents, 1837, no. 1; Patentes XI, *AASF*; and Bloom, "Mexican Administration," *OSF*, Vol. II, 10, 130 & 181.

Pérez who had been sent to New Mexico by President Antonio de Santa Anna to help fulfill the latter's plans to centralize his government and collect more taxes. José Ángel Gonzales, a *genízaro*, led the rebellion that resulted in the defeat and killing of Pérez. Gonzales declared himself governor for several months until his military defeat by Armijo. Armijo then received the appointment to succeed the recently killed Governor Pérez.[2]

In his reply of 18 July, Vicar Ortiz advised Armijo that he had received 400 pesos for New Mexico's civil government after speaking to the Mexican President about his land's endemic poverty. He found it regrettable that he could not get more. During the previous year, he added, he himself had received no payments from the federal government for his salary and expenses.[3]

By June of 1839, Ortiz was in Durango on his way back home when Bishop Zubiría personally renewed his vicarship *in capite* for another two years, and by July he was back in Santa Fe. On 21 August, he wrote to the federal government that after the first wagons of an American trade caravan had passed through Santa Fe, he had conferred with Governor Armijo about 6,633 pesos in the civil department's treasury that belonged to the parish and that Armijo had sequestered. The latter, he said, had promised to repay half of the amount anon and the rest in the following year.[4] As the year 1840 began, this and other events to come posed a decade of added challenges for the Vicar.

He was now forty-three years old and entering old age by the standards of those times, but age did not interfere with his many varied activities, including his arduous travels at home and abroad. But now a brief interlude.

---

[2] The Chimayó Rebellion occurred for the same reasons that gave rise to similar rebellions in Texas, California, and other Mexican states around the same time. The northern frontier of Mexico had grown tired of President Santa Ana's increasingly heavy-handed government and wanted to return to the more liberal constitution of 1824. The Texas rebellion resulted in Texas's independence. A. Chávez, *But Time and Chance*, 51-59; and Janet Lecompte, *Rebellion in Río Arriba, 1837* (Albuquerque: University of New Mexico/Historical Society of New Mexico, 1985). Lecompte's book is the best study on the 1837 rebellion.

[3] Accounts, LXXII, *AASF*; and Bloom, "Mexican Administration," *OSF*, Vol. II, 181.

[4] Accounts, LXXVI, *AASF*.

Digression to Another Relative

Several years prior to the Vicar's fourth decade, a flashy gambling establishment, the likes of which centuries-old New Mexico and its drab capital had never seen before, suddenly came to life in one of the town's adobe alleys. Today, its vicinity is called Burro Alley. Stranger still for those times, its owner and operator was a woman. Her name was Gertrudis Barceló, but she left her mark in the annals of that period with the added sobriquet of La Tules. Her fame is greater than ever today. Since Vicar Ortiz enters the picture now and then as a family friend, and no less because so much outlandish nonsense has been published about her personal character and her family, a review of the woman and her activities is not out of place.

Around the year of 1815, a certain lady named Dolores Herrero and her husband Juan Ignacio Barceló came up to New Mexico from Sonora in New Spain to settle in the village of Valencia in the southern parish of Tomé. She brought with her a son, Trinidad, and two daughters, Gertrudis and María Luz, all three bearing the surname Barceló. Also relevant to this history are some second-generation recollections from Don Amado Chaves, a prominent gentleman of his day, and his first cousin Doña Amada Baca, whose common grandparents were related to La Tules by marriage. Writing at the end of the nineteenth century, Chaves and Baca furnish some helpful clues, which have to be sorted out with a critical eye. For example, Don Amado stated that the Barceló, whose intimate family details he and his cousin no longer knew, had come from Sonora to settle at the Valencia homestead of his own grandfather.[1] That they had chosen his grandfather's Valencia hacienda for their

---

[1] Amado Chaves Papers, New Mexico State Records Center and Archives (NMSRCA), Santa Fe.

home is altogether credible, since Don Amado would have learned this from his father, Colonel Manuel Antonio Chaves of Civil War fame, and from his mother, Doña Vicenta Labadía (later spelled Labadié). And, what is more likely, the Barcelós had settled in the homestead of the latter's own father, Don Pablo Labadía, and not in any of the Chaves spreads that lay on the west side of the Río Grande River.

But, first, the question arises, why did they, after leaving a much more prosperous and civilized life far down south, choose such a rural site in backward and isolated New Mexico instead of going all the way to Santa Fe? As both the capital and the northern terminus of the Chihuahua Trail, the town offered better social and other opportunities for herself and her family. Apache raids in Sonora were legendary and made life extremely dangerous. Perhaps they did not consider the Indian attacks in the Tomé area as much of a problem. Maybe, as well, Juan Ignacio feared persecution from the local rebels in the years following the Miguel Hidalgo Revolution of 1810 and decided to move his family, along with a cache of gold and silver, to safe, faraway New Mexico. A kindred supposition is that he had run a gambling saloon in some rich mining center; how else to explain how one of his daughters had both the expertise and wherewithal to open such a casino in an isolated land, which had never seen such a thing. A more likely supposition is that he made his money in one of the many mining enterprises that were paying off in Sonora. Naturally, mining communities attracted gaming houses, so the whole family would have been exposed to the activity.[2]

Also pertinent is the subsequent arrival of a secular priest from Chihuahua in 1821, the very year of Mexican independence. Don José Francisco Madariaga y Serrano took over the Tomé parish of 6 July from the last Franciscan padre of the mission, the aged Fray José Ignacio Sánchez, whom Father Madariaga would bury three years later. He also brought along a younger brother, Juan José, who at his marriage in 1829 declared that he was a native of Chihuahua.[3] From his friendliness with the Barceló family, one might conclude that this priest had previously known its members in the rich mining environments in Mexico. A year after his arrival, on 20 October 1822, he took the premarital depositions in Valencia of María Luz Barceló and Rafael Sánchez, subsequently marrying them on 3 November.

---

[2] The Barceló family is still prominent in many of Sonora's old mining communities. The Barceló surname is found in Spain in Cataluña and Valencia, later moving into the Balearic Islands.

[3] M-56, Burial-54, Tomé, Diligencias Matrimoniales, 1829, no. 54, *AASF*.

The bride deposed that she had lived in Valencia "since a tender age," while a local witness testified that he had known her for seven years – hence the supposition that her family arrived in 1815. Another local witness was Pablo Labadía, 36 years old and noted here for being the future maternal grandfather of Amado Chaves and his cousin. But in the previous matrimonial investigations, Don Francisco Ignacio Barceló was not mentioned as already deceased.[4]

The following year saw the wedding of the older Barceló sister, Gertrudis, the future Doña Tules of Santa Fe. On 20 June 1823, Padre Madariaga took depositions of a Manuel Sisneros of Tomé, the son of Don Hermenegildo Sisneros, deceased, and Doña María Rita Lucero. (The groom's parents are mentioned here because his sister, María Rosa de los Reyes, was the wife of Pablo Labadía.) However, Padre Madariaga, for whatever reason, did not record the bride's parents in depositions. Also, he married the pair on the very same day. As with other marriages, the respective parents were not entered in the Tomé marriage book, a faulty practice by Madariaga or his scribe. The marriage took place right after the investigations and in the groom's own church, and not the bride's because the she was already four months pregnant.[5]

Only seven weeks later, a really surprising third wedding took place in Valencia, and under the most baffling circumstances. On 6 August 1823, Madariaga recorded the marriage of a Pedro Pino with the two daughters' own mother, whom he now called Doña Dolores Barceló (not using her maiden name Herrero as was the custom). Nor was she designated as a widow. Still more unusual and altogether contrary to Church regulations, Padre Madariaga made the premarital investigations three full weeks afterward, on 1 September. Here Don Pedro Pino deposed that he was forty years old and a native of Belén residing in Valencia, but his own parents' names were not recorded. As for the bride, she was now designated as Doña Dolores "de Herrera (sic)," as well as *the widow* of Juan Ignacio Barceló! Here, for the first and only time, her previous husband is mentioned as being dead. Moreover, the priest had two witnesses testify that Doña Dolores had *always* lived in Valencia, which falls in line with his use of her common New Mexican surname, "de Herrera."[6]

---

[4] DM, 1822; M-56, Tomé, *AASF*.

[5] DM, 1823, no. 82; M-56, Tomé, *AASF*; and A. Chávez, *New Mexico Families*, 202.

[6] M-56, Tomé; DM, 1823, no. 43, *AASF*. Italics are the authors.

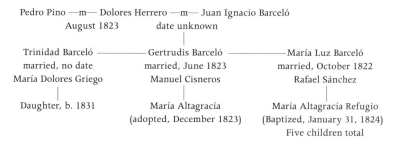

Genealogical chart of the family of Gertrudis Barceló's family showing the adoption of María Altagracía.

There is a very possible solution to the puzzle. Evidently at the insistence of a strong-willed woman like Doña Dolores, and also because of their lifelong acquaintance, Padre Madariaga married her to Pedro Pino without having all the necessary documentation. But weeks later, possibly fearing that the bishop of Durango would scrutinize the matrimonial investigations at some point, he drew up the belated depositions which not only stated that the bride was a widow, but also made her look like a lifelong resident of New Mexico.

The first marriage, that of Rafael Sánchez and María Luz, Gertrudis's sister, produced five baby girls between 1824 and 1833, the second to last child dying shortly after she was born. The very first child, María Altagracia Refugio, baptized on 31 January 1824, requires mention because some years later she would become confused with another María Altagracia adopted by her grandmother and aunt, Gertrudis Barceló. Also of interest is the fact that the baptizing priest was the newly ordained young Padre Martínez from Taos who was substituting for Madariaga during the latter's absence in Mexico. Here Martínez spelled the maternal surname as Varzelón and Varzelona, and the grandmother's as Herrero. In all the other baptisms by Madariaga, he or his scribe wrote her name always incorrectly as Herrera, escept for once correctly as Herrero.

As for Gertrudis Barceló and her Sisneros husband, they had two baby boys. The first one was born on 17 October 1823, five months after his parents' wedding. He died a month later, to be followed on 19 January 1825 by a brother, who also lived only five months. In these two baptisms the grandmother's name was spelled Herreros and Herrero.[7] After this, Doña

---

[7] B-71, Bur. 54, Tomé, *AASF*.

LADY TULES.

Gertrudis Barceló (La Doña Tules) from Harpers Monthly Magazine, *April 1854. Photo courtesy Museum of New Mexico, Neg. No. 50815.*

Gertrudis bore no more children, evidently the reason for their later adopting a girl, a not uncommon practice among Hispanic families.

Nine years after their marriage Dolores and her Pino husband moved to Santa Fe. Sometime in December of 1832, they sent a baby girl, who had been "exposed at the house of Doña Dolores Barceló, residents of Santa Fe," to be baptized at Tomé where she was christened María Altagracia on 22 December.[8] Here it appears that the Pinos had sent the baby there to be

---

[8] B-72, Tomé, *AASF*.

reared by their childless daughter (and step-daughter) Gertrudis.

As for her now residing in the capital, it is very likely that Don Pedro Pino of Belén was closely related to the famous Pino people of Santa Fe. He could have been one of the five unnamed sons whom the noted Don Pedro Bautista Pino, New Mexico's 1812 Deputy at the Cortes in Spain, had engendered in the 1790s at Tomé with his second wife. Or else he was one of many nephews living in the Tomé-Belén area. Hence Don Pedro Pino was either a brother or a first cousin of a prominent Santa Fe lady, Doña Gertrudis Pino, who was the ex-Deputy's daughter by that same second wife, and who in 1816 became the second stepmother of Juan Felipe Ortiz.[9] Here is a possible family connection, if remote, between Vicar Ortiz and La Tules.

But when, more or less, had La Tules and her Sisneros husband followed her mother and stepfather to Santa Fe? Already by November of 1827, her brother, Trinidad, had moved to northern New Mexico in the capacity of superintendent of education for Governor Antonio Narbona.[10] He seems to have been living at Don Fernando de Taos in 1831 when a female child of his was baptized there on 7 July. Here Padre Martínez designated the mother as María Dolores Griego, duly naming her parents, and Trinidad's, as Ignacio Barceló and María Dolores "Guerrero" for Herrero.[11]

The Griego wife's parents had been married in Santa Fe in 1789, and this can explain why Trinidad and his wife later claimed some land in Pojoaque near Santa Fe in 1837.[12] All this suggests that the Barceló matriarch and her Pino husband had been residing in Santa Fe for some years prior to the birth of Trinidad's daughter's in 1831.

Gertrudis Barceló and Manuel Sisneros could have also moved up to Santa Fe after this date, along with her sister with her own family, although the evidence for this comes after the fact. On 6 February 1838, a Santa Fe child of unknown parentage was christened María, her godparents being Manuel Sisneros, (Gertrudis' husband) and Dolores Griego (Trinidad's wife).[13] This child could have been another by Gertrudis Barceló.

It is likely that Gertrudis' gambling establishment had been in existence for several years, so as to be described as the flourishing and most lavish casino that it already was in 1838-1840. The very first descriptions

---

[9] A. Chávez, *New Mexico Families*, 159-60, 328, & 330.

[10] A. Chávez, *But Time and Chance*, 30.

[11] B-48, Taos, *AASF*.

[12] DM, 1789, no. 27, *AASF*; and Ralph E. Twitchell, *The Spanish Archives of New Mexico, Vol. I* (Cedar Rapids: The Torch Press, 1914), no. 148.

[13] B-48, Taos, *AASF*.

that exist, both of the gambling hall and of Doña Gertrudis herself – Doña Tules (Miss Trudy) as she was endearingly called by all and sundry – chiefly came from two American travelers, Matthew Field and Josiah Gregg.

"Matt" Field, who called her "Doña Toulous," started out by referring to her, and with no tone of sarcasm, as "the great lady and *monte* dealer of Santa Fe" and later on as "the supreme queen of refinement and fashion" of what he called "fashionable society" at her gaming establishment. He had first seen her, a lady of middle age, riding in her "gaudy" carriage with a smiling black-eyed young beauty at her side whom he took to be her niece, "an adventurous belle," recently arrived from Chihuahua. Then at the casino itself he saw Governor Manuel Armijo with some of his officers, and also some young men who were the flirty niece's admirers. Field described all the lush interior furnishings – which were by far more lavish than to be found in any Santa Fe residence. As for Doña Tules herself, he now described her as "not handsome" but with an intelligent mischievousness in her eye which sufficed "to make the countenance agreeable." Likewise, her neat figure and bearing were "not graceful," so that her waltzing with the young Americans would have made her stand out at any high function in Washington. Her "gambling bank," as Field called it, was not in her residence, which stood in another part of town. Card games of *monte*, which she dealt herself, and the fandangos or dances, along with the "Pass whiskey" (El Paso brandy) that was sold were the only amusements offered at her bar.[14]

Another traveler from the East, Dr. Andrew Randall, who was on his way from Ohio to California, wrote in his 1849 journal that he had "stood and watched the celebrated Madam Tules deal [monte]. She has a marked countenance, I presume the look of a Female Gambler, for I see no reason why they should not be marked like the other set [male gamblers]."[15]

Years later Amado Chaves recalled from family hearsay that La Tules had been "very beautiful and intelligent," as she well could have been before reaching middle age. She was a great expert in dealing *monte*, he went on to say, and for a time was the mistress of Governor Armijo, whom she ruled with a velvet hand; but she gave him up after a revival preached in Santa Fe by a Padre Francisco Madariaga of Tomé. If such an affair did take

---

[14] John E. Sunder, editor, *Matt Field on the Santa Fe Trail* (Norman: University of Oklahoma Press, 1960), 207-13.

[15] Diary of Dr. Andrew Randall, 19 April 1849, Cincinnati, Ohio – Santa Fe, New Mexico. Original in the California State Library, Sacramento, California; copy in the Fray Angélico Chávez Library, Palace of the Governors, Santa Fe. Underline in the original.

place, it had to be brief, since Armijo moved from Albuquerque for his second term late in 1837, and Padre Madariaga passed away at his parish on 17 November 1838.[16] Quite possibly, the Armijo-Tules romance was all rumor that folks like Don Amado passed down to historian Ralph Emerson Twitchell and others. It was also around this time, again according to Amado Chaves, that La Tules's Sisneros husband left her and went to live in Manzano where he died. (And here Don Amado misnamed him José, instead of Manuel Sisneros.) He also said that the latter had been excommunicated for some reason by the bishop, who would have been Jean Baptiste Lamy. But this again looks like rumor of later times, since Bishop Lamy had been in Santa Fe for only three weeks following his arrival in August 1851, prior to his trip to Durango, from where he returned in January 1852, the very month when La Tules died. Or, perhaps, Don Amado confused a later such incident when Lamy did excommunicate his own Chaves father over a real estate dispute concerning the Guadalupe chapel in Santa Fe.[17]

With respect to Doña Gertrudis's personal appearance, Amado Chaves wrote that he was told about it by an 87-year-old American gentleman named Carlos Conklin, whose mother-in-law had been a very dear friend of La Tules. Conklin remembered her as a very fine and attractive woman, about middle-sized with very large eyes and black hair, and weighing about 140 pounds.

Altogether different because of its blatant religious prejudice is what the better-known American traveler, Josiah Gregg, published in 1844. Here he introduced La Tules as a "roamer" of loose habits who had lived in Taos some twelve or fifteen years before. She had then moved to Santa Fe where conditions were more favorable for her trade, which, he claimed, was prostitution. In Santa Fe she started her gambling place, and through it had prospered so well that "now she is known as Señora Doña Gertrudis Barceló."[18]

This canard, as it obviously is, was in tune with other things Gregg wrote about New Mexico's people and clergy. Still other such descriptions and passing references by others who came later are best left for La Tules's last years and her final demise twelve years later. These same commentators had a problem about some young women whom she had reared, and because

---

[16] Bur. 54, Tomé, AASF; Twitchell, *Old Santa Fe: The Story of New Mexico's Ancient Capital* (Santa Fe: The Santa Fe New Mexican Publishing Corporation, 1925), 338-39.

[17] Marc Simmons, *A Life of Manuel Antonio Chaves: The Little Lion of the Southwest* (Chicago: The Swallow Press, Inc., 1973), 117-20; and Amado Chaves Papers, NMSRCA.

[18] Gregg, *Commerce of the Prairies*, 169.

Gambling Saloon in Santa Fe, New Mexico from Harpers Monthly Magazine, *April 1854. Photo courtesy Museum of New Mexico, Neg. No. 14963.*

of them she would be labeled as a madam.

One soldier, who was not an officer and doubled as a correspondent for a St. Louis newspaper, had a more studied description of La Tules. Richard Smith Elliott, while subject to a bigoted attitude toward Mexicans, seems to have admired La Tules, for he correctly noted that she came from Sonora and "notably struggled with the world – a sublime spectacle – a great *woman*, struggling with adversity! She, by dint of successful gambling, amassed a considerable fortune; preserving all the while, a reputation for chastity as distinguished as her extraordinary successes." He noted that when he saw her she was "a little *passe*" but had been in youth "very beautiful and very much admired."[19] While criticizing Gregg's account of La Tules, Elliot intended to write a biography of her. Elliot, incidentally, wrote a detailed ac-

---

[19] Richard Smith Elliott (pen name John Brown), *The St. Louis Reveille*, 21 August 1847 as printed in Mark L. Gardner and Marc Simmons, editors, *The Mexican War Correspondence of Richard Smith Elliott* (Norman: University of Oklahoma Press, 1997), 211. Italics in the original.

Plaza view looking east, Santa Fe, New Mexico, circa 1868. Photo by Nicholas Brown, courtesy Museum of New Mexico, Neg. No. 38025.

count of her playing *monte* not in a palatial hall but in a small dust-filled, earthen floored, crowded "tavern...in the plaza."[20]

During this later period Vicar Ortiz comes more fully upon the scene in connection with the influx of American merchants, the outbreak of the Mexican War, the subsequent American occupation of New Mexico in 1846, and with further comments by American newcomers on La Tules in her gambling hall on Burro Alley.

---

[20] Elliot to the Editors of *The Reveille*, Santa Fe, 22 April 1847 in Gardner and Simmons, War Correspondence, 165. Published in The St. Louis Daily Reveille, 6 June 1847.

Troublesome Times

New Mexico was fast emerging from a centuries-long isolation during this period of its history. Not only were naïve outsiders like Gregg beginning to comment upon the scene as the Santa Fe Trail began introducing new peoples with new ideas in government and commerce, but there were also signs of a more ominous nature. First of all, the year 1840 brought Vicar Ortiz and his peers serious worries of invasions that were altogether different from the traditional Indian raids. These, by immemorial custom, had been taken in due stride. But now, far away to the southeast, where New Mexico's Río Bravo was said to flow into the sea as the Río Grande, some American colonists had successfully rebelled against Mexico in 1836 and set up a republic of their own which they called Texas. This was the historic name of the Hispanic colony that had the mission and garrison of San Antonio de Béjar as its center for many decades. This new English-speaking republic, by an act of 19 December 1836, began claiming all the vast territory east of the Río Grande, from its mouth in the Gulf of Mexico all the way to its northernmost source in what is now Colorado. This, of course, included a good portion of New Mexico, including its capital.

What concerned Vicar Ortiz and his peers most was the threat of seemingly boundless Texas encroachment, with New Mexico as the evident goal. Agents from the republic even traveled to Santa Fe to organize a county in that name.[1] Still more overt was a message from Texas President Mirabeau

---

[1] David Lavender, *Bent's Fort* (Lincoln: University of Nebraska Press, 1972), 21.

Buonaparte Lamar that attempted to convince New Mexican citizens to be-
tray their country in favor of Texas.[2]

Texan braggadocio aside, Lamar was partially attracted to New Mexico
due to the activities of Josiah Gregg, who led a successful 1839 caravan from
Arkansas to Santa Fe. The Texas President reasoned that his new and debt-
ridden government would benefit from Santa Fe trade via a southern route.[3]

Although Texas had declared independence, Mexico, which included
New Mexico, did not recognize the claim. Texas was merely a department in
rebellion. Now the Texans were seeking to spread their rebellion to New
Mexico and the threat was imminent. In 1839 and 1840 federalists in Nuevo
León and Coahuila made two attempts at seceding from Mexico. Centralist
forces defeated them on both occasions. But Texas' aid to the aborted rebellions, although covert, was obvious to Mexico.[4]

Hence, to Vicar Ortiz and his brethren, whose homeland had been a
Catholic Hispanic enclave under Spain and recently under Mexico for almost two and a half centuries, this first threat by an Anglo-Protestant power
was most disconcerting. On 2 February 1840, Vicar Ortiz issued a circular
warning his clergy and people about the danger, while begging their prayers
in the matter. He further commented on the ingress of Protestantism in the
persons of eastern Americans who had been coming to New Mexico in recent years. Besides publishing several Durango decrees of March and May
on Church discipline, he issued another warning on 22 July about an impending Texan invasion.[5] While no such invasion had ever occurred, the
prospects must have weighed heavily on his mind, Mexican and New Mexican patriot that he was, over and above his position as church and civic
leader.

A more personal attack took place around this time in the early 1840s,
and not surprisingly, by one of those Americans to whom the vicar had
referred in his circular. Josiah Gregg used Vicar Ortiz as his vehicle of sarcasm in recounting a story of an Indian legend, which the vicar was fond of
recounting to his parishioners. Gregg intended to expose the gullibility of

---

[2] "Mirabeau Lamar to the Citizens of Santa Fe, Friends, and Compatriots," Austin, 14
April 1840, in Charles Adams Gulick, Jr., *The Papers of Mirabeau Buonaparte
Lamar From the Original Papers in the Texas State Library* (Austin: The Univer-
sity of Texas Press, 1972), Vol. III, 370-71.

[3] Thomas E. Chávez, "The Trouble With Texans: Manuel Alvarez and the 1841 'Invasion,'" *New Mexico Historical Review* (NMHR), (April 1978), 134.

[4] Weber, *The Mexican Frontier*, 266.

[5] Patentes, XI, XIX, *AASF*.

"The Padre Wins." Photo courtesy Museum of New Mexico, Neg. No. 78351.

his parishioners and the priest that he called, "the blind and reverential one."

Many years before, during the Pueblo Revolt of 1680, so the legend ran, the Indians of San Felipe Pueblo had protected a Franciscan padre from the general massacre suffered by the friars in that fateful year. This padre repaid their kindness when, upon seeing that they had run out of water atop of their mesa, he cut both of his wrists to furnish them with all the water they needed.[6]

This story, while having its basis in history, also departed fantastically from the actual facts, as folklore and tradition like to do.[7] While it is quite possible that Vicar Ortiz and his listeners believed the story to be true, Gregg, as an avowed Protestant, believed the figurative account of Moses striking forth a torrent of living water out of a solid rock. But he reacted with dis-

---

[6] Gregg, *Commerce of the Prairies*, 177. This tale was still being told in San Felipe Pueblo in 1950, and continues today.

[7] A. Chávez, "The Inter-Relation of History and Folklore," *New Mexico Folklore Record*, (Vol. 5, 1950-51), 1-3.

dain to what he deemed a silly Mexican Catholic superstition. Such "traditions" wrote Gregg "tend to obstruct the advancement of knowledge" and "is a part of the superstitious blindness of these people."[8]

The year of 1840 ended with new internal problems for Vicar Ortiz, which involved some young priests whom Bishop Zubiría had recently ordained. These problems would continue to plague him from then on. One such instance occurred in December 1840, when a newly ordained young priest, José Manuel Gallegos, incurred the wrath of Governor Armijo when he injudiciously insulted the wife of one of the governor's minions. The case was blown so far out of proportion that Ortiz had to step in on Gallegos' behalf, even when threatened with bodily harm by one of Armijo's officers. Armijo summarily exiled the young priest to Abiquiú. Ortiz countered that the Governor had acted injudiciously for not investigating the charges before acting. The vicar also sequestered Gallegos at an undisclosed site for the time being. Armijo reconsidered his action and acquiesced. But that same night ensign Tomás Martínez, brother of the minion who brought the initial complaint, broke into Ortiz's house, drew his sword and berated the vicar for helping Padre Gallegos. Ortiz, genteel person that he was, probably was scared out of his wits. But the episode shows how the otherwise mild-mannered vicar was not afraid to back up his priests when the situation called for it.[9]

Another incident, albeit of a different nature and which Ortiz handled differently, occurred during this same year of 1840. It concerned another young padre, José de Jesús Luján, whom the bishop had transferred to Chihuahua from his post at Picurís Pueblo in New Mexico. This time it was not a civil official who interfered but Padre Martínez of Taos who had always envied Ortiz because of his vicarial office.

Martínez ran the northern districts of Taos, Picurís, and Lo de Mora as if he were their own dependent "vicar" and resented any intrusion on his domain. Martínez protested and contended that Ortiz had no authority in the area – only around Santa Fe. Ortiz insisted on his authority in two letters but went no further. He was well aware of the fact that crossing the headstrong Martínez would produce nothing but further troubles. Ortiz referred the matter to the bishop, explaining in letters to him that he had used restraint in order to keep the peace.[10]

---

[8] Ibid.

[9] Accounts, LXXIII, *AASF*; and A. Chávez, *Très Macho – He Said*, 10.

[10] Accounts, *AASF*; and A. Chávez, *But Time and Chance*, 42, 49-70.

"Father Ignatio Moved By The Spirit." Photo courtesy *Museum of New Mexico,*
Neg. No. 78352.

A tougher case was that of another young padre, José Tomás Abeytia, who during November 1841 became involved in serious disputes at the Isleta parish and then refused to leave the scene on Vicar Ortiz's orders. Ortiz stood his ground, at first in a conciliatory manner by requesting Abeytia to go to Durango and present his case before the Bishop. When Abeytia refused, Ortiz used the civil arm to forcibly ship him to that city early in the following year.[11]

Between January and August 1841, Ortiz was also busy writing circulars to the faithful about Church support following the federal government's abrogation or tithes. What he had feared most came to pass during the course of that summer and early fall. Men whom he descibed as "Texan adventurers" invaded his beloved homeland.

Mirabeau Lamar, the President of Texas, sent an army of 320 men and fourteen wagons, ostensibly to open a wagon road from Austin to Santa Fe. Its leaders had clear instructions to seize New Mexico and form a new government to join Texas. Delayed at the start, the expedition became lost en route, suffered Comanche attacks, and subsequently ran out of food. As they wandered into New Mexico in small desperate groups, the worn, weary, and thirsty Texans were more than happy to surrender to Armijo's ragged militia or even to New Mexican shepherds.[12]

New Mexicans took euphoric delight in their "victory" and thanked God the Texans had been defeated.[13] On 7 October, Ortiz requested masses of thanksgiving to be celebrated in all the parishes following the defeat of

---

[11] Accounts, C-1, *AASF*.

[12] Manuel Alvarez Diary, *Benjamin Read Collections*, NMSRCA. The main force of 200 men surrendered on 7 October 1841. Other groups came into New Mexico's outlying communities, reported Alvarez, in the following manner. On 15 September at Anton Chico, three men; on 18 September at Las Vegas, eighty-five men; on 30 September at Las Gallinas, twelve men. Also see T. Chávez, *Manuel Alvarez, 1794-1856: A Southwestern Biography* (Niwot, CO: University Presses of Colorado, 1990), n. 40, 206-207.

[13] T. Chávez, "Trouble," *NMHR*, (April 1978), 133; Weber, *The Mexican Frontier*, 267. Some contemporary accounts written from the Texan point-of-view are Thomas Falconer, *Letters and Notes on the Texan-Santa Fe Expedition*, F. W. Hodge, editor, (Chicago: The Rio Grande Press, 1963); George Wilkens Kendall, *Narrative of the Texan-Santa Fe Expedition* (Austin: The Steck Co., 1935), Vols. I & II; and Franklin Combs, "Combs' Narrative of the Santa Fe Expedition in 1841," *NMHR*, (July 1930), 304-14. Falconer was a British scientist who wanted to see the American west and northern Mexico. He joined the expedition to get to Mexico. Combs, son of General Leslie Combs of Kentucky, was also a guest of

the Texans.[14]

The state of euphoria ran so high that a folk play surfaced in which the great victory was dramatized. The play praised Armijo and lambasted the Texans, calling them insolent and greedy, while accusing them of "profaning" the land of "the proud Mexican people." Because of their "foolhardiness," Armijo's army captured the Texans. The play *The Texans*, written sometime between 1841 and 1846, was clearly an expression of the kind of pride and relief felt by many New Mexicans.[15]

The mission registers of baptisms and marriages of the spring in 1841 indicate that Ortiz had been obliged to take the parish of Cochití Pueblo and its environs under his wing once again. Following his action with regard to Padre Abeytia, he advised his clergy in a letter of 6 June 1842, about the current federal law on church properties. He also mentioned his forthcoming personal consultation with the bishop in this matter (and perhaps the Abeytia case). This would indicate that he made a trip to Durango shortly afterward, returning by November when Governor Armijo referred him to the requirements contained in a decree of President Santa Anna on the same subject.[16]

Once again, he had the pleasure and satisfaction of writing another message to his priests and people concerning the Texan adventurers. On 5 July 1843, he requested more masses to be offered in thanksgiving for their second summary defeat. Actually, the only Texan "defeat" came at the hands of Captain Philip St. George Cooke and the First United States dragoons he commanded. Cooke was acting in accordance with United States policy to keep the Santa Fe Trail open at least to the international border at the Arkansas River. On 30 June 1843, Cooke spotted Colonel Jacob Snively and 107 Texans who had been raiding in New Mexico. Cooke demanded and

---

the expedition. For a different contemporary view see T. Chávez, editor, *Conflict and Acculturation: Manuel Alvarez's 1842 "Memorial"* (Santa Fe: Museum of New Mexico Press, 1989), 49-61. Alvarez, the United States Consul in Santa Fe, was nearly killed by a mob led by "Tomás Martin," the governor's nephew, "most intimate friend and confidant" who may have been the same hothead who broke into Vicar Ortiz's house to attack the padre. See 56, infra.

[14] Accounts, C-1; Patentes, XI, *AASF*.

[15] Aurelio M. Espinosa, *Folklore of Spain in the American Southwest: Traditional Spanish Folk Literature in Northern New Mexico and Southern Colorado*, J. Manuel Espinosa, editor (Norman: University of Oklahoma Press, 1985), 219-24.

[16] Patentes, XII, *AASF*.

received the Texans' surrender. He then disarmed and disbanded the raiders.[17]

Around this time Ortiz also passed on the bishop's plea for alms on behalf of the persecuted Christians of China and on 6 August 1843 instructed the pastors on parish contributions which he had to report to the Durango chancery.[18] There is no report of how much New Mexicans donated, if anything, for the persecuted in China.

Then something dramatic happened in Santa Fe in which Ortiz was not directly involved but which again illustrates his policy of remaining passive when any resistance would prove fruitless. Previously, Padre Martínez of Taos had been involved in a serious feud with Governor Armijo over large land grants the latter had been making to foreigners. On 6 July 1843, Armijo complained to Ortiz about secret meetings being held by Martínez. The governor wanted Martínez to come to Santa Fe with an explanation. But by 6 August the Vicar reported to Armijo that Martínez had not left Taos. The same thing happened when Armijo accused young Padre Gallegos of attending such meetings, but there are no details about the subsequent consequence. However, matters came to a head when the departmental assembly met in Santa Fe, with Vicar Ortiz presiding, to elect a deputy to the National Mexican Congress. Padre Martínez was the unanimous choice when Armijo appeared with a squad of soldiers in front of the Palacio Nacional, today's Palace of the Governors, where the meeting was being held. Pointing his baton of office at Ortiz, the Governor demanded that Diego Archuleta be named the deputy instead, and Ortiz quickly acceded to his demand. Martínez subsequently pursued the matter in his ongoing feud with Armijo, but for Vicar Ortiz it was apparently a closed case.[19]

The year 1844 then began with Vicar Ortiz announcing his intention to visit the distant pueblo of Zuni every two months thereafter, saying that those unfortunate Indians had just about returned completely to what he termed their "ancient barbarity."[20]

If these problems of arduous and distant travel were not enough, Ortiz once more had a tiff with Padre Martínez after appointing Padre Gallegos to Picurís with its attached missions of Lo de Mora. Instigated by Martínez,

---

[17] Louise Barry, *The Beginning of the West: Annals of the Kansas Gateway to the American West, 1540-1854* (Topeka: Kansas State Historical Society, 1972), 478 & 487; and T. Chávez, *Alvarez*, 83-86.

[18] Loose documents, 1843, no. 3; Patentes, XII, LXXI, *AASF*.

[19] A. Chávez, *But Time and Chance*, 67-68.

[20] Patentes, XI, XIX, *AASF*.

the parishioners protested the change in pastorship, and once again Vicar Ortiz wrote the bishop for support, waiting to act until the bishop made a final decision in the matter.[21] Solely to preserve the peace, Ortiz allowed Martínez to retain the Mora valley settlements, which Martínez considered as his very own preserve. In fact, he had gone so far as to challenge Ortiz's overall vicarial jurisdiction in New Mexico. When the bishop responded, Ortiz calmly wrote back, quoting the episcopal papers that proved his appointment as the bishop's vicar for all of New Mexico.[22]

More internecine troubles of this sort were to follow, presaged by the appearance in the following year, 1845, of a new young priest by the name of Nicolás Valencia. He may have been a New Mexico native, but from certain indications, he could well have been born in the area of El Paso if not farther south in the Mexican republic. What is known is that the fellow, while in temporary charge of Sandía Pueblo following his arrival, was already insisting on having a permanent parish of his own. Vicar Ortiz curtly told him to stay at his post until the bishop came on a visitation and made his own decision. After this, Valencia persisted in his independent way of doing things, which eventually led to his suspension and ultimately to a schism, which he caused among the southern parishes in Río Abajo.[23]

It could well be that sum of all these clerical problems is what prompted Bishop Zubiría to announce his second visitation to New Mexico in 1845. This pastoral journey turned out to be very much like the first one in 1833, as were his final comments and instructions to the clergy. Conditions had not improved, and now there was the growing influx of Anglo-Americans, most of them not of the Catholic faith. Moreover, there was still a shortage of priests, since only the personnel had changed but not their numbers in the twelve years since his last visit. Where there had been ten secular priests and five old friars, now at the start of 1845, there were fourteen secular priests and no Franciscans, the last one having died five years before.[24]

Since most of these secular priests were to become involved in some of the future crises in the vicar's career, their respective persons bear identification. First, there were José Francisco Leyva y Rosas and José Vicente Montaño, the only Mexico-born *curas* left. Of the older New Mexico na-

---

[21] Patentes, XXIX; Accounts, C-1, *AASF*.

[22] Accounts, C-1, *AASF*.

[23] A. Chávez, "A Nineteenth-Century New Mexico Schism," *NMHR*, (January 1983), 35-54.

[24] A. Chávez, *But Time and Chance*, 79-80.

tives, there were the vicar himself and his two cousins, Fernando and Rafael Ortiz, besides the most assertive Antonio José Martínez of Taos. The others were all younger natives. Three of them have already been mentioned: José Tomás Abeytia, José Manuel Gallegos, and José de Jesús Luján. Four others were Antonio de Jesús Salazar, Juan de Jesús Trujillo, José de la Cruz Vigil, and Eulogio Váldez (the latter two fated to die within five years).

In this, his second visitation, Bishop Zubiría added two more recently ordained natives who had evidently accompanied him from Durango. They were José Antonio Otero and José de Jesús Cabeza de Baca, both of them from prominent families in the Río Abajo. The bishop also brought along a mature Franciscan with a learned background, Fray Mariano de Jesús López, for the purpose of reviving the ancient Franciscan custody of New Mexico. Unfortunately, the friar would pass away within two years or so.

From Zubiría's final instructions of July and August 1845, when as a parting note he urged the local clergy to re-read and carry out his long and detailed decrees of 1833, little has survived to gauge any resurgence in spirit among both clergy and people.[25] One solitary item mentions that a very old and almost defunct confraternity of the Blessed Sacrament, a religious lay group, now combined with a much older one of La Conquistadora, had just experienced a sharp revival. Its greatly augmented membership, with its list of paid dues, was headed by Governor Armijo and Vicar Ortiz.[26] By itself, a confraternity's revival does not indicate much in regard to a religious resurgence, but this strong attraction and adherence of the people to their pious organizations was to be a subject of severe criticism in the future by a foreign ecclesiastical regime.

In the year following Bishop Zubiría's return to Durango, Vicar Ortiz had another problem on his hands. The young Padre Luján, mentioned before, while temporarily without a parish and hence, according to the regulations of those times, without the faculties to hear the confessions of females, happened to be in Tomé when some women insisted upon his hearing their confessions. He finally acquiesced, subsequently feeling remorse for what he had done. He took his problem to the pastor, Padre C. de Baca. The latter could not absolve Luján for his foolish infraction of canon law, having to defer to the bishop for the proper faculties to do so. The matter must have come before the bishop who, according to an Ortiz letter of 5 February 1826, ordered Luján to travel to Santa Fe and there brush up on Church law under

---

[25] Loose documents, 1845, nos. 2 & 13, *AASF.*

[26] Accounts, LXXIX, *AASF.*

the vicar's supervision. Luján agreed and, after some weeks of study, was examined by Padres Gallegos and C. de Baca. Vicar Ortiz, heeding Luján's pleas, allowed him to say Mass on stated days, but withheld all other privileges until the bishop himself made a decision on the matter.[27] Years later, a foreign and unfriendly clergyman twisted this incident to make it a morals' case, with Ortiz as an accessory to Luján's alleged immoral lapse.[28]

In his role as vicar and assemblyman, Ortiz had more serious matters to worry about in this particular year of 1846. A far greater change than all those problems that he had experienced so far was in the offing. It was occasioned by the outbreak of war between the United States and Mexico and the subsequent American occupation of New Mexico which, over and above its own significance, provides a more intimate view of Vicar Ortiz.

For more than two decades, the people of New Mexico and their civil and church leaders, particularly in Santa Fe and Taos, had become acquainted with Anglo-Americans of every stripe. The influence of these newcomers to New Mexico had grown apace with the increase of trade on the Santa Fe Trail. Some of them settled in the region and became Mexican citizens, and a goodly number of them married native women. Through their social contacts and trade dealings with these *extranjeros*, or foreigners, Vicar Ortiz and his fellow countrymen had come to suspect that the American way of life had something to offer. While the Mexican Republic came first as a matter of sentiment, its succession of unstable governments had failed them in their hopes, economic and otherwise.

Yet there was a lurking suspicion or fear that the United States, which they looked upon as a bigoted Protestant nation, would suppress their ancestral Catholic religion. Their civic leaders, knowing how certain resident *Americanos* showed more vim and know-how in civic and economic enterprise, rightly feared that under United States rule the newcomers would make themselves masters of their land in every way. This serves to explain the conduct of Vicar Ortiz and his compatriots in 1846 and the years immediately following. Subsequent events and the written observations of some Anglo-Americans at the time help sketch a vivid image of the vicar and his people as these new arrivals saw them.

The year 1846 had started out normally enough in Santa Fe. But by summer, Ortiz had most alarming news for New Mexico's pastors. On 4 July (a date that certainly had meaning to him), he warned his priests that United

---

[27] Ibid.
[28] See pages 194-195 herein.

States' forces were already in "Texas" and would soon be invading New Mexico. On 7 August, Ortiz wrote his priests that the American troops were already at the gates. Some of the priests, he noted, had already started to leave New Mexico for this reason, and he pleaded with the others to remain with their flocks.[29] However, judging by the parish records, it looks as though none of the padres fled for any appreciable length of time.

On 10 August, Governor Armijo asked Ortiz for money from the funds of pious societies so he could feed his own troops. Ortiz replied that the only two confraternities left, the combined Blessed Sacrament and La Conquistadora, had only 400 *pesos* that had already been lent (most likely to Armijo). He personally could give the governor the only 261 *pesos* that he had in cash. He also mentioned what could be raised from the sale of a dozen silver trays with their lids that he owned, as well as from 1300 sheep and 150 head of cattle (whether his or belonging to the parish). All of it, he wrote his governor, would be donated "for the independence and liberty of the Mexican nation."[30] Ortiz probably did not know that just seventeen years before his birth, or 66 years before he wrote his offer to protect Mexican independence, New Mexico, including his own ancestors, had paid a tax to help win the independence of the United States.[31]

Vicar Ortiz's offer was never fulfilled, for within a week of Armijo's request, Brigadier General Stephen Watts Kearny, the Commander of the United States Army of the West, entered Santa Fe unopposed and his men raised their national flag in front of the Palacio Nacional. This easy victory had come about because Governor Armijo, who had assured Vicar Ortiz and the citizens of Santa Fe that he would fight to the last man, had dismissed the civilian militia and fled south with his sixty regular dragoons. Armijo was later accused of having accepted a large bribe in the capital from an American merchant named James Magoffin. Representatives of the United States had visited Governor Armijo on more than one occasion. As soon as news of the outbreak of the war reached Santa Fe, Manuel Álvarez, the United States consul, visited the governor to convince him to capitulate, but he had little success with Armijo. Magoffin and Captain Philip St. George Cooke

---

[29] Accounts, C-1, *AASF*.

[30] Accounts, LXXVI, *AASF*.

[31] Cavallero de Croix to Governor Juan Bautista de Anza, 12 August 1781, no. 827, Microfilm roll 11, frames 272-74; and Felipe de Neve to Anza, 16 January 1783, no. 850, Micorfilm roll 11, frame 511, and Neve to Anza, 14 January 1783, no. 850a, Microfilm roll 11, frame 621, *Spanish Archives of New Mexico* (*SANM*), NMSCRA.

then visited Armijo under a flag of truce. The two emissaries of Kearny, whose well-equipped army was then marching toward Santa Fe, delivered a conciliatory letter on the afternoon of 12 August 1846. That night another secret meeting was held that included Armijo, Álvarez, and Henry Connelly, a Santa Fe Trail merchant. None of these men ever alluded to a bribe being delivered as legend has stated. Connelly described Armijo as being "in painful doubt and irresolution."[32]

Whatever the motive, Armijo's action prevented the slaughter of many of his poorly armed countrymen by the modern rifles and field pieces of the American troops. On 20 August he gave a reason for his capitulation in a letter from Manzano to Mexican Colonel Mauricio Ugarte who was in El Paso del Norte.

> ...all the other soldiers (the local militia) have turned against
> me...with respect to the people of the department, I believe
> that in general they are pro-American.[33]

Armijo could have been telling the truth. Colonel Ugarte himself reported three days later on Armijo's message saying that the clergy, all the political and judicial authorities, and the troops who had surrendered had sworn solemn obedience to the new government.[34] Consul Álvarez reported to his superiors that he found the Mexican officials other than the governor, and especially his advisors, disposed to surrender. He further wrote that the underlings, "not holding such high places, nor so responsible commissions and yet exposed to the same dangers, were rather easily won over."[35]

Nevertheless, Vicar Ortiz must have been stunned by Armijo's turnabout even as his genteel clerical heart began quaking with fearful apprehension. The vicar fled Santa Fe after having begged his priests ten days before not to flee the country! And yet, only a few days earlier, when he had

---

[32] T. Chávez, *Álvarez*, 108; T. Chávez, "Don Manuel Álvarez (de las Abelgas): Multi-talented Merchant of New Mexico," *Journal of the West*, (January 1979), 28; and Henry C. Connelly, 29 September 1848, as quoted in William A. Keleher, *Turmoil in New Mexico, 1846-1868* (Santa Fe: The Rydal Press, 1952), 31.

[33] As quoted in George Rutledge Gibson, *Journal of A Soldier Under Kearny and Doniphan, 1846-47*, Southwest Historical Series, Vol. IV, Ralph P. Beiber, editor (Glendale: The Arthur H. Clark Co., 1935), 201-02, n 345.

[34] Ibid.; and Bloom, "Mexican Administration," *OSF*, Vol. II, 366-79.

[35] Manuel Álvarez to Secretary of State James Buchanan, 4 September 1846, Consular Dispatches, Santa Fe, Records of the Department of State, Record Group 59, National Archives (Microfilm copy in the Fray Angélico Chávez Library, Palace of the Governors, Santa Fe).

hoisted the American flag at Las Vegas, General Kearny assured the people that his country respected all religions, and hence that their faith would not only be left undisturbed but fully protected as well. This is what George R. Gibson, one of Kearny's men, wrote on 20 August 1846: "The principal priest returned this evening, having fled to the mountains [very likely Río de Tesuque]. He is a fat jolly fellow... ."[36]

Lieutenant William W. Emory, a topographical engineer who traveled to New Mexico after Kearny, related the same incident later at greater length:

> The same afternoon, just as twilight closed, the vicar of the department, a huge lump of fat, who had fled with Armijo, came puffing into town, and soon presented himself to the general. The interview was amusing. His holiness was accompanied by two young priests [his assistant Padre Luján and perhaps his seminarian half-brother, Eulogio Ortiz]; one of them showed the highest state of alarm and agitation. The vicar assured the general he had been persuaded to run off by the women of his family [step-mother Gertrudis Pino and half-sister Ana María Ortiz]. The general told him, sharply, he thought it would have been much more in keeping with his office to stand by his flock, than listen to the unreasonable fears of two women. He then told the general that at another time he would give him the reason for running away on the approach of the American army.[37]

What explanation Vicar Ortiz gave Kearny later, if he did indeed give a reason is unknown. Perhaps he and the much younger clerics had feared that they would be promptly executed by the bigoted soldiers, something that they knew had happened in Mexico at the hands of certain revolutionaries. Soon they were to discover that Kearny's men consisted of quite a large number of Catholics, including some of the officers. Kearny himself betrayed a sense of kindly humor in his interview with Vicar Ortiz and, despite its touch of sarcasm, he and the Vicar became good friends. There can be no doubt that the latter invited the general to his house for a good dinner and repeated toasts. It was the same Spanish conviviality that, as shall be described in the sketch of Padre Leyba y Rosas, Kearny had experienced days before at San Miguel del Vado.

---

[36] Gibson, *Journal*, 214-15.

[37] Ibid., 215n.

The day after Ortiz's first meeting with Kearny, the general, although not a Catholic as one might expect from his Gaelic surname, went to Sunday mass held at the old *parroquia,* parish church, of San Francisco with a large number of his officers and enlisted men. These could have been mostly Catholic, since in every war from those times to this day, the American Catholic "minority" has furnished U. S. combat units with at least a third of the officers and men. Kearny wanted to demonstrate to the local populace that Catholicism not only existed in the United States but that he and his non-Catholic officers were also religiously tolerant. But the incident is of particular interest here because of what was said about Vicar Ortiz. Henry Smith Turner penned this rather confused account:

> The mass was performed by the vicar, a large fat looking man *and he is grossly misrepresented by rumor:* it seems a desecration of the temple of God, that such men be permitted to officiate as priests: but these people [the clergy] may be misrepresented – that they are pure I scarcely believe *yet they may not be so abandoned as they are said to be* – the reports we receive are *from ignorant [civilian] Americans generally, with whom want of veracity and violent prejudice are the conspicuous trait of their character. A truthful American is rarely seen here.*[38]

The italics are added to point out the cruel gossip rampant among certain puritanical American civilians in Santa Fe about the native clergy – what Bishop Lamy and his aide Father Machebeuf promptly picked up five years later after the arrival in New Mexico. At the same time, the comments illustrate the confusion of an earnest and honest soldier in his initial contact with his civilian countrymen in a strange land. American military observers were generally more objective and free of bigotry than their civilian counterparts, and therefore that much more believable even when their comments are not quite flattering.

Evidently referring to the same occasion, Captain St. George Cooke noted, "There was some music, of violin and triangle, and no spoken service."[39] Here he was referring to the mumbled Latin mass without a sermon to the congregation. The latter was to be one criticism later used by Bishop Lamy

---

[38] Henry Smith Turner, *The Original Journals of Henry Smith Turner with Stephen Watts Kearny to New Mexico and California, 1846,* Dwight L. Clarke, editor (Norman: The University of Oklahoma Press, 1966), 73

[39] Gibson, *Journal,* 218n.

against Vicar Ortiz that he preached only once a year for a large fee. (This meant at the patron feast of St. Francis in October.) For, sad to say, preaching in New Mexico had in places died out earlier, chiefly due to the fact that the old Franciscans had replaced it with catechetical instructions to their Indian congregations outside of Mass. Still, this was not excuse enough for omitting instructive sermons from the Spanish folk. It seems as though the secular clergy from Durango and the newer native priests had also ignored the practice, except for Padre Martínez of Taos, who made himself deservedly popular as a constant orator.[40] Furthermore, since Sunday collections were unknown, the pastor took a cut of the collection taken up for the annual parish fiesta. Hence, this is where Bishop Lamy, as will be seen, was wrong in attributing the practice to Vicar Ortiz alone.

Unbeknownst to himself, Vicar Ortiz continued to be the subject of further portraitures, which would have less value had he assumed a pose. On 30 August 1846, General Kearny once again attended Sunday Mass with some of his men. According to Lieutenant Emory, the officiator was "a very grave, respectable looking person, of fair complexion." By now he had revised his initial estimate of "a lump of fat." He also commented that the music was good, of two violins and a guitar, and was the same tunes heard at the *fandangos* or dances, "but not a word was uttered from the pulpit by the priest, who kept his back to the audience, the whole time uttering prayers."[41] Interestingly enough, four days later Lieutenant Emory likewise described the gracious pastor at Santo Domingo (who was the vicar's first cousin, Rafael Ortiz) as "a fat old white man." Apparently, obesity as well as fair complexions seem to have run within the immediate clan.[42]

Elsewhere, the same lieutenant made this observation regarding the Santa Fe vicar:

> The priest, who was a very grave respectable person, of fair complexion, commenced the service by sprinkling holy water over the congregation [The Asperges before Mass]. When abreast of the general, he extended his silver waterspout [the aspergillum] and gave him a handful.[43]

[40] A. Chávez, *But Time and Chance*, 31 & 41.

[41] Ibid.; and William H. Emory, *Notes of a Military Reconnoissance [sic] From Fort Leavenworth, in Missouri to San Diego in California...* (Washington, D. C.: Wendell and Van Benthuysen, Printers, 1848), 34.

[42] Emory, *Notes*, 38.

[43] Gibson, *Journal*, 227; and Emory as quoted in Gibson, 227-28n. For a slightly different version of Emory's quote see Emory, *Notes*, 34.

This rite had come down from Spanish church-state times when the royal governor even had a special throne near the altar. In New Mexico, contrary to the Mexican government's secularism, the ritual seems to have been carried over to the republican governors for Vicar Ortiz to continue rendering the ancient royal honor to Kearny as the current "chief executive." Then Emory continued:

> Though not a word was uttered, the whole service was grave and impressive; and I thought it was the very religion for the people present; and much more decent and worthy of God's temple, than many of the ranting, howling discourse we have at home. All appeared to have just left their work to come to church. There was no fine dressing or personal display that will not be seen on weekdays. Indeed, on returning from church, we found all the stores open, and the market women selling their melons and plums, as usual.[44]

All of this had shocked the puritanism of the Anglo-American civilians, but for Vicar Ortiz and his faithful who did not have a Reformation past, the freedom of the New Testament had not been supplanted by the strict restrictions of the Hebrew Testament to which Protestantism had reverted. Nor was one's "Sunday's best" obligatory for these people when confronting the Lord at worship. Henry Turner also noticed this when he went to church, remarking that the place was very crowded:

> The Mexican portion of the congregation, women, especially, appear devout. Everything very difficult to comprehend considering the dissolute character of the life they lead [according to his civilian compatriots]. Not one woman in the church is supposed to be virtuous – still everyone performed their religion with apparent devotion...[45]

Josiah Gregg had made a similar observation some years before, namely, that no people were "more punctual" in attending public worship and performing the external rites of religion:

> ...they had to hear Mass before undertaking a journey, but the religious exercises seldom had the character of true devotion, since folks tittered and chattered in the act of crossing themselves or at formal prayer.[46]

---

[44] Ibid.

[45] Turner, *Journals*, 75.

[46] Gregg, *Commerce of the Prairies*, 179.

Here civilian Gregg's puritanical pants were showing, while military Turner's estimate of the vicar and the common people was more objective, even if confused by what he was hearing from his own countrymen.

There is still more about Vicar Ortiz. Two days before the Mass described on 28 August 1846, General Kearny had given a ball. The people did not begin arriving until the church bells gave the signal, and from four to five hundred people attended, which indicates that it must have been held outside, on the town plaza. This unholy association of church bells and a worldly dance must have shocked observer George Gibson, who commented:

> Amongst them [was] the principal priest, who received great attention from the general, who no doubt sought this opportunity to satisfy the Church, the great lever in Mexico by which all important transactions are effected.[47]

Gibson, who seems to have acted as chaplain to the troops, was most unfair to General Kearny who seems to have had more of an Anglican view of things and therefore was not using religion for political ends. Gibson himself, who incidentally always referred to the natives as "Spaniards," was echoing Josiah Gregg's general notion that they were entirely priest-ridden, while implicitly shocked by the sight of a priest in his black cassock punctuating such an unchurchly spectacle as a public dance. Young Mrs. Susan Magoffin, a delicate Protestant military wife who, like Turner, was also disturbed by the anti-Mexican and anti-Catholic gossip in Santa Fe, left a distaff view of the vicar that is not so much catty or cruel as it sounds, given the context of her entire diary. This was at another ball held on 11 September given by the army officers and the leading native and American citizens. Vicar Ortiz likewise attended as Mrs. Magoffin described:

> El Señor Vicario was there to grace the gay halls with his priestly robes [the black cassock] – he is a man rather short of stature, but that is made up in width, which not a little care for the stomach lends a hand in completing the man.[48]

With such a disadvantage, Vicar Ortiz must never have participated in the dancing itself, as some younger padres were accused of doing. But one must keep in mind that these were communal folk dances. Gregg himself had observed during the years 1831-1840 that the priests attended the *fan-*

---

[47] Gibson, *Journal*, 225.

[48] Susan Shelby Magoffin, *Down the Santa Fe Trail and into Mexico*, Stella Drumm, editor (New Haven: Yale University Press, 1926), 119.

dangos and *bailes,* and, to his credit, he did not impugn their sexual mores.[49] Gibson, who merely repeated what he heard, brought in the clergy:

> The priests, who are of the people, share all their vices and
> virtues. They are generally present at fandangos and pay
> their compliments to the ladies like other Christians, and
> get disgustingly tipsy. In fact a priest present at this affair
> collapsed from drunkenness while dancing. They picked
> him up and took him to the door, where he eased his heart
> by a simple operation and then went home.[50]

This was only hearsay, but even if such a padre had acted in that way, it could not have been Vicar Ortiz who, besides being too unwieldy to trip the light fantastic, was well used to his El Paso wines and brandies. Moreover, Gibson and his fellows had seen only four New Mexico padres since their arrival. Hence his sweeping condemnation of all the clergy belongs strictly to the general anticlerical prejudices of their civilian countrymen. As for the specific incident in Santa Fe that could have been true, it had to be a younger fellow who perhaps had been plied with liquor then being distilled in Arroyo Hondo north of Taos, and popularly known as Taos Lightning. Drunkenness at this time was not a problem among the native people, as Gregg himself admitted, writing that the New Mexicans (the *ricos* only) used but little wine at meals, an exclusive product of El Paso del Norte. He added that they were "little addicted to inebriety and its attending dissipations" and noted later in his book, the high cost of spirituous liquors that placed them beyond reach of the lower classes.[51]

We know that New Mexico had produced no wines thus far because the grapevines that Father Francisco Domínguez had observed back in 1776 did not survive the cold, dry winters. But now, Gregg testified that the local

---

[49] Gregg, *Commerce of the Prairies,* 170.

[50] Gibson, *Journal,* fnt., 217.

[51] Gregg, *Commerce of the Prairies,* 110-11, 171. For "Taos Lightning," see Janet Lecompte, *Pueblo, Hardscrabble, Greenhorn: The Upper Arkansas, 1832-1856* (Norman: University of Oklahoma Press, 1978), 78-88. Most of the whiskey came from the distillery of Simon Turley who traveled to Taos in 1830. Shortly afterward he opened a store and distillery on Arroyo Hondo Creek, some twelve miles north of Taos. Prior to the Mexican War, Turley was primarily selling liquor on the upper Arkansas River to traders to use to their advantage in the Indian trade. Although more research needs to be done it appears that the American "grog shops" invigorated Turley's sagging business and made him one of New Mexico's richest men at the time.

vines were being pruned like shrubs and then covered up with earthen mounds during winter weather, instead of being strung out on supports. This new practice, which was conceived by some nameless genius (perhaps a French Canadian who traveled to New Mexico earlier), presaged a future wine industry that had just begun at Bernalillo as noted by Lieutenant John Abert. Zebulon Montgomery Pike, while under house arrest in 1807, noted vineyards all around Albuquerque. This same officer observed that the native people, while they were inveterate gamblers, were extremely temperate with regard to meat and drink, and that the worst insult for anyone was to be called a drunkard, a *borrachón*.[52]

Returning to Gibson's views about the priests' and people's vices, Henry Turner repeated his story in a letter to his Catholic wife:

> I have no respect for the priesthood in this country, and I think it a desecration of God's temple, that a priest of New Mexico should be permitted to officiate in one. I have learned that the church of New Mexico had been excommunicated [another piece of outlandish gossip!]. I hope the information is not correct, if one-half of what is reported of the priesthood is true. It is notorious [!] that they are the greatest debauchers, gamblers, and drunkards of the community. A priest at a fandango, a few evenings ago, became so much intoxicated as to fall from his seat. The practice of the priesthood of this country is no reflection whatever on the Catholic religion, because they corrupt it does not follow that the church is so, unless they are upheld and sustained by the church in this corruption.[53]

Here, obviously, Turner's closing remarks were meant to assuage his wife. The entire paragraph is quoted to show the kind of anti-native gossip, which was rampant at the time in the middle of the nineteenth century among American civilians, and something that now had overwhelmed his credulity. His sweeping statements show how much he had departed from his first doubts concerning the credibility of his countrymen.

But if drunkenness was not a grave problem in New Mexico at the time, gambling was an inveterate habit among all classes, rich and poor, and even the young. Nor were the clergy exempt. When Gibson first described Vicar

---

[52] Lieutenant John W. Abert, as quoted in Emory, 455n & 464n.

[53] Turner, *Journals*, 142.

Ortiz as a fat fellow, he also added that he "bets high at *monte*, loves good liquor, and attends all the *fandangos* of the respectable people and public places."[54] Lieutenant Abert, as has been seen, observed that all the natives were inveterate gamblers, though free of the vice of drunkenness, while W. W. H. Davis, another visitor from the United States, also remarked that, "Gambling in its variety, prevails to an alarming extent among all classes of people...."[55] Gibson had been surprised to see a Jew frequenting the gambling tables, going on to say that "Here they have no such things as professional gamblers, for all classes are addicted to this vice, and there is nothing disreputable about it."[56] Young Richard Elliott had a different observation. Nine months after Kearny's entry into New Mexico's capital, he noted that many "grog-shops" had opened and he added,

> Many of the grog-shops and gambling 'hells,' are kept by enlisted soldiers! Others have soldiers for their barkeepers and attendants! Gambling tables are kept by officers of the army for soldiers to bet at! So we go; and these things are all known to the commanding officer!

Elliott then concluded,

> We have actually, as to morals and manners, become contemptible in the eyes of this most contemptible of all people – the Mexicans![57]

The correspondent could only compare his indignation over his colleagues to the only thing his bigoted mind's eye thought worse. And this was published in a St. Louis newspaper, the *Daily Reveille*.

From all these reports, it is quite obvious that those gentlemen with money, whether native or newcomers, frequented the *monte* games at the saloon of the famed Gertrudis Barceló, among others. Meanwhile the local folk livened up their otherwise dull lives, even on Sundays to the Puritans' discomfiture, with their betting at games that Gregg named for posterity: *los gallos, el coleo,* and *los toros.*[58] The first were the ordinary cockfights, or else a contest on horseback which Indians now call "chicken-pull." The sec-

---

[54] Gibson, *Journal*, 214-15.

[55] W. W. H. Davis, *El Gringo or New Mexico & Her People* (Santa Fe: The Rydal Press, 1938, originally published in 1857), 56-57.

[56] Gibson, *Journal*, 268.

[57] Elliott to the Editors of *The St. Louis Daily Reveille*, 29 April 1847, in War Correspondence, 187-88. Printed in the *Daily Reveille* on 2 June 1847.

[58] Gregg, *Commerce of the Prairies*, 167-80.

ond was the bulldozing of steers by twisting their tails, a forerunner of the modern rodeo method of twisting the neck instead. The third was the turning loose of bulls for "teasing," something like the famed bull-runs of Pamplona in Spain, now annually mimicked in the Pueblo of Jémez. Much more common, for being so simple, was a game called *mitotes*, a word of Indian origin, which appears in old documents. The name was used for a type of dance as well as a game played with reeds, possibly cast in the manner of dice. Historians have been unable to identify the game further. It took the place of *naipes*, or Spanish cards, which the poor could not afford.

It is doubtful that Vicar Ortiz ever bet at these coarser types of entertainment, but sufficient evidence tells us that he did place his chips at the Barceló *monte* tables on occasion. Gibson and Emory both left accounts, besides one by G. Douglas Brewerton, which requires its own treatment later on. Nor was it such a damaging indictment, since for the vicar and his priests, gambling was not proscribed in scripture. As to his personal character, Gibson provides a subsequent appraisal: "This evening with Mr. Giddings, I called upon the priest, who received us kindly, and found him agreeable. He is the fat, jolly fellow mentioned in a preceding page, and talks as if he snuffed to excess or was burdened with the flesh."[59] This was a left-handed compliment, but a change in Gibson's attitude.

An interesting item that Gibson also records is the funeral that took place on 3 November 1846 of a young "Spaniard" who had been a cadet at the Chihuahua military school and who was buried with military honors by the American soldiers. This was a generous gesture to a fellow soldier that is so typical of the American military spirit to this day. "The procession was unusually large, headed by the priest [Ortiz] in his robes in the usual Catholic style, the first time I had seen him heading a funeral."[60] The deceased cadet, according to the Santa Fe burial records, was one Ignacio Sena, who was interred inside the old chapel of San Miguel, the total fee being thirty *pesos* for this extra privilege. Gibson's last mention of the vicar is on 22 November 1846, when referring to a "theater" put on by the military at the Government Palace. "The *vicario* was present, as well as many of the best women, all of whom enjoyed it."[61]

---

[59] Gibson, *Journal*, 254.

[60] Ibid., 265-67. Gibson may have been confused about where the Mexican military school was located. In this case, not in Chihuahua but in Chapultepec in Mexico City.

[61] Ibid., 273-74.

Concerning the vicar's alleged gambling, we bring up an outlandish account if only to expose it for the fiction that it was – and is. G. Douglas Brewerton, who claimed to have passed through New Mexico at this time in late 1846 and 1847, wrote an account that was published six years later in *Harper's Magazine*.[62] From a brief biography of the author in a modern edition of his work and no less from the tone of his writing, one can tell that he was giving full play to his imagination as much as to his personal prejudice. With reference to Santa Fe's gambling saloon, he said that most noticeable at the gambling table sat, "a Mexican priest who, in clerical garb of his order, with cross and rosary most conspicuously displayed," was engrossed in a game of chance; moreover, his bad luck was marked by "oaths as shocking and blasphemous as ever issued from human lips," and so forth.

Now Brewerton did not know enough Spanish to make this last assessment, nor did he realize that a secular priest wore only a plain black cassock without any dangling cross and rosary of whatever size. He had made up similar fictions in other northern towns and, as in this case, had the padres wearing the garb of Franciscan friars when these had already disappeared from the scene. Evidently, Brewerton conjured up engravings that he might have seen of friars like Friar Tuck in the tales of Robin Hood, and concluded that all priests dressed that way.[63]

To sum up, at this significant American juncture, Don Juan Felipe Ortiz was indeed a short, stout man, his obesity striking different observers in different ways, with most of them also noting that he was jolly and agreeable. His native contemporary and friend, Don Francisco Perea, remembered him as a red-headed gentleman noted for his most friendly and agreeable disposition.[64] As has been demonstrated thus far, neither his obesity nor his easy-going nature had stood in the way of his many duties, whether civil or vicarial. Under these fleshly and jolly aspects he had his dignity and other laudable qualities whereby he commanded the complete trust of Bishop Zubiría along with the reverence and affection of all kinds of persons of good will.

Appearances aside, Ortiz was a New Mexican who had received an education in distant Durango and returned to his homeland to minister to his own people. He was a good priest and obviously built upon his family's

---

[62] G. Douglas Brewerton, "Incidents of Travel in New Mexico," *Harper's Monthly Magazine* (April 1854), 589.

[63] Ibid.

[64] Bloom, "Mexican Administration," *OSF*, Vol. II, 181

support for the humble Church in New Mexico. While the distant observer is tempted to see this man through the ethnocentric views of men like Gregg, his humility and his ability to work among his people are evident in his attendance at social as well as ecclesiastical functions. No stretch of the imagination is needed to picture this man comfortably walking among the flat-roofed adobe structures and along the often dusty and muddy streets of Santa Fe. He would not progress very far in his hometown, for he knew everyone and everyone knew him. He lived in a town that one traveler described as looking like a fleet of flat bottom boats on the Mississippi River. The population ranged from two to three thousand people, a very miniscule portion of whom were from the United States. Padre Ortiz, with his natural personality, could easily converse with virtually anyone in Santa Fe not only about mundane maters like the weather but also about relatives, friends, and probably every failure and success of anyone whomever. He was, in short, an integral part of the community despite his travel and education.

The vicar's relationship with the new American government was of far more importance than his personal characteristics. Within ten days after his peaceful entry into Santa Fe on 18 August 1846, General Kearny had set up a semi-civil regime under a military code that bears his name. He then appointed as governor a Santa Fe Trail merchant named Charles Bent along with a staff made up of native as well as Anglo-American officials. Bent was a long-time trader, resident of Taos, former business partner of ex-Governor Armijo, and married to a member of the Taos Jaramillo family. It is at this time that Vicar Ortiz wrote Bent a note of felicitation on his appointment, with gracious thanks for some unspecified favors that he had received from the new governor.[65] No doubt, in conjunction with most of all the native leaders, he had already become an American citizen by swearing allegiance to the United States. All this was during the period of peace and contentment that reigned in the capital when the American military had little else to do than put on skits and attend balls with the local gentry.

While involved in these same activities, Ortiz attended his duties as vicar as if nothing unusual had happened. On 17 September 1846, after receiving some minor complaints from the Isleta Indians against their pastor, he delegated Padre Gallegos of Albuquerque to look into the matter. The

---

[65] Accounts, LXXVI, *AASF*. For Bent's marriage see David Lavender, Bent's Fort (Lincoln: University of Nebraska Press, 1954) 176 and 421, n 13. No records exist of his marriage. He was living with Maria Ignacia Jaramillo and had a son by her. Clearly, in his mind, he was married to her.

pastor at Isleta was Padre Mariano López, a lone Franciscan whom Bishop Zubiría had brought the year before with the hope of restoring the New Mexico custody of Franciscans. Fray López would not last more than two years before his death. In this connection, it is of interest to note that López had sent Ortiz some old mission registers because, he wrote, the old Franciscan archive at Santo Domingo no longer existed.[66] There are also indications that just prior to the American occupation, Ortiz had finished making some repairs on his *parroquia*, for, according to later testimonies, the *Castrense* chapel on the plaza's south side had been serving as a surrogate parish church for some time prior to Kearny's arrival.[67] Ortiz had made some earlier renovations right after he became vicar in 1832. He moved into the 135-year old convent attached to the south side of the *parroquia*. No doubt the building was not up to the standards of Ortiz's tastes, so it was probably at this time that the convent and church were disconnected, an act that required the demolition of the convent's entire northern section and leaving an open space between the two buildings.[68] In any event, these earlier renovations were completed by 1846. Lieutenant J. W. Abert described the residence as "having a fine portail (sic)" in front and as "one of the best dwelling houses in the city."[69] His 1846 drawing of the *parroquia* shows a part of the residence with a fenced portal and white washed-facing wall. Three years later Richard H. Kern made a drawing from basically the same angle. While the latter's church is not as clean lined and somewhat run down, the portion of the residence that is depicted looks to be in very good shape. The fence no longer exists, but the other features conform to Abert's drawing.[70]

Meanwhile, General Kearny left for California with his staff and some of his soldiers, leaving a strong garrison in Santa Fe. His stops at the different Río Abajo parishes as he traveled south along the Río Grande were marked by the same good will among the pastors and people that existed in the capital. But then something most dramatic happened to disturb the peace as

[66] Accounts, C-1; M-19, Isleta, (end of book), *AASF*.

[67] James H. Defouri, *Historical Sketch of the Catholic Church in New Mexico* (San Francisco: The McCormick Brothers, 1887), 51-52; and Ellis, *Lamy's Cathedral*, 88-89.

[68] Ellis, *Lamy's Cathedral*, 88-89.

[69] Abert as quoted in Emory, 455n. For Abert's drawing of the parroquia, see 454, facing.

[70] Both Abert's and Kern's drawings are in David J. Weber, *Richard H. Kern: Expeditionary Artist in the Far Southwest, 1848-1853* (Albuquerque: University of New Mexico Press, 1985), 138 & 58.

the year of 1846 drew to its end. It could have been a bloody disturbance had it not been nipped in the bud by Governor Bent and Colonel Sterling Price, the garrison's commander, and, some say, through Doña Gertrudis Barceló, who picked up all kinds of talk at her gambling bistro.

It turned out that some prominent citizens, as well as some young hot-headed *caballeros* who had declined to swear allegiance to the new country, had been plotting to overthrow Kearny's government at Christmas. They would kill all the Anglo-American civilians in Santa Fe as well as the native officials allied with them. They were heedless of the fact that they stood no chance with the well-armed American garrison if their insurrection took place. Chief among these resistors were Diego Archuleta, Armijo's quite able protégé mentioned earlier, who expected to become the new general, and Tomás Ortiz, the vicar's much younger half-brother who envisioned himself as the new governor. These citizens of Mexico correctly considered themselves at war with a foreign occupying force. They planned a revolt for December, but it aborted when word leaked out and Archuleta and Ortiz fled south.[71]

Because of his half-brother's part in the plot, Vicar Ortiz had a share in it in the minds of the accusatory Anglo-American civilians, a not uncommon mistaken assumption based simply on blood relationship. Tomás Ortiz was not only a younger brother by different mother, but, like his fellow-plotter Archuleta, he is said to have graduated from the Chapultepec Military Academy in Mexico City. This alone would make a radical difference in the outlook of both men. In one of historian Ralph Emerson Twitchell's questionable footnotes, several other young men are named, along with the old Mexico-born Padre Leyba of San Miguel del Vado, as having met in the vicar's own residence to concoct the bloody strategy. Twitchell's source was the reminiscences of a very old man.[72] Similar to this are some of the recollections of old Don Demetrio Pérez concerning Bishop Lamy's arrival in Santa Fe that will be discussed later.

A more likely scenario is that the followers of Archuleta and Ortiz, besides some other worthy youngsters caught up in patriotic fever, felt that they had nothing to lose. What is more, they became allied with a group of men in Taos and Chimayó who believed as they did and had planned and effected a similar uprising against the local government nine years earlier.

---

[71] Ralph E. Twitchell, *The History of the Military Occupation of New Mexico, 1846-51* (Denver: Smith-Books, Co., 1909), passim; and T. Chávez, "Álvarez," JOW, 29.

[72] Twitchell, *Leading Facts*, Vol. II, 232-33n.

The plot was discovered in time, while the main conspirators made their escape. Later rumors had it that Tomás Ortiz was seen sneaking away from the vicar's house. If this is true, it could mean that he had been hiding under the protection of his mother, Gertrudis Pino, and his sibling Anamaría Ortiz, both of whom lived with the vicar.

The remaining conspirators revised their plans, which bore fruit in January 1847, when Kearny's appointed governor, Charles Bent, was assassinated in his home in Taos. Bent's Jaramillo brother-in-law and four others also died violently in the Taos area. Simultaneous revolts broke out in Arroyo Hondo north of Taos and in Mora north of Las Vegas. With news of the violence, Colonel Price marched his army north from Santa Fe over the snow-covered trail to Taos. He encountered organized resistance at La Cañada and Embudo and eventually defeated the Taos resistors in a violent battle at Taos Pueblo.

The apprehended resistors were brought to trial in Taos and Santa Fe. The assassins of Bent and the others were tried for treason. Fifteen men were hanged and more might have received the same fate had it not been for an objection to the process. Padre Martínez questioned how Mexican citizens could be charged for treason when they were resisting an occupying force during a state of war. On 12 April 1847, Padre Martínez wrote to Manuel Álvarez, the former United States Consul in Santa Fe, complaining of the lack of justice and asking the ex-consul to petition Colonel Price on behalf of the accused.[73] The question of the propriety of conviction for treason went all the way from New Mexico to Washington, D. C. before Colonel Price was instructed to use some discretion. As a result no more executions were held.[74] In Santa Fe, the American officer who been appointed the defense attorney succeeded in convincing the courts that the plotters had in their minds acted as sincere patriots of their native country rather than as traitors with regard to the United States.[75]

Lewis H. Garrard, a teenager from Cincinnati, Ohio, arrived in Taos just in time to witness the trials. Traveling for his health, his sense of fairness suffered no malady, for he wrote in disgust about the initial convictions: "Treason, indeed! What did the poor devil know about his new allegiance?"

---

[73] T. Chávez, "Álvarez," JOW, 29; and Padre Antonio Martínez to Manuel Álvarez, 12 April 1847, no. 182, The Benjamin Read Collection, NMSRCA.

[74] T. Chávez, "Álvarez," JOW, 29; T. Chávez, Álvarez, 113-14; and E. Bennett Burton, "The Taos Rebellion," OSF, Vol. I, 176-209.

[75] A. Chávez, But Time and Chance, 82-86.

He further wrote that he left the courtroom "sick at heart," and added, "Justice! Out upon the word, when its distorted meaning is the warrant for murdering those who defend to the last [their] country and their homes."[76]

Gossip against some of the native priests continued apace in connection with the plot. Besides Padre Leyba, already mentioned, there were Padre Martínez and Padre Gallegos as well as Vicar Ortiz, all of whom had been completely absolved of all blame for complete lack of proof by the above-mentioned trials. What lent strength to the false accusations, no doubt, was the fact that these four clergymen had been outstanding members of New Mexico's Assembly under Mexico prior to Kearny's arrival. Moreover, even some native politicians were still blaming Padre Martínez unjustly for having instigated the bloody revolt of the Chimayosos and Taoseños in 1837. After the outbreak of violence in Taos, the local scuttlebutt had Padre Martínez behind the whole thing when, on the contrary, he had not only risked his life to stop it but housed Colonel Price and saved some lives. He also gained a lasting friendship of Colonel Price.[77]

Yet, the same rumors kept rolling apace and gathering new moss, contrary to the old saying. Some years later, Davis, who boarded with a Baptist minister when he first traveled to Santa Fe, wrote from what he heard in the local rumor mill, that Vicar Ortiz and Padre Gallegos had been the main plotters, while the other priests had been preaching open rebellion from the pulpits. Vicar Ortiz himself, under the pretext of celebrating the Guadalupe fiestas at La Joya in Río Arriba, had actually gone there to incite the people, as did Gallegos in Albuquerque.[78] As for the evolution of this furor, a basis can be found in a confusion of names alone. First, there had been a layman in the 1846-47 plot that resulted in Bent's death whose name was José Manuel Gallegos. Secondly, the priest at San Juan at the time was the vicar's cousin, Fernando Ortiz, who may or may not have expressed anti-American sentiments at his Guadalupe fiesta on 12 December.

Vicar Ortiz began the new year of 1847 with a letter to his clergy on 2 January 1847 containing nothing but spiritual counsels that were followed by other mundane circulars transmitting the Church directives from Durango. Nowhere is there so much as a hint on his part of his having been accused of sedition during the previous two weeks.[79] Meanwhile, Colonel Price had

---

[76] Lewis H. Garrard, *Wah-to-yah and the Taos Trail* (Norman: The University of Oklahoma Press, 1974), 172-73.

[77] Loose documents, 1847, nos. 1 & 2, *AASF*.

[78] Davis, *El Gringo*, 94-95 & 238; and Twitchell, *Military Occupation*, 175-80.

[79] A. Chávez, *But Time and Chance*, 87-88; and A. Chávez, "Schism," *NMHR*, 43.

appointed a native, Donaciano Vigil, to succeed the murdered Bent as interim governor, and here began a steadily growing problem with which Vicar Ortiz had to endure – not from any Protestant American civilians as such, but from some of his own Catholic *paisanos,* countrymen.

According to Twitchell, who does not specify the reason, Governor Vigil, a believer in United States' ideals, thought that the Mexican Church's influence needed to be curtailed. He even had the gall to suspend Ortiz from his church office. From Ortiz's reactions during Vigil's term, 1847-48, one surmises that Ortiz paid no heed to the governor's opinion or action. He well knew that Vigil had no authority, under the American form of government, to interfere in purely clerical affairs. But such had been the case with the old Spanish royal governors and the more recent Mexican *jefes.* What is more, Padre Martínez of Taos shared the same mentality despite his avowed enlightenment with regard to democratic principles of the American republic. Also, some local magistrates elsewhere were using their offices to meddle in parish matters. Worst of all, another major official by the name of Antonio José Otero, whom Kearny had appointed as one of New Mexico's three Territorial supreme court justices, would soon help create a schism of two parishes along the Río Abajo.[80]

With regard to Vigil's motive for suspension of Vicar Ortiz, there exists an indirect reference to the act from a response that Padre Martínez wrote to the governor. The letter concerned Padre Nicolás Valencia, the brash young fellow who first appeared demanding a parish from Vicar Ortiz in 1845. Some time after this, Bishop Zubiría while on his visitation had appointed Valencia the pastor of Belén for a trial period, but soon thereafter, following his return to Durango, the Bishop removed the young priest because of what he termed habitual disobedience. Valencia, however, continued functioning as Belén's pastor with the backing of the local magistrate and his council, who bodily expelled the bishop's new appointee, Padre José Antonio Otero. Nor could Vicar Ortiz enforce the bishop's will because of the opposition, presumably abetted by Vigil in the capital, although most of the parishioners sided with the bishop. The result was that Zubiría, through his vicar in Santa Fe, suspended Valencia from his priestly faculties, but this had no effect for the reasons given, and the vicar's troubles worsened.[81]

---

[80] Twitchell, *Military Occupation,* 221.

[81] For a more detailed story of Valencia's schismatic activities, see A. Chávez, "Schism," *NMHR,* 35-44.

Returning to Padre Martínez's answer to Vigil's query, he severely criticized Vicar Ortiz for being against canon law even though he was doing so in the bishop's name. Martínez also blamed the vicar for his handling of the Padre Abeytia case at Isleta some years earlier. All of this was because the proud Martínez who had always been envious of Ortiz's high office.[82]

Vicar Ortiz had no knowledge of Martínez' criticism. He also had no idea that the Valencia case would grow much more serious toward the end of 1849 when Valencia in Belén joined forces with another maverick priest from Mexico City who had recently arrived in the parish of Tomé across the river. This fellow, Benigno Cárdenas, first made his appearance in August 1847. On 6 September, Vicar Ortiz circulated a warning issued by the Franciscan Province of the Holy Gospel in Mexico City, stating that Cárdenas was an apostate and fugitive friar who should not be allowed to function as a priest. As a fugitive Cárdenas was under suspension and shorn of all his sacerdotal faculties by his Minister Provincial in Mexico. A nonconformist, Cárdenas obviously flouted church canons and regulations. Another warning came from Bishop Zubiría in November, who said that Cárdenas carried forged papers pretending to be from some other Mexican bishop. Zubiría also ordered him to leave New Mexico. In the meantime, the ex-friar had ingratiated himself with the magistrate and civil council of Tomé, which in turn ousted the lawful pastor, José C. de Baca. At the point when Vicar Ortiz seemed to be finding some recourse from some upright Americans in Santa Fe, Valencia joined forces with Cárdenas to create a schism in the Church. To make matters worse at this time, none other than Kearny's appointed chief justice, Antonio José Otero, confirmed the actions of the officials of Tomé and Belén. Ironically, this near namesake of Padre Otero also happened to be his first cousin.[83]

The whole affair was a losing battle for Vicar Ortiz even after Governor Vigil's term ended, when the reins of the civil-military government were assumed from late 1848 to the first months of 1851, first by Colonel John M. Washington and then by Colonel John Monroe. It was probably early in 1850 that Vicar Ortiz finally succeeded in ending the schism and in having Cárdenas expelled from the region. He accomplished this principally because he found help with an attorney named Richard R. Weightman who later, as a delegate to Congress in Washington, brought up the violations

---

[82] Ibid.

[83] Arie Poldervaart, "Black-Robed Justice in New Mexico, 1846-1912," *NMHR* (Vol. 22, 1947), 45; and Twitchell, *Military Occupation*, 175-80.

regarding the separation of church and state that had taken place in New Mexico. This same Mr. Weightman, who was a pugnacious lawyer later involved in a political killing, likewise provides a sharp picture of the entire affair of Tomé and Belén, including the un-American antics of Justice Otero. While he inveighed against Colonel Monroe, it is clear that he meant that the whole mess was started earlier by Governor Vigil.[84] Weightman was a staunch supporter of statehood for New Mexico while Justice Otero, Colonel Monroe, and Governor Vigil all advocated territorialism. The phenomenon of early American politics in New Mexico being mixed up with ecclesiastical matters in New Mexico is a subject that still needs study.[85]

Up to this point in his long career, our rotund vicar's life had been more than sedentary even as his gentlemanly ways and peaceful character were being tested to the limit. Bishop Zubiría in Durango was kept well apprised of events in New Mexico, always backing his vicar, and this appears to have been the main reason for undertaking his third arduous trip north to visit New Mexico in 1850. On 22 April, Vicar Ortiz transmitted some circulars from Durango, one of them bearing the news of the bishop's planned trip in May. Upon his arrival and throughout his personal inspection of all the parishes, Zubiría found little by way of improvements over what he had observed in 1833 and 1845. But his chief concern at this very time was repairing damage caused by those whom he termed the "schismatic" Valencia and Cárdenas, all of which he mentioned in directives to the clergy as well as in notations he inserted in some of the parish registers.[86]

But neither the bishop, when he left New Mexico in November 1850, nor Vicar Ortiz had the least notion that the ecclesiastical jurisdiction of Durango had already come to an abrupt end – officially that is – during July of this same year. They could not have known that Rome had created the Vicariate Apostolic of New Mexico, appointing a French priest named Jean Baptiste Lamy as its first bishop. Bishop Lamy, with his own French so-called Vicar Joseph Machebeuf, would suddenly announce their impending arrival exactly a year later, in July 1851.

---

[84] Ibid.

[85] See Robert W. Larson, *New Mexico's Quest for Statehood, 1846-1912* (Albuquerque: The University of New Mexico Press, 1968), 67-72.

[86] Loose documents, 1846, no. 13 and 1850, no. 2; Patentes, XII, LXXI; and M-7, Belén, all in *AASF*.

Guadalupe Church, Santa Fe, New Mexico, May 1880. Photo by Ben Wittick courtesy Museum of New Mexico, Neg. No. 15847.

Part II

A New Dispensation

Toward mid-July of 1851, Don Juan Felipe Ortiz received some surprising and totally unexpected news from young Padre Otero of Socorro. He immediately composed a letter to his clergy and had some *cordilleras* (chain circulars) copied from it, these letters to be sent with dispatch in different directions. Each pastor receiving a copy would then enter the contents in his parish book of *Patentes* (official communications) and then forward the missive to other parishes in his district as listed on the margin. Besides many copies of such *Patente* entries, one of the Ortiz originals has survived and reads as follows:

> Brethren, today at one o'clock in the afternoon I received a letter from the Señor Cura of San Miguel del Socorro, Don José Antonio Otero, in which he includes the one which his Most Illustrious Lordship of this new bishopric of the Territory of New Mexico has sent him from the Villa of El Paso del Norte in the Mexican Republic, the tenor of which is the following. Sr. Cura of San Miguel del Socorro, Paso del Norte. 1 July 1851. The Holy See has designed to place under my pastoral care the new Bishopric of New Mexico. In the coming week I shall continue my journey toward those churches; and although I have already sent notice to the Señor Vicario of Santa Fe, in case it should get lost on the way, I direct this one to you so that you may be informed, and so that you may give notice to the Señores Curas [in the Río Abajo], for I wish to see all the churches of my

bishopric even when passing through. May God our Lord grant you his grace, and with this wish goes the pastoral blessing of your Bishop. Juan, Vicar Apostolic of Santa Fe.

Then Ortiz continued.

Which message I hasten to bring to your knowledge, so that each one of us may comport ourselves with our new Ordinary as our duty requires, reminding you for a better understanding [of this delay] that notice which his Most Illustrious Lordship mentions having sent to the Vicar of Santa Fe has not reached me. This Circular, after it has been entered in the proper book, will be dispatched with safeguards by the same clergyman, and with the utmost speed possible, to the next place on the route, and from the last point let it be returned to Santa Fe. 14 July 1851 – Juan Felipe Ortiz – with "Señores Curas"on the margin. Also listed on the margin are the parishes of San Ildefonso, Cañada, Abiquiú, Taos, and Picurís.[1]

This amply demonstrates that Vicar Ortiz was not in any way disturbed by the news of the arrival of the new Bishop Jean Baptiste Lamy, as his detractors have always held. He was ready to receive the new bishop with all the reverence due a lawful prelate while counseling his priests to do the same. More than that, he immediately began contacting the civil and military authorities in Santa Fe, and his parishioners to help him prepare a reception such as the capital had never seen. This reception is described in the reminiscences of Demetrio Pérez, who was the vicar's sixteen-year old clerk or amanuensis the time. (He was, by the way, the son of the Mexican governor assassinated back in 1837.) These memoirs, like so many such composed in advanced years, have their serious defects, as when Pérez wrote that Vicar Ortiz had previously received notice during July from Bishop Lamy while the latter was still at San Antonio de Béjar in Texas, and when he claimed that he had also read about the new bishop in newspapers from the eastern states.[2]

---

[1] Juan Felipe Ortiz file, no. 2, *AASF*. Translated from Spanish.

[2] Demetrio Pérez, "Rasgo Histórico," in "Bruce T. Ellis, editor, "New Notes on Bishop Lamy's Years," *El Palacio*, (Vol. 65, no. 1, 1958), 27. For Pérez's father see A. Chávez, *New Mexico Families*, 429.

As to the first error, clearly Lamy's letter of 1 July 1851 written at El Paso del Norte was the first news Ortiz received through Padre Otero. As to the second error, Don Demetrio confused this occasion with a particular newspaper item of 1853, which will be discussed in its place. What we can be sure of is that the young Pérez was the one who copied the *cordilleras* mentioned before, and that, as he claimed, he had written a letter on the subject to Bishop Zubiría in Durango at his master's dictation.

But what Pérez remembered most vividly, and therefore correctly, was what would impress a teenage youth the most – the part played in the grand reception by the military. For young fellows anywhere there is nothing so impressive as soldier parades with a military band playing amid cannon salutes. After telling how much Vicar Ortiz was elated by the prospects of having a resident bishop, and whereby church order and the education of youth would profit the most, Pérez remembered best how he and his master had gone up to Fort Marcy on a hill overlooking the city. They went to the fort between seven and eight o'clock that evening on 14 July 1851, to see a Lieutenant Colonel William T. H. Brooks. This officer happened to be a Catholic and spoke Spanish well, and soon he and the vicar began planning a colorful and noisy reception for the new bishop.[3]

From what happened later on, Vicar Ortiz had no trouble enlisting the cooperation of the civil authorities as well. What stuck most vividly in young Demetrio's mind were the military activities which, as shall be shown, wonderfully complemented the descriptions of both Lamy and Machebeuf.

As for Vicar Ortiz himself, all of this was not enough. Despite his obesity, he rushed south a hundred miles to Tomé to welcome his new bishop personally. For this we have Bishop Lamy's own casual statement, which has been carefully passed over by his biographers in order to denigrate Ortiz. The Frenchman wrote, "*El Señor Vicario* of Santa Fe came to attend us *a cente milles*, one hundred miles from the capital."[4] The one parish on the *Camino Nacional* (the *Camino Real* of previous royal Spanish times) and about a hundred miles south of Santa Fe, was that of Tomé where young Padre José C. de Baca was the pastor. Here Lamy and his party were fêted royally by pastor and people, as they had been at every parish stop along the way according to what both Lamy and Machebeuf wrote. To crown this celebration, the vicar from Santa Fe lent his presence. The new bishop impressed Ortiz so much that he hastily betook all his stodgy poundage back to the

---

[3] Ibid., 27-28.
[4] Jean B. Lamy file, 15 August 1851, no. 12, *AASF*.

capital in order to oversee the final preparations for the grandest reception of them all.

Several days later, according to Pérez, in early August of 1851, Lamy and his companions reached Albuquerque and lingered there awhile for a much-needed rest. This, he said, was what Lamy wrote to Ortiz in a note specifying the approximate date of his arrival in Santa Fe — on August 8th or the 10th between nine and ten o'clock in the morning, "if I remember correctly," Pérez added.[5] A bit of self-doubt like this one lends the statement some credence, and it could well be that Lamy's party spent the night of August 8th at La Ciénega so as to reach Santa Fe in the late hours of the following morning, which it did on 9 August.

The day after the Albuquerque note arrived, Pérez wrote that Vicar Ortiz gathered all the faithful in his parish church to announce the bishop's impending arrival, urging them all to sweep and decorate the streets. A committee would be named to escort him from the town's outer limits to the residence Ortiz had prepared for him. By evening, Pérez continued, the route had been made ready for a distance of more than three miles! While this looks like an exaggeration, Lamy and Machebeuf both stated that at previous parish stops the people had gone far out of their towns to escort them under flowery arches. More specifically, Pérez said that the Calle de San Francisco, to its juncture with the street leading to the Guadalupe chapel, had been swept clean and, then, strewn, for the most part, with rugs and flowers, while arches had been erected at short distances apart. The same treatment was given from Guadalupe along the *Camino Nacional*. Moreover, the fronts of houses on both sides were decorated with tapestries and framed pictures of saints.[6]

According to the most enthusiastic descriptions by Bishop Lamy and Father Joseph Machebeuf, their party reached Santa Fe on Saturday, 9 August, around eleven o'clock in the morning in magnificent weather. They were met three miles out of town by a great cavalcade of citizens and by civic officials riding in their fancy carriages. Here he was invited to ride in the gubernatorial carriage with the territorial secretary – not the governor himself as both Frenchmen wrote, since he was away at the time. At the western edge of town, from which point the streets were lined with cut evergreens (junipers and piñons) all the way to the parish church. The populace came out to help escort the honored guests to the *parroquia,* and amid

---

[5] Pérez, "Rasgo," 28.
[6] Ibid.

Bishop Jean B. Lamy, Santa Fe, New Mexico, circa 1860s. Photo courtesy Museum of New Mexico, Neg. No. 35878.

the continuing booming of cannon from the fort.

At one point the bishop, as he must have done for the long processions at the previous parish stops, donned his full choir regalia of purple *soutane* and *mozette* (cassock and capelet) and lace *rochet* (prelatial surplice) showing below the latter. On his purple *mozette* glittered his pectoral cross, which was distinctly French for being shaped like a *fleur-de-lis* as it appears in his portraits. The cross was suspended from a golden chain.[7]

Machebeuf, while exaggerating certain details and figures, also noted Indians [from Tesuque most likely] dancing in their colorful costumes. This could very well be true since, up until some decades ago, the Tesuque Indians, whose nearby pueblo had been attached to the Santa Fe parish from the very beginning, had always joined the Hispanic folk of the Capital in their festive celebrations.[8]

In connection with all that has been said, further details furnished by Don Demetrio Pérez are of particular value. He most vividly recalled how Colonel Brooks had stationed his troops and placed five fieldpieces near the Guadalupe chapel at the western edge of town. As soon as a lookout on top of this chapel's front south-corner tower (as it appears in old photographs) caught sight of the approaching coterie of horsemen and carriages, the colonel called his men to parade attention. As the procession came within sight, he ordered the first cannon salvos to be fired. Upon arriving at the chapel, the bishop and his companions stepped down and entered it in order to chant a *Te Deum*. For this rite, Bishop Lamy had sufficient help from two other priests with him besides Machebeuf, and whom the latter had mentioned weeks before in passing as a Pole and a Spaniard. Pérez identified the two as Padres Alejandro Grzelachowski and Antonio Servero Borrajo, besides a young layman with them named Gustavo Noël, and whom Lamy had referred to as a musician.[9] Hence the venerable chapel must have resounded with a stentorian foreign clamor it had never heard before.

As soon as the new arrivals emerged from the chapel, the more orderly procession into town began, the ranks of soldiers falling in lines behind them and ahead of the gentry's carriages bearing their honored guests. At this time the bell on the Guadalupe tower had begun clanging, struck on its rim with a stone or metal bar, and all the bells at the other four churches in

---

[7] Lamy file, 15 August 1851, no. 12; Paul Hogan Collection, 28 August 1851, no. 10, both in *AASF*.

[8] Horgan Collection, J. B. Machebeuf letters, 29 September 1851, *AASF*.

[9] Pérez, "Rasgo," 29.

J. P. Machebeuf. Photo courtesy Museum of New Mexico, Neg. No. 112696.

town took up the metallic refrain.[10] At the same time, as the Lamy and Machebeuf wrote, the guns at Fort Marcy added their smoky pounding in the triumphant din. As for the four other churches, which Pérez mentioned, they were the *parroquia* of San Francisco, the *Castrense* or Our Lady of Light, and the San Miguel and Rosario Chapels at the opposite ends of town, all of which Machebeuf named in the proper locale.

Thus far, Vicar Ortiz had not taken part in all this pageantry, as might be presumed. According to church protocol, he had to wait fully vested at the main entrance of his parish church for the prescribed reception of a major prelate with the liturgical requisites of bell, book, candle, and the holy water sprinkler. Don Demetrio also observed that Ortiz's assistant, Padre Luján, and other priests from nearby towns also waited with Ortiz at the church entrance. Here the old man's memory seemed to falter concerning the other clergy besides Luján, for neither Lamy nor Machebeuf mention other welcoming padres except Ortiz. But then they also failed to include Luján as well as the other priests who came with them, and hence Pérez could be right about the additional clergy, the closest ones being from the Santa Cruz-Santa Clara valley.

The liturgical reception in the parish church ended with the service of Solemn Benediction and another *Te Deum*, all of it loudly accompanied by fiddle and guitar music which shocked Machebeuf as it already had the earlier Protestant foreigners. For these, they said, were the very same instruments (and to them the same tunes) played at the dances. Following this, the honored guests and all the carriage officials and gentry were escorted to Vicar Ortiz's own residence for a sumptuous banquet.[11]

It is in this particular connection that Bishop Lamy directed his paeans of gratitude toward the Mexican vicar's person. In letters written on 15 and 28 August 1851, he told how the old *vicaire* "is extremely generous" and weeks before had offered his own *belle maison* for the episcopal residence, when the Mexican and American citizens proposed acquiring another house for the bishop. Hence Ortiz's offer must have been made at Tomé when he went there to meet Lamy. After all, Lamy wrote, Ortiz's house was much superior in every way as well as being close to the parish church. As for the magnificent dinner that Ortiz had prepared for the grand occasion, and which

[10] Ibid.

[11] Horgan Collection, Machebeuf letters, 29 September 1851, *AASF*; Emory, *Notes*, 34; Gregg, *Commerce of the Prairies*, 159; Gibson, *Journal*, 227-28n; and Magoffin, *Down the Santa Fe Trail*, 138.

was attended by all the Catholic and Protestant authorities, it was almost as good as any such repasts in New Orleans. Meanwhile, Lamy added, Ortiz went to live with his family.[12]

Even Machebeuf, almost two months later while criticizing all the native clergy, was still expressing his admiration in this regard. The old vicar, he commented, introduced the bishop to his own house, which he had decorated like "a veritable episcopal palace." As for the banquet, all the authorities without distinction of race and creed attended the "magnificent dinner" which made his party totally forget their long and tedious journey "across the Texas desert."[13] Don Demetrio Pérez recalled that the vicar's half-sister, Anamaría Ortiz, and other members of the family had been living with him. Hence they also had to move to one of the several other homes owned by the family. The house which Lamy occupied and which stood on the site of the present cathedral rectory was quite large since, as Pérez also observed, rooms had been provided for the Frenchman José P. Machebeuf, the Spaniard Severo Borrajo, who was a Doctor of Theology, and Alejandro Grzelachowski.[14]

Had Josiah Gregg been present on this occasion, as he had been at Vicar Ortiz's first reception of Bishop Zubiría back in 1833, he would have been more shocked by this enthusiastic participation of his own countrymen and coreligionists. At that time the processions and other rites, such as the kissing of the bishop's ring, had made him remark with disgust that the native people believed it to be "the second coming of the Messiah – only a heightened picture of what occurs every day in the intercourse between the rancheros and the common padres of the country. The slavish obsequiousness of the lower classes towards their pampered priests is almost incredible."[15] We might add that these countrymen of 1851 were more enlightened than he in this regard; but there still existed a goodly number among these civilian newcomers who kept Gregg's prejudices very much alive from having read his book in addition to other like-minded publications.

Sad to relate, it is to these cultural bigots living in Santa Fe to whom Bishop Lamy, and especially his friend Machebeuf, would be lending an

---

[12] The French term *parents* means relatives and not parents as others have translated it, and much less his "mother" as Lamy's biographer Paul Horgan wrote. Lamy file, 15 August 1851, no. 10; and Horgan, *Lamy*, 110.

[13] Horgan Collections, Machebeuf letters, 29 September 1851, *AASF*.

[14] Pérez, "Rasgo," 29.

[15] Gregg, *Commerce of the Prairies*, 179.

eager ear, and then would begin adding their voices to the same tune practically in unison.

Only six days had passed since the glorious reception when Bishop Lamy's euphoria began to evaporate, as we learn from his two letters just cited and a third one of 2 September. In fact, they seem oddly out of place among those most enthusiastic descriptions of the grand reception and the lavish praise he had showered on the now ex-Vicar Ortiz. After stating that there were more than sixty-five churches or chapels in all of New Mexico, and no more than fifteen priests – and that the so-called Mexican people were attached to their religion but in great part forgetful of its true practice, "God knows who is at fault." He added a loud sigh: "Oh, if we only had here some young priests zealous and devout." Shifting briefly from French to Spanish, he hinted to the New Orleans prelate, whom he was addressing, that he would tell him how bad things really were when they met in Baltimore.[16]

Two weeks later he wrote much the same to the bishop of Cincinnati; here is where, while yearning for "good" priests and "zealous missionaries," he criticized Ortiz himself (and implicitly the native clergy in general) for their neglect of preaching except for a fat fee once a year. A few days before he had been more explicit in a letter to France, when he said that there were four Protestant ministers in town who had thus far failed to seduce the faithful. But he offered no criticism for this failure of theirs – rather he went on to say that the native padres "were for the most part incapable and unworthy."[17] To sum up, Lamy and his bosom friend Machebeuf must have kept mulling over these matters between themselves, for the latter repeated Lamy's criticisms in almost identical terms. Machebeuf went further in saying that of the fifteen priests "six were burdened with age and without the least energy, and the others devoid of zeal and scandalous to a degree you could not imagine." Alas, he continued, what could one expect from "a Mexican clergy, which dreaded a reform of their morals."[18]

Here one can legitimately question how these two French newcomers could have come to know so much about all of the local priests' characters, their ages and state of health, down to their personal morals, since neither of the two men had been out of Santa Fe since their arrival. Thus far they had

---

[16] Lamy file, 15 August 1851, no. 12, *AASF.*

[17] Ibid., 2 September 1851; Horgan Collection, 28 August 1850; Extracts, nos. 9 & 15, *AASF.*

[18] Horgan Collection, Machebeuf letters, 29 September 1851, *AASF.*

Rev. Antonio José Martínez (1793-1867), pastel-charcoal over photograph. Photo courtesy Museum of New Mexico, Neg. No. 174508.

met only a fraction of the seventeen, not fifteen, priests who were in active service: Padres Otero at Socorro, C. de Baca at Tomé (and here perhaps Rafael Chávez from Belén across the river), Gallegos in Albuquerque, José Vicente Montaño (probably at Isleta at the time), Rafael Ortiz in Santo Domingo, and now ex-Vicar Ortiz and his assistant Luján in Santa Fe. Most of these were relatively young men, except for the vicar who was not so aged, much less decrepit, and his first cousin, Rafael Ortiz at Santo Domingo. As Bishop Zubiría had noted before, Rafael Ortiz was the only infirm padre. Ortiz, in fact, would pass away within eight months.

Besides, as just pointed out, there were seventeen active priests in all, which are listed here according to their respective ages: José Francisco Leyva (ca. 65), Antonio José Martínez (58), Juan Felipe Ortiz (54), Rafael Ortiz (54), Fernando Ortiz (54), José Vicente Montaño (ca. 50), Juan de Jesús Trujillo (ca. 42), José de Jesús Luján (40), José Tomás Abeytia (38), Mariano de Jesús Lucero (ca. 38), Antonio de Jesús Salazar (36), José Manuel Gallegos (35), Ramón Salazar (34), José de Jesús C. de Baca (32), José Antonio Otero (29), Rafael Chaves (ca. 29), and Vicente Saturnino Montaño (ca. 29).

To these an eighteenth priest must be added: Nicolás Valencia, who was still under Bishop Zubiría's suspension for his crimes in Belén, where he was officiating privately for some folks who clung to him. Valencia would form a baffling association with Bishop Lamy and his new vicar, Machebeuf. In fact, he could well be one of the critical sources from whom the two Frenchmen had just gotten their negative assessment of the native clergy.[19] Now, all of these priests had been Vicar Ortiz's subjects with whom he had always dealt amicably for the most part, excepting the habitual jealousy of Martínez and the tiff with the younger Abeytia many years before. As for Valencia, he had already caused problems for Ortiz. Finally, when compared to Bishop Lamy's age of 37 (born on 11 October 1814) and Machebeuf's of 39 (born on 11 August 1812), half of the local priests were of the same age or younger.[20]

Going back to the query as to how did these two recently arrived men presume to know so much, and with such conviction, about the local padres, particularly concerning their private lives, which requires a quick resume.[21] At Galveston Lamy and Machebeuf met another French bishop, Jean-Marie Odin, who told them the most lurid stories about the gross immorality

---

[19] A. Chávez, "Schism," *NMHR*, 37-39, 45.

[20] Horgan, *Lamy*, 12 & 16.

[21] For more detail on this question see A. Chávez, *But Time and Chance*, 95-96; and *Très Macho*, 25.

of the people of New Mexico and their clergy in particular. He even tried to dissuade Lamy from going on to his destination, urging him to return to Europe for priests of better caliber. Odin had never been in New Mexico, hence he was relaying prejudiced accounts which were rampant at the time, and which had kept growing apace ever since Texas had unsuccessfully claimed New Mexico as a part of Texas.[22]

As if all this were not enough, Lamy and Machebeuf had now fallen victims to exactly the same misguided gossip which was current in Santa Fe among a goodly number of its American residents, whether Protestant or Catholic. This is no empty surmise, for during the week following their triumphant entry into Santa Fe, they must have been invited to soirees and dinners at the homes of newcomers of whatever creed, as had occurred ever since down to the present. Priests coming to labor in New Mexico first gravitated to the company of their own kind, as is most natural. From these people they heard talk, whether malicious or in jest, about the native population; then some of these priests innocently relayed such talk to some local person, forgetting that they were addressing one of those natives. Concerning Lamy himself, he casually mentioned in his very first letter, as to how he had obtained a small organ from a Protestant minister just the day before he celebrated his first Pontifical Mass on 15 August 1851. This incident has been skipped over by his biographers. He must have met the reverend gentleman at one of those teas or dinners, and one wonders what the latter told him.[23]

Nor can one exclude, to be totally fair, what Lamy and Machebeuf could have heard from native Catholics like the Kearny-appointed Judge Otero who was perhaps the chief justice whom Lamy had mentioned as a visitor. Otero was the same man who supported the schismatic Valencia against Ortiz's legitimate authority. Also, he could have talked to Donaciano Vigil who, as governor, had tried to suspend Vicar Ortiz in connection with the schism. Finally, there is that sneaky Valencia who could have secretly contacted Lamy and Machebeuf to ply them with further mischievous gossip. This last observation is a broad conjecture at first glance, which will come into sharper focus shortly.

Lamy's first Pontifical Mass is of particular significance, over and above the small organ just mentioned, which was masterfully played by the young Frenchman Noël whom Lamy had brought along from Texas. Some German

---

[22] Horgan, *Lamy*, 91-93.

[23] Lamy file, 15 August 1851, *AASF*.

Catholic residents who did the singing accompanied Noël. According to Don Demetrio Pérez, the organist's full name was Gustavo Antonio Noël. Also according to him, Bishop Lamy had asked Ortiz what kind of choir he had, and Ortiz replied that there were only some inexpert violinists, while young Pérez did the singing. Lamy told Pérez to consult with Noël and have him unpack the little organ, which they had brought along. This last story is a mistaken impression further muddled in Pérez's recollection of the event. Pérez further added that a German individual ("un Señor Alemán," a German gentleman and not a Mexican with this surname) helped make up a choir of three voices, presumably with Pérez and Noël at the keyboard. In connection with Noël, who later opened a school, he mentioned a fellow named Augustine Heyne, perhaps the German voice alluded to above.[24]

Pérez remarked, with what looks like nostalgia, that Bishop Lamy and clergy assisting him, looked splendid in the beautiful Spanish-style vestments of those days – vestments to be heard about again in ex-Vicar Ortiz's coming disputes with the bishop. Lamy, Pérez also claimed, had held rehearsals for the unaccustomed pontifical rites for two or three days prior to the Assumption Feast on the following Sunday. (Actually, 15 August fell on a Friday that year of 1851.) Padre Borrajo was the master of ceremonies and the instructor during the rehearsals. Pérez did not mention the other participants who played the part of deacons and chaplains, but there were a sufficient number of candidates from among Ortiz (most likely as archpriest), Machebeuf, Grzelachowski, Luján, and seminarian Ortiz supplying the other roles.[25]

As for Don Juan Felipe Ortiz himself, despite the misgivings and false estimates being expressed by Lamy and Machebeuf at the time, all factual evidence points to the fact that he continued on very good terms with Bishop Lamy, who in turn must have dissembled his unjust suspicions. Ortiz himself, of course, as well as the other native padres, had no idea at all that so much evil against them was being written abroad by the two Frenchmen. While his own exalted office as vicar had come to an end, having been replaced by Machebeuf as the bishop's right-hand man, he had been left in peaceful possession of his family-endowed *parroquia*, and with the same Padre Luján continuing as his assistant.

What Lamy wrote at this time, saying that he and Machebeuf had been left alone in Santa Fe, is in reference to the fact that the clerical trio he had

---

[24] Pérez, "Rasgo," 29-31.

[25] Ibid.

San Francisco Street view looking west from the walls of the Cathedral, Santa Fe, New Mexico, 1880. Photo courtesy Museum of New Mexico, Neg. No. 11353.

brought along from Texas had already been dispersed. The Polish Grzelachowski had just been assigned to the Indian Pueblo parish of San Felipe, while the Spaniard Borrajo evidently returned to Texas. This is assumed because his name never appears in the parish or mission registers, and he shows up thereafter at San Elizario, an El Paso village in Texas and hence a member of the Galveston Vicariate at the time.[26]

At this time also, a signal event took place when Bishop Lamy acquired the old *Castrense* chapel on the plaza for the purpose of turning it into a parish for the English-speaking civilians, as well as the Catholic personnel at Fort Marcy. He had considerable trouble getting it from the civil authori-

---

[26] Lamy file, 28 August 1851, no. 15; San Felipe registers, Catholic Directory, 1855, *AASF.*

ties who had been using the building as a storehouse and sometimes for holding court trials. Actually, he had no right to it just because it had been a Catholic chapel, as will be explained later on when Vicar Ortiz's own real estate acquisitions come into question. But, wrote Lamy and Machebeuf, most of the Mexicans were on his side, as well as many of the influential American Protestants (who presumably could not see a place of worship desecrated). The acquisition accomplished, Machebeuf began restoring it for the intended English-language parish.[27]

But what is of utmost importance to note here is that ex-Vicar Ortiz made no objection to Machebeuf's re-establishment of *La Castrense*. While within the territory of his own parish, it did not affect the spiritual and ethnic entity of his Spanish-language *parroquia*. Instead, the new church would furnish a welcome and needed opportunity for the English-speaking Catholics and the soldiers from the garrison to hear sermons and make their confessions in their own tongue.

What has been said all along concerning Ortiz brings us back to the lamentable fact that all of the writers on Bishop Lamy have categorically maintained that the ex-vicar and his fellow native priests had begun questioning the new bishop's credentials from the very start, while the ordinary folk labored under a suspicious regard for his person as an alien. Nothing could be further from the truth. Paul Horgan, for example, incorrectly wrote that "Ortiz, and the local clergy over whom he presided, suddenly maintained that Lamy was not the bishop of Santa Fe, and refused to recognize him as such." Worse yet, "Ortiz had shown no zeal for his duties, and under his regime his clergy had lost theirs. But in the matter of change of bishops, he was suddenly zealous, legalistic, and rudely stubborn."[28]

Now, as has been seen, Ortiz had been a dedicated priest all his life, moderately legalistic in his correct dealing with one or the other of his priests who had been disobedient, and far from stubborn – almost to a fault. If any of his clergy had become lazy, or worse, it was no fault of his. So far, he had been cooperating with his new prelate, although he must have rued the cessation of his long vicarial standing as would be most natural. In short, neither his inner feelings nor his outward conduct changed all of a sudden to set him in direct opposition to his legitimate superior.

---

[27] Lamy file, 2 September 1851, no. 14; Horgan Collection, Machebeuf letters, 29 September 1851, *AASF.*

[28] Horgan, *Lamy*, 113-14.

To conclude at this point, what had originally started the foregoing false assumptions were a couple of innocent statements made fifty years later by the good Archbishop Jean B. Salpointe in his book, *Soldiers of the Cross*. Salpointe, incidentally, never overplayed Lamy's heroism nor blackened any of the native priests. Basing his innocuous assertions on the French clerical lore of his day, he commented that the populace and clergy of New Mexico, unused to strangers and suspicious of them, had likewise been suspicious of Bishop Lamy and his vicar. As a result Lamy decided to undertake a long and perilous trip to Durango. Then, depending again on the same lore, Salpointe stated that Lamy made this journey with a single lay companion, as shall be seen shortly.[29]

The fact is that both the local people and their priests had long become acquainted with alien strangers of every type. Their numbers and identities have been detailed in many histories of the era and Frenchmen had been coming to the area, at least, as early as the seventeenth century.[30] But as proof for his erroneous contention Horgan cited definite data against Ortiz which were decidedly damning. Unfortunately, these "facts" came from the gravest of canonical charges – and he bent the truth, to put it mildly.

And now to that famous Durango journey which, according to Horgan and others, Bishop Lamy undertook because of the alleged sudden enmity displayed by ex-Vicar Ortiz and his people. Salpointe wrote that "Dr. Lamy, *it is said*, made the long journey from Santa Fe to Durango, having only a servant as a companion."[31] Salpointe relayed a turn-of-the-century clerical tradition, and without the least intention of deceiving anyone. However, subsequent worshippers of Lamy's hallowed memory took it to mean that he

---

[29] Jean Baptiste Salpointe, *Soldiers of the Cross; Notes on the Ecclesiastical History of New Mexico, Arizona, and Colorado* (Albuquerque: Calvin Horn Publishers, 1967, originally 1898), 198.

[30] Jean l'Archévèque, Jacque Grolé (Grolet), and, maybe, Pedro Meusnier who were with Diego deVargas's resettlement at the end of the seventeenth century. The Mallet brothers traveled overland from the "Illinois country" to Santa Fe in 1739 and were precursors to the many Frenchmen who would end up in New Mexico intermarrying with the local families. Certainly, the many French fur trappers who moved into New Mexico to add to its colorful history in the immediate three decades before Lamy's arrival were well known to the local populace. Names such as St. Vrain, Robidoux, Beaubien, and Patie hint of the many Frenchmen who preceded Lamy and Machebeuf. For l'Archévèque, Grolé and Meusnier see A. Chávez, *Origins of New Mexico Families*, 129, 193, and 229.

[31] Salpointe, *Soldiers of the Cross*, 198. Italics are the authors'.

undertook this 1900-mile dangerous journey, practically alone, because of Ortiz's refusal to accept him as his bishop. For example, Willa Cather has him leaving alone in her novel. Thus the conclusion to use the trip as an example of their hero's bravery. All of this inspired Horgan to dedicate more than a chapter to the lonely journey, detailing every step along the way by employing and enhancing the travel accounts of earlier writers who had gone to Mexico.[32]

The hard facts are that in those times no one was foolhardy enough to undertake such a trip without an armed escort party; not even the simplest-minded man in Santa Fe would have willingly volunteered to accompany Lamy as his sole companion. Even from Belén south to Socorro, but most especially from Socorro down through La Jornada del Muerto all the way to El Paso del Norte, attacks by the marauding Apaches were a constant menace. Too often small parties of travelers, even if well armed, were found massacred.

Of greater import here is the part played by ex-Vicar Ortiz in the entire affair. For weeks since Bishop Lamy's arrival on 9 August 1851, down through his happy first Pontifical Mass on the 15th, and followed by his acquisition of the military chapel, Ortiz had shown nothing but good will toward his bishop. What one gathers from all the primary sources, is that it was around this time, if not before, that Lamy must have asked him why the old Texas villages of El Paso del Norte, including today's Ciudad Juárez as well as the recently settled Mesilla Valley north of there, should not come under his own jurisdiction as vicar apostolic of New Mexico. Bishop Odin, that garrulous prelate of Galveston, whom Lamy met on his way to New Mexico, dumped the El Paso settlements on the new bishop. Those settlements now included the American garrison of Fort Franklin, today's El Paso.

Actually, by Vatican law and procedure, Odin had no right to take such action. His own Vicariate of Texas, comprising the original Spanish and then Mexican Tejas closer to the Gulf coast, and now a part of the United States, had been formed by Church decree by separating the area from the Mexican diocese of Monterrey. But, even though American Texas had subsequently extended its limits far northwestward to include the El Paso settlements on its own bank of the Rio Grande River, the Vatican had thus far refrained

---

[32] Horgan, *Lamy*, 132-40. Cather merely states that the local clergy refused to recognize his authority without the proper paperwork so "Latour," her Lamy, left on "a journey of a full three thousand miles" with a horse and a pack-mule. See Cather, *Death Comes for the Archbishop*, 22-23.

from separating this area from the Mexican diocese of Durango. Yet, as ignorant of Church law as Odin appeared to be, Lamy gladly accepted his act, subsequently hailing himself as the "shepherd" of these towns when he reached them in June of 1851 while en route to Santa Fe.[33]

As for the Mesilla Valley, it was still Mexican territory and would not become a part of New Mexico until the Gadsden Purchase two years later. No settlements had existed there until recently, following the American occupation of New Mexico when some New Mexican families, who did not care to live under American rule, had moved there to live in Mexico. Here they had founded the towns of Mesilla and then Las Cruces with additional migration to El Paso del Norte families from both the Texan and Mexican sides. These places, too, still belonged to the diocese of Durango in Mexico. Incidentally, ex-Vicar Ortiz's first cousin Don Ramón Ortiz, described as "an intelligent, shrewd man" who "exerts greater influence than any other man in the State of Chihuahua," was the pastor of El Paso del Norte. He had been delegated by the Mexican government to recruit New Mexican families for settling in the Mesilla Valley. However, to his frustration, he and his pushy propaganda were not too well received by New Mexico's officialdom, native or otherwise.[34]

Hence, when Bishop Lamy brought up the entire matter before the ex-vicar, the latter had to inform him that his own jurisdiction as vicar for Durango included what was New Mexico proper, not the newly-settled Mesilla area nor the district of El Paso and Ciudad Juárez. The whole rightfully belonged to the Durango diocese of Bishop Zubiría, and his cousin Padre Ramón Ortiz was still the rightful pastor and vicar for that bishop. It was this information alone, not any ill will on the part of Ortiz and his people that prompted Lamy to go to Durango. Lamy still labored under the mistaken belief that Zubiría could, and should, relinquish these places to him. Nor, to repeat, had he severed his amicable relations with Ortiz precisely for this reason, although something else totally unrelated might have come up to confuse Ortiz in the meantime, as will be seen.

For in that same letter of 15 August 1851, in which he had been praising

---

[33] Lamy file, 29 June 1851, no. 8, Horgan, *AASF*; and Horgan, *Lamy*, 93.

[34] Benjamin M. Read, *Historia Ilustrada de Nuevo México* (Santa Fe: Compañia Impresora del Nuevo México, 1911), 289-90; Reverand Hiran Walter Read, October 1851 as quoted in Lansing B. Bloom, ed., "The Reverend Hiran Walter Read, Baptist Missionary to New Mexico," *NMHR*, (Vol. XVII, no. 2, 1942), 142; Fidelia Miller Puckett, "Ramón Ortiz: Priest and Patriot," *NMHR*, (Vol. XXV, no. 4, 1950), 286-87.

the ex-vicar most gratefully, Lamy added this postscript: "Within a few days I leave for Durango with the old vicar, five hundred leagues of travel, a great part desert and dangerous." Nor did the letter contain anything about any personal dissension between the two; nor did he mention any questioning of his authority by anyone. On the contrary, as Lamy continued in the same letter, the native faithful were a Catholic people who showed their utmost respect toward their prelate, and humble folk "so good and so docile" as he wrote in a subsequent letter of 2 September.

Of greater significance is the fact that his friend Machebeuf made no mention of such dissension, as one might expect from him. Machebeuf tended to look for every excuse to blame the native priests. Even when attacking Ortiz five years later in Rome, he wrote that Ortiz "offered to accompany him [Lamy] to Durango for a better understanding with Monsignor Zubiría concerning his jurisdiction."[35] He wrote nothing at all about any bad relations at this point. Furthermore, right after Lamy left for Durango, Machebeuf wrote that "the interests of the diocese [vicariate rather] had obliged him to undertake a journey to see the old Bishop [who] had been in charge, the Mexican vicar [Ortiz] having also left." Thus finding himself alone in Santa Fe, he continued that he was busily engaged in exercising his faulty Spanish while "granting dispensations, etc., until the bishop returned by Christmas."[36]

Even five years later in Rome, when ranting against several of the native priests who in the meantime had criticized Lamy for giving his own French vicar free rein, Machebeuf did not mention any problems with Ortiz or any of the other New Mexican priests. Instead, he wrote that Lamy had no other reason for going to Durango than:

> ...solely with the hope of making arrangement with Monsignor Zubiría about following the same procedures as much as possible, to obtain information about the mores [not morals], the customs of the land, and to present the ecrits [papal documents], to a venerable prelate who had preceded him – Monsignor [Lamy], then, had not made the trip except of his own will [underlining his] concerning affairs of the Holy See, to give official notice to Monsignor of Durango about the nomination [of Lamy for New Mexico]."[37]

---

[35] Horgan Collection, Propaganda fide, Defense, 1856, *AASF*.

[36] Horgan Collection, Machebeuf letters, 29 September 1851, *AASF*.

[37] Horgan Collection, Propaganda fide, Defense, 1856, *AASF*.

Don Demetrio Pérez, in his own hazy recollection about this episode, said that Vicar Machebeuf, upon returning from his first visitation of the outlying parishes, had told Lamy that the native pastors were unwilling to recognize his authority because they had not been notified of the change by Bishop Zubiría. It is plain to see that the old man was wrong in his recall, since neither Lamy nor Machebeuf wrote that they had been out of Santa Fe to date, while the latter would not have failed to bring up such a rebellious attitude of the native priests. Then, Pérez continued, Lamy invited Ortiz to accompany him to Durango, thus nullifying his previous statement while echoing both Lamy's postscript and Machebeuf's several declarations previously quoted. What is more, according to Pérez, Ortiz offered the bishop his own carriage and Lamy accepted the offer; a few days later both men started out together, accompanied by some well-armed men for protection against the "Indian barbarians."[38]

This matter of an armed escort rings true, but not the one of their leaving together, for there is definite evidence that Ortiz left Santa Fe some days ahead of Lamy, as hinted also by Machebeuf's indefinite remark about the old vicar "having also left" [before they did]. Other evidence comes from Santa Fe parish registers which record Ortiz's last burial on 28 August and his last baptism on 30 August, following when his assistant Luján took over the ministrations as "pastor in charge." Hence, Ortiz must have left a day or two later, that is, before 3 September, when a significant wedding took place in his church. It was on this day that Padre Luján witnessed the marriage of ex-Vicar Ortiz's own half-brother, Don Tomás Ortiz (who was a young rebel leader in 1846) and a woman named Refugio Baca. One would expect that Don Juan Felipe would have tarried long enough to do the honors himself. What raises a question in this regard is that Padre Luján, in recording the wedding, wrote that Bishop Lamy had dispensed the couple from a close double relationship, which they had as first and second cousins. Such cases had always gone to Durango for resolution, and this appears to look as though the ex-vicar avoided taking part in the wedding because he feared that a mere "vicar apostolic" did not enjoy the power of granting a dispensation of such serious import. On the other hand, Lamy's action is another indication that he and the locals were working together.

It appears that Ortiz could well have left at this time in order to confer with his cousin Ramón in El Paso del Norte, both on this matrimonial matter and the larger one of territorial jurisdiction. As to how he traveled the record

---

[38] Pérez, "Rasgo," 31.

is silent, and there is no indication whether Lamy accepted Ortiz's offer to use his carriage.

As for Bishop Lamy himself, he was still in Santa Fe on 2 September, the eve of that Ortiz-Baca wedding, when he penned a letter to his former bishop in Cincinnati. Here he told him about his educational plans, and that a chief justice and other major officials who were already pledging their support had visited him. He also conveyed the particulars of his acquisition of the military chapel, which Machebeuf was now repairing: "I hope to say mass in it in three months when I come back from Durango." In both projects, he wrote, the good Mexican people and the American authorities were most helpful. It is true that in this connection he did express his desire for younger and more zealous priests, while criticizing the elderly Ortiz for his neglect of regular preaching. He wrote nothing about any quarrels between him and Ortiz, much less opposition from the native clergy or misgivings on the part of the faithful.[39]

According to Machebeuf in his letter of 29 September, Lamy had already departed for Durango, six weeks after his arrival in Santa Fe, and thus should be halfway on his journey. This would place his departure around the 21st, but he left much earlier in the month because he passed through Padre Otero's parish of Socorro on the 12th, when he issued another matrimonial dispensation for a local couple.[40] Hence he left about a week after Ortiz. As to how he set out, we do not know. If he did with one single servant or companion, it was only as far as Albuquerque or Tomé, where he joined a well-armed party of horsemen or an escorted caravan of wagons or pack mules.

There is an interesting advertisement in the *Santa Fe Gazette* in 1851, in which the owner of the mail caravan to El Paso del Norte gives the new passenger and freight rates, announcing that he now has better passenger

---

[39] Lamy file, 2 September 1851, no. 14, *AASF*. Machebeuf's most recent biographer, Lynn Bridgers, acknowledges that there is some controversy over whether or not Lamy went to Durango because of his bad reception but does not try to give an answer. Lynn Bridgers, *Death's Deceiver; The Life of Joseph P. Machebeuf* (Albuquerque: University of New Mexico Press, 1997), 89. Steele does not hesitate to provide an answer to the issue. He writes, "Lamy realized that he needed the acquiescence of Bishop Zubiría, so he and Vicario Foreneo Ortiz set out for Durango." Thomas J. Steele, editor and translator, *Archbishop Lamy: In His Own Words* (Albuquerque: LPD Press, 2000), 8-9.

[40] DM, 1851, no. 76, *AASF*.

coaches, additional freight wagons, and new teams of superior horses.[41] Whichever mode of transportation Lamy took, and since he was only a week behind Ortiz, he and the latter might well have come together at Padre Ramón Ortiz's rectory in El Paso del Norte. From there they may have joined another escort party through the Apache-infested territory south as far as Chihuahua, and thence without any such needed protection the rest of the way to Durango. All that is known is that both reached this city sometime late in October and that both were the simultaneous guests of Bishop Zubiría.

Pérez wrote that the Durango bishop came out to welcome them both in the company of civil and other church dignitaries. Either he got this from Ortiz later or else he let his imagination assume such a scene, since he does not say that he accompanied his former master.[42] Here he adds, and this is confirmed from other sources, that Bishop Zubiría proved himself most hospitable to a fellow bishop and an old friend who had served him so long and so well as his personal vicar. He already knew of Lamy's appointment as vicar apostolic of New Mexico, from a letter of 10 April, which Lamy wrote to him from San Antonio in Texas. However, thus far, Zubiría had not received any official lead-sealed parchment from Rome separating that area from his own diocese. This was because, as discovered later, the Vatican secretaries had accidentally sent it to the bishop of Sonora. The two Roman parchments with their white and yellow ribbons bearing their stamped leaden "bulls," which Lamy brought along, were evidence enough for Zubiría. One of the documents created the New Mexico Vicariate, and the other named Lamy as its prelate. Consequently, by 1 November, the Durango chancery drew up a large four page official document whereby Bishop Zubiría acknowledged the new situation. Toward the end of the document Zubiría also declared that Ortiz had ceased being his vicar for New Mexico, while at the same time urging the faithful of New Mexico to render their complete and willing obedience to their new bishop.[43]

Thus the Durango bishop, strictly obedient to the Vatican decrees, most graciously conceded what was New Mexico proper to Bishop Lamy, just as instructed in the documents presented to him. On the other hand, Zubiría

---

[41] *The Santa Fe Gazette*, 6 November and 4 December 1851.

[42] Pérez, "Rasga," 31-32.

[43] The original document, besides the two parchments which Lamy took to Durango and, in which, Zubiría makes reference to Lamy's episcopal consecration in Cincinnati, as scribbled on the back of Lamy's appointment, are with that of the Vicariate's creation. See, Lamy file, Bullae, 1851; and Zubiría document, 1 November 1851, *AASF*.

declared most emphatically that, without similar decrees from the Holy See, he did not have the authority to relinquish the Doña Ana-Mesilla district that was still Mexican territory. Nor could he relinquish the settlements in El Paso, Texas that Lamy told him had been turned over by the Texas Bishop Odin. Zubiría explained that Odin's jurisdiction extended only to the southern part of Texas that Rome had separated from the Mexican diocese of Monterrey. Disappointed, Bishop Lamy started back for Santa Fe, his headstrong canonical ignorance stirring his anger all the way back.

Whether or not he and ex-Vicar Ortiz left Durango together is unclear. What seems more likely, is that the latter tarried in Durango for a good while, and then with his cousin at El Paso del Norte, for it was months before he returned to Santa Fe. Lamy himself also spent some days at the American garrison of Fort Franklin (the nucleus of what would become the present city of El Paso). Here he chanced to meet Lieutenant Emory, now a major, who wrote that Bishop Lamy impressed him as an "excellent man" who told him that his Durango trip had been for the purpose of adjusting "the territorial limits of their respective dioceses."[44] This was yet more evidence, and from an external source, that contradicts Salpointe's innocent statement about Lamy's Durango trip having been prompted by the New Mexico people's distrust of strangers, or Horgan's own blind insistence on having the enmity of the native clergy as the real motive.

While at Fort Franklin, Lamy had another adventure which was soon to turn sour, and therefore make his Durango trip all the more bitter. Here a certain Mexican priest, that scamp Benigno Cárdenas, no less, made such a good impression that Lamy promptly accepted him to work in New Mexico. But Lamy soon had to drop Cárdenas after they reached Socorro, for Padre Otero told him that Cárdenas was a heretical fugitive friar who had caused a most unfortunate schism in Tomé not too long before.[45] This bad judgment and gullibility on his part must have added fuel to his disappointed if not angry mood, and one to which he would give hasty vent shortly after reaching Santa Fe on 10 January 1852. As gathered from parish registers, ex-Vicar Ortiz did not return to Santa Fe until March.

The year of 1852 began badly with the marring of Bishop Lamy's relationships with some of the native clergy and then ended with a pair of turbulent incidents involving two of Ortiz's friends and former subjects. The first had to do with Padre Leyva y Rosas of San Miguel del Vado, the second

[44] Horgan, *Lamy*, 146.
[45] A. Chávez, *But Time and Chance*, 98-99; and "Schism," *NMHR*, 45-46.

Cathedral, Durango, Mexico, circa 1905. Photo courtesy Museum of New Mexico, Neg. No. 65315.

with young Padre Gallegos of Albuquerque. Other such incidents would occur during the intervening spring and summer months while Lamy was away on his first trip east, to a bishop's council in Baltimore. His friend Machebeuf went on a destructive rampage that laid the foundation for all the serious troubles that would ensue and persist for years to come.

But what has to be noted here, and strongly emphasized, is the fact that Don Juan Felipe Ortiz stayed completely clear of this entire year of troubles, quietly administering his beloved old *parroquia* without uttering a word or lifting a finger. No doubt, he was heeding Bishop Zubiría's advice that anything that happened outside his own parish was no longer any of his business. Zubiría followed his own counsel, by the way, by never interfering in another diocese, as when some New Mexico priests went to him with their complaints. Besides, it was Ortiz's nature to avoid violent confrontations of any sort as much as possible.

The case of Padre Leyva at San Miguel del Vado was the opening round, but, before describing it, a diversion is required about something of particular interest which took place in Santa Fe just a week after Lamy came back from Durango, for the absent ex-Vicar Ortiz was intimately, if indirectly, involved in the affair.

A Funeral and Controversey

Death finally came for Doña Tules in 1852, just a few days after Bishop Lamy had returned from Durango. Ex-Vicar Ortiz would not return for more than another month, as parish registers indicate. He stayed in Durango to visit with old acquaintances and did likewise at El Paso del Norte where his first cousin, Padre Ramón Ortiz, still served and had his sisters living with him. Hence it was Ortiz's Santa Fe assistant, Padre Luján, who gave the dying woman the last rites and recorded her burial on 17 January 1852.[1]

Don Amado Chaves recalled from family talk that Doña Tules never believed in confession. Nevertheless, a dear friend of hers, Doña Guadalupe Tafoya, the mother-in-law of Mr. Conklin mentioned before, had persuaded her to send for the priest, who then heard her confession and gave her Holy Communion. Whether all the foregoing is true or not, she did indeed receive the last rites. Some fourteen months before, on 30 October 1850, she made and personally signed her last will. Here she named Vicar Ortiz as one of the three executors.[2] Some of the document's details regarding her heirs and legacies are best left for later on, particularly those concerning the young woman whom she reared. That woman's connection to Tules's saloon still tingles the popular imagination along with her mistress.

Her grand funeral was more of a tribute to her well-earned popularity than what the critics later considered her ill-received wealth. It was attended by the native officials and gentry of means, the assimilated Americans in

---

[1] Burials, Santa Fe, 1852, *AASF.*

[2] Chaves Papers, NMSCRA. The document is a very poor translation of the original, now lost.

business and government, the officers and men from Fort Marcy, and the many poor who gratefully remembered her generous acts of charity. Incidentally, Don Amado Chaves said that many priests came from other towns, and that her sister (whom he miscalled Dolores) had been the distributor of her alms to the needy. After the Requiem Mass everyone formed a very long procession to the cemetery, led by Bishop Lamy himself in his white mitre and black cape, while Father Luján brought up the distant rear in tears. The processional order comes to light from Machebeuf, who was not there but could have heard about it later from his American friends, as he did other matters or gossip. Years later, in 1856, while he was lashing out at the native priests who had stood up to his mean treatment of them, he accused Luján of having been the deceased woman's lover. Machebeuf claimed Lujan's indiscretion as the reason why he had chosen to walk at the tail end of the procession without even wearing a surplice over his cassock, while shedding the bitterest of tears.[3]

Even if this canard has some truth in it regarding the procession, Luján could well have had one big reason to cry. By not conducting the services himself as the interim pastor for the absent Ortiz, he had been cheated of the enormous burial fees that Bishop Lamy appropriated for himself. The unusually vast sum in dollars became the object of a grave scandal in the eyes of another American critic. Like Brewerton years before, William W. H. Davis depended on Josiah Gregg's book for his denigration of La Tules and the native folk in general. In her will she charged her brother Trinidad, her sister María Luz, and the latter's daughter Refugio to take care of the funeral expenses. These were the *demandas* (fixed church fees) which she had computed at thirty dollars apiece for any extra ceremonials. Then these sorely-bereaved heirs, following the custom of the local *ricos* in outdoing one another in pomp and circumstance, acceded to Bishop Lamy's own more excessive "demands" when they asked him to conduct the services, for never before in Santa Fe's long history had anyone been buried by a lord bishop.

Hence Davis found a handy reason to be shocked when he came to learn, from Lamy's signed bill, that the total fees amounted to more than sixteen hundred dollars! It started out with the first thousand dollars as the "rights of the bishop." Then followed other charges of fifty dollars each for the number of *pasos* (stops with rites along the route), besides additional charges such as extra candles and the tolling of all the bells, which Davis said "were in proportion" to the Bishop's fee. Such extravagances among the well-to-

---

[3] Horgan Collection, Propaganda fide, defense, 1856, *AASF*.

do, which in our day have been taken over by morticians, have long been a source of confusion.[4] Finally, it is of further interest to note that Bishop Lamy, while he reduced the Hispanic clergy's regular fees in his first pastoral letter issued at the end of this very year of 1852, was careful to add that the fees for any "ceremonies of pomp" should be worked out between the petitioners and the celebrant.[5]

At this point a look at Doña Tules' 1850 will is necessary to garner some information in regard to her heirs, in particular the girls whom she reared. Doña Amada Chaves said that there had been three of them, one of whom was her niece. The niece had to be Refugio, María Luz's first child whom she had long ago adopted in Tomé and who married a Santiago Flores in Santa Fe on 17 August 1841 and now had a child named Delfinea, who is also mentioned in the will. Over and above her many properties, La Tules left all her wealth in cash to her brother Trinidad, her sister María Luz, and the latter's daughter Refugio, to be divided equally among the three. Santiago Flores, as Refugio's husband, was to bring up and educate two girls, whose names were Rayitos Gutiérrez and Carmel Sisneros, until they were twenty-five and as long as they were single, whichever came first. Are these the two young ladies adopted by La Tules whom Doña Amada cited along with her niece?

First, Rayitos Gutiérrez, whom La Tules identified as a girl that she had reared since infancy and who was residing with her. From her marriage in Santa Fe on 16 February 1852, only a month after her stepmother died, her full name is given as María Consuelo de los Rayos (Mary the Solace during lighting). This was a Spanish title for the Virgin Mary applied to female infants, a favorite one in those times and even within memory, and which in practice was shortened either to "Consuelo" or "Rayitos." She was recorded as the natural daughter of a Petra Gutiérrez of Santa Fe, while the groom was Lorenzo Labadíe, the son of Pablo Labadíe and Rosa Sisneros of Tomé. Lorenzo was the maternal uncle of Doña Amada and Don Amado who kept referring to him and Rayitos with much pride.

Carmel Sisneros was the second young woman whom La Tules identified as another girl living with her at the time. On 2 December 1851, two months after the will was drafted, Carmel married an American in Santa Fe named Henry Derr. Here the bride was recorded as Carmen Sisneros, a "fa-

---

[4] Davis, *El Gringo*, 186; and A. Chávez, "Doña Tules, Her Fame and Her Funeral," *El Palacio*, (Vol. 57, August 1950), 227-34.

[5] A. Chávez, *But Time and Chance*, 104.

miliar" of Don Manuel Sisneros and Doña Gertrudis Barceló.[6]

Now, the priest who married them was Lamy's vicar, Machebeuf, while the former was in Durango. Hereby hangs another tale, which also concerns the same Padre Luján who was having his tiffs with the autocratic vicar at this very time. Later, Machebeuf accused Luján of having had a pretty girl living with him and vigorously opposing her marriage to a certain fellow who in turn appealed to the bishop so that the wedding could take place. Both the time and the circumstances point to the marriage of Carmen with Henry Derr, a non-New Mexican whom Luján must have distrusted for being a vagrant – like a couple of others who are about to be mentioned. None of the parish registers records any children from this union.[7]

Neither the much younger Rayitos nor Carmen could have been one of those women described by Doña Amada. They would have had to be of Refugio's age, more or less. Doña Amada furnishes some juicy gossip, which had been passed down in her family about one of these two elder women. While La Tules was down in Mexico on one of her trips, she said, that one of those two girls had a female child by an American who frequented the gambling saloon. The father left the country upon learning that La Tules was on her way back. Learning from the young mother who the culprit was, La Tules tried in vain to locate him. While La Tules was on another trip south, the same girl started having an affair with another American. When La Tules returned, the girl was pregnant again. Now keeping a watchful eye on her, one day she spied the lover sneaking into the girl's room through a window. Leaving two men to guard the place, she went and got the priest. Then, while both of them stood watching the window and La Tules with a pistol in her hand, the fellow came out and was apprehended. He promised to come back later to arrange a wedding, but La Tules with her pistol insisted on the marriage right then and there, and so the padre married the couple. Here Doña Amada ended her tale by telling Don Amado that she knew who the parties were.

If all this gossip is partly true, the young woman in question was none other than Petra Gutiérrez, while her daughter Rayitos was the fruit of either one of her affairs with the two Americans. Also, Petra could well have been the pretty adventurous belle whom Matt Field had seen riding with La Tules in her carriage, and later as the flirt at her saloon, but mistakenly identifying her as the niece Refugio. Don Amado claimed that the groom of

[6] Marriages, Santa Fe, *AASF*.
[7] Ibid.

the shotgun wedding was a Colonel Washington, and that his daughter "Rayitos Washington" later became the bride of his uncle Lorenzo Labadíe, whose descendents were living in Santa Rosa.

Despite Amado Chaves's claims, the father of Rayitos could not have been the Colonel John M. Washington who became New Mexico's military governor in 1848-1849. There was a Louis Washington in Santa Fe who married a Marcelina Salas around 1836. If he was indeed Petra's lover while also a married man, that shotgun wedding could not have happened. Nor could Father Ortiz, who was always a stickler when it came to canon law, have performed the wedding under any such circumstances. And could Rayitos have been that baby María, of unknown parentage, who had been baptized in 1838 with Manuel Sisneros as her godfather? Or was it the other girl, Carmen, perhaps the result of Petra's first pregnancy by the American who left the country?

As for Petra Gutiérrez herself, she is not mentioned in Doña Tules' will. Perhaps she was already dead, or else she had left the family by getting married to someone. There is a Doña Petra Gutiérrez, the daughter of Don Gabriel Gutiérrez and Doña Dolores Sisneros, who had married an American named James Giddings on 6 May 1842.[8] Her mother's Sisneros surname tempts one to suspect that the lady was somehow related to the husband of La Tules, something that cannot be ascertained as of now. Moreover, there were other women in those days who bore Petra's full name. For example, on 14 February 1847, a María Petra Gutiérrez buried a natural infant at Tomé, while an adult female of the same name was later buried in Santa Fe on 7 December 1857. The latter was listed as the daughter of a José Gutiérrez and his wife Rosario Crespín.[9] As for the third adopted daughter of La Tules cited by Doña Amada, besides the niece Refugio and the wild Petra, she could have been a Rafaela Barceló, recorded as an adult "familiar" of Doña Gertrudis Barceló when she was buried in Santa Fe on 29 April 1851, only six months before the latter made her will.[10] Besides, there could have been other such adoptions, like the infant Altagracia from Santa Fe baptized in Tomé far back in 1832.

Another biased tale of the period again came from young Brewerton who in 1848 had traveled with Kit Carson from Los Angeles to Taos. He claimed to have made his way from there to Santa Fe. He kept a journal, but

[8] Ibid.

[9] Burials, 54, Tomé; Burials, Santa Fe, *AASF.*

[10] Burials, Santa Fe, *AASF.*

years later after returning back East, and having become a news writer as well as a Baptist preacher for a spell, he exaggerated whatever notes he had with the wildest flights of imagination which only a cub reporter and religious fanatic could concoct. He recalled the Barceló place as a stinky saloon, morally pestiferous, having a roulette table, and with cash and weapons all over the place. As for La Tules herself, her face bore "the impress of her fitful calling being scarred and seamed" by her "unbridled passions." Then he went on to repeat Gregg as his bible of indignation. La Tules was already dead when he wrote, so he criticized her elaborate funeral which, he said, had been made possible by her illegitimate wealth. Here he added that he remembered her as being tastelessly dressed, all her fingers loaded with rings, and her neck adorned with three heavy gold chains, the longest of which had a massive crucifix of some precious metal.

His bitterest gall was reserved for that unnamed gambling priest he supposedly saw in the saloon. Brewerton damned the priest in a long sentence redolent of a preacher's pious prattle. He described him as a person "who would go from the curses of this hell to the house of the living God, and there stand in his sacerdotal robes and say to his people, 'Go in peace, thy sins are forgiven thee!'"[11] Had this priest been Vicar Ortiz, he surely would have remembered him as being quite fat, which he omitted. Or was this individual Ortiz's current assistant at the *parroquia*, or else some padre from another town? Whatever, it all looks like a made-up story because, as mentioned earlier, Brewerton described the fellow as a friar of a religious order with cross and rosary in full view. There were no Franciscans or other orders of priests in New Mexico at the time. The old Franciscan friars who were allowed to remain were already dead at this time. The remaining secular clergy, like Ortiz, wore only a plain black cassock with no monastic paraphernalia of any sort.

As said long before, it was La Tules' adopted daughter's presence in the gambling saloon at one time or another which caused others later on, while aping Gregg and Davis, to continue labeling La Tules as a whore and a madame. Sad to say, even a modern New Mexican author like Paul Horgan, who admired Gregg and wrote his biography,[12] also quoted Davis in running down the native population as a morally corrupt lot in a paragraph devoted

---

[11] George Douglas Brewerton, *Overland With Kit Carson; A Narrative of the Old Spanish Trail in '48* (New York: Coward-McCann, Inc. 1930), 185-89, 191-92.

[12] Paul Horgan, *Josiah Gregg and His Vision of the Early West* (N.Y.: Farrar Strauss Giroux, c1979).

to La Tules in his biography of Bishop Lamy. He also quoted some early visiting Anglican bishop who, evidently having Davis in mind, commented on the extravagant funeral of this "notorious prostitute and gambler [as being] utterly disgraceful to Bishop Lamy." Here Horgan, to whitewash Lamy, suggested that it was Vicar Ortiz who had been behind it all.[13] As has been seen, Ortiz had not yet returned from Durango and would not do so until March. Upon his return, Ortiz would find his friend Doña Gertrudis dead and buried and the dear Barceló family totally dispersed.[14]

In addition, the new French bishop's formal and strange policies were changing the old Spanish church life that Ortiz had known. He was still loyal to Lamy, as he had shown himself to be when he received him that previous August with all the pomp he could muster among his flock as well as civil and military authorities, and more so now at the recent urging of his former Mexican prelate. But little did he know that this loyalty of his would be stealthily sloughed off by the new French regime within a year. His resulting disappointment, which tends to collapse a mind as old as his was, would make his life more miserable day by day until he, too, passed away.

---

[13] Horgan, *Lamy*, 186.

[14] In fact, the Barceló family names no longer appear in the Santa Fe church registers from this time on.

A Problem of Bias

Don Juan Felipe Ortiz, by failing to return home earlier, missed a grand windfall that had been provided by his wealthy friend Doña Tules in her will. Instead, the bequest became Bishop Lamy's good fortune. As it looks, Lamy deliberately deprived Padre Luján, who was the pastor in charge, of all that welcome extra cash. What is more, the same poor Luján would suffer still worse indignities in this connection from Machebeuf's lies four years later.

Thus within a week of Lamy's arrival, La Tules died and was buried. Now his friend Machebeuf was anxious to pour some stories into the bishop's ears. Machebeuf told him how Padre Luján at the *parroquia* had scorned his own authority as vicar general by refusing certain directives that Lamy had left just before leaving for Durango. Lujan declared that Machebeuf was not vicar general. Nevertheless, Machebeuf wrote years later, that "he often had to suffer [Luján's] insults and effronteries until Lamy's return from Durango."[1] This was to be expected when, as soon as the bishop left, Machebeuf assumed complete episcopal authority, while Luján, with his master Ortiz also away, took pleasure in vexing a fussy fellow who would not hide his scorn for him. Hence, there must have been other instances of the sort, like the one narrated by Salpointe fifty years later. He wrote that while Luján "had invited" Machebeuf to celebrate Sunday mass after Lamy's departure, Machebeuf tried to preach "after the priest had introduced him not too warmly." Machebeuf delivered such a fiery sermon that the congregation wondered whether the preacher was a Jew or a Protestant! But after mass

---

[1] Lamy file, Horgan Collection, Defense 1856, no. 17, *AASF*.

one old crone assured her fellow worshipers that he had to be a Catholic from the way he made the sign of the cross![2] The story as it stands sounds like one of Machebeuf's boastful accounts which had evolved into its current form with each telling thereafter; but it was just the kind of stuff which Horgan used to insult the native folk by exclaiming: "But what an index of the primitive mind and local experience all this revealed!"[3] Certainly there were many people in the congregation with much more intelligence than that old crone, or Machebeuf for that matter. To give one outstanding example, Machebeuf considered himself a true vicar general, always appending "V. G." to his signatures, general, as though he enjoyed full jurisdictional powers during his bishop's absence. But in his day, a mere vicar apostolic such as Lamy was, even though a duly consecrated bishop, did not rate any such vicar general until after his credentials had been accepted, which is to say upon his return from Durango. Nor, incidentally, could he designate a particular church as his "cathedral." When, at this very time, he wrote to France about the English-language parish that he had established in the old *La Castrense* or military chapel, Machebeuf boasted about his true vicar general's standing in what he termed the newly founded "cathedral" that Bishop Lamy would find ready for use on his return from Durango.[4]

Returning once more to Lamy's arrival on 10 January 1852, the complaints against Luján were tame in comparison with what Machebeuf had to tell his travel-weary friend concerning old Padre Leyva of San Miguel del Vado. Sometime during a late November night just past that aged Mexican pastor had been thrown by his horse while dead drunk and suffered a badly injured leg.[5] Right away, as is evident from the parish registers of San Miguel, Machebeuf transferred Father Grzelachowski from San Felipe to replace Leyva.[6] Bishop Lamy, as has been described, was in the proper grim mood to react to Machebeuf's account of the scandal, which must have been as vehement in its hate-filled delivery as others he later wrote about in his letters and in his defense in Rome later in 1856. As a result, despite his weariness from the Durango trip and with only one week of rest even if financially sweetened by the Barceló funeral, Lamy traveled to that distant parish of San Miguel on the Pecos River, and there he soundly excoriated the poor

---

[2] Salpointe, *Soldiers*, 196-97.

[3] Horgan, *Lamy*, 147-48.

[4] Horgan Collection, Machebeuf letters, 29 September 1851, *AASF*.

[5] Lamy file, 1 February 1852, no. 1, *AASF*.

[6] San Miguel, registers, *AASF*.

pain-wrecked old Leyva. The bishop deprived the priest of his parish and suspended him from his priestly functions. However, as a kindly person at heart, Lamy must have been a bit moved by the sight of the old fellow's miserable condition and his poverty, for he allowed Leyva to keep part of the parochial benefice, and this is very much to Lamy's credit.[7]

Upon his return to Santa Fe, he described the whole tawdry event to Bishop Purcell of Cincinnati, saying that he was resolved to discipline, in exactly the same strict manner, with all of the other bad priests whenever he "caught them in the act." Someone in San Miguel must have told him that old Padre Leyva had distinguished himself as a legislator during both the Mexican and American regimes, for here he made a sarcastic remark about it.[8] What Lamy now wrote about Leyva and the other padres in general clearly indicates that the Bishop had finally come to believe all the old Odin gossip which he had heard repeated and expanded since his very first days in Santa Fe. Now Machebeuf had thoroughly convinced him of it all with the Leyva example, including other specifics he had gathered in the meantime about certain problems among the other native clergy.

There is another source of the malignant gossip. This source has to do with that maverick priest Nicolás Valencia. It was at this very time, following his return from Durango and his punitive excursion to San Miguel del Vado, that Lamy accepted Valencia's services and sent him down to San Felipe where Grzelachowski had been before Machebeuf transferred him to San Miguel to replace Leyva. All this, despite the fact that up until this moment Valencia had not only been under Bishop Zubiría's suspension for more than five years, first for his habitual disobedience and then for the schism he had created with Cárdenas, but had kept exercising priestly functions in the general Belén area. He, thus, incurred the most grievous status of "irregularity" as defined by canon law. All this poses a big mystery, but one not entirely beyond solution.

Whether or not Valencia was a native of New Mexico cannot be entirely established. No child with his full name appears in the extant baptismal records of any parish. Years later, a hint comes from Valencia and the Jesuit pastor of Albuquerque who buried the former's mother in Atrisco. His mother appears to have been an Antonia María García. The Jesuit pastor did not

---

[7] Lamy file, 1 February 1852, no. 1, *AASF*; and Horgan, *Lamy*, 148 and 150. Horgan misread the text to claim that Lamy went to the extinct pueblo of Pecos and the town of this name.

[8] Ibid.

name her in his house journal, but hers is the only Atrisco interment entered in the parish burial register for that same week.[9] This alone would
make Valencia a native of the Río Abajo area of New Mexico where the
Valencias and Garcías abounded. But, from his conduct since his first sudden appearance in 1845, initially in his cool relations at this time with ex-
Vicar Ortiz and later with his gross ill treatment of native priests Otero and
C. de Baca during the Belén-Tomé schism, he could well have been a nonconformist outsider, possibly born in El Paso del Norte or points farther
south in Mexico. He very likely descended from the New Mexico Valencias
and Garcías who had not returned with Governor Diego de Vargas in his
1693 re-colonization of New Mexico.[10] Valencia also must have been a very
odd fellow in so many ways that, as has already been seen, Bishop Zubiría
had to suspend him in that very first year of 1845 for what the bishop called
his habitual disobedience, or disdain for all discipline. All of this, and the
schism he subsequently caused, leads one to speculate on a couple of most
interesting incidents mentioned in the following year of 1846, immediately
following Kearny's takeover of New Mexico for the United States.

Lieutenant Emory wrote that on the night of 29 August 1846, a priest
came to warn General Kearny about a Mexican Colonel Ugarte who was marching north from El Paso del Norte with a force of five hundred men. But this
intelligence did not seem to have bothered the general. Just a week later,
when Kearny and his party, while en route to California, were the guests of
a Don José Chaves at Los Padillas, a priest was present who invited them all
to a mass he celebrated in the chapel the following morning. Here, Emory
wrote,

> The eccentric person we met at yesterday's dinner offici-
> ated. Priest, fop, courtier, and poet were curiously com-
> bined in one person. Proud of his pure white hand, he flour-
> ished it incessantly, sometimes running his fingers through
> his hair, in imitation of some pretty coquette, and ever and
> anon glancing in one of the many looking-glasses with
> which which the church was decorated. After Mass, to our

[9] "Diario de la Residencia parroquial de la Compañía de Jesús, Albuquerque, N. M.,"
5 February 1871, various volumes 1867-1966, Archives of the New Orleans
Province of the Society of Jesus (ANOPSJ), New Orleans, Louisiana. Courtesy
of Father Thomas J. Steele, S. J. Also see Burials, Albuquerque, 20 January
1971, *AASF*.

[10] A. Chávez, *New Mexico Families*, 109, 301 (for Valencia), and 181-85 (for García).

surprise, he delivered an eloquent discourse, eulogizing the grandeur, magnanimity, power, and justice of the United States.[11]

Emory gave a masterful portrait of an effeminate man, whether homosexual or not. Now, the man just cited in both of the foregoing instances had to be Valencia, who was still officiating, despite his suspension, for some followers of his in the general Belén area. The description does not fit at all the manly characters of any of the pastors in the Río Abajo. These would have been Otero, C. de Baca, Gallegos, and old Rafael Ortiz. None of them, even if they had passively accepted the American occupation as a fact, would have sneaked up to Santa Fe that August night to warn Kearny about Ugarte. Nor would they have been so eager to eulogize the United States with such flamboyant passion. Moreover, Valencia later joined Cárdenas, another odd character, in creating that turbulent schism, which had been sanctioned at least quietly by the short-lived Vigil-Washington-Monroe regimes in Santa Fe. Supreme Court Justice Otero, as an aside, positively abetted that schism. Finally, there is Bishop Zubiría's statement on 9 November 1850, when after reviewing Valencia's former capers said that the fellow's late aberrations had come as a result of "the civil change" in government with the aid of certain irreligious persons.[12] In other words, Valencia had taken the principle of American religious freedom to mean his own release from ecclesiastical supervision whcnever it best suited him. Now, with the advent of a totally new ecclesiastical regime, he saw an opportunity for personal advancement while getting even with the native padres.

All of this looks like a very wide and wild surmise, yet it is one which cannot be merely shrugged off as such, particularly within the context of Valencia's summary acceptance by Lamy and Machebeuf as a worthy priest. Here the question arises: Had this weasel secretly contacted the two Frenchmen during that first August week after they arrived, as he had General Kearny that August night of five years before, in order to ingratiate himself through more lurid gossip? At the very least Lamy and Machebeuf began repeating the gossip and, to Machebeuf's particular delight, they learned more tales concerning the native priests' alleged relationships with females? Or did Valencia wait until Lamy passed through the Río Abajo on his way to Durango, and then travel up to Santa Fe to see Machebeuf, perhaps, a kindred soul, who not only provided fertile ground for Valencia's tidbits about

---

[11] Emory, *Notes*, 33, 40-41.

[12] M-7, Belén, 9 November 1850, *AASF*.

clerical adulteries, but found in him a person he could recommend to Bishop Lamy as soon as he returned. Machebeuf apparently rationalized that Valencia was a fine priest who had been unjustly persecuted by the former Mexican bishop and his former vicar, Ortiz, as well as by all the other native clergy. Otherwise, why did Bishop Lamy so readily accept his services at this very time under such conditions?

Here also, someone may counter, Ortiz should have told the bishop about the rascal's past history, as Padre Otero had recently done at Socorro concerning Cárdenas's past history. Perhaps he did tell Lamy and the bishop, under Machebeuf's baneful influence, refused to listen. Or else Ortiz, as said before, had resolved to remain completely uninvolved as he had in the recent case of Padre Leyva at San Miguel. Whatever the reason, Lamy sent Valencia to replace Grzelachowski at the Pueblo of San Felipe when the latter was transferred to San Miguel. Valencia then received the assignment to replace Machebeuf at Santo Domingo Pueblo. Months later Lamy would make Valencia the pastor of Socorro to replace Padre Otero, the very man whom Valencia had illegally ousted from Belén with the new American government's backing!

One other problem remains unsolved with regard to Bishop Lamy's strange action in this matter. While he could remove Valencia's suspension imposed by his predecessor, the latter's past crime of schism and his current canonical irregularity were something that the Holy See reserved to itself for absolution.

Whether or not Lamy ever had recourse to Rome in this matter, either before he went to Durango or at any other time thereafter, there is no evidence in the Vatican Archives as there is for other minutiae of this sort.[13] What is more likely, Lamy considered himself empowered to resolve any case howsoever grave the nature. As for ex-Vicar Ortiz in his *parroquia*, he must have pondered these things in his heart while saying nothing for as long as his own parochial bailiwick was not disturbed.

The good, but canonically misinformed, bishop most likely spent the rest of February preparing his agenda for a national Bishop's Council in Baltimore, which he was to attend that spring. Among these points, no doubt, were the bad things about the native padres which, in that Spanish aside with his other information in French, he had previously promised the New

---

[13] Finbar Kenneally, O. F. M., *United States Documents in the Propaganda Fide Archives; A Calendar*, Vol. I-VII, (Washington, D. C.: Academy of American Franciscan History, 1972), passim.

Orleans prelate as a juicy topic of conversation when they met at the Council.[14] Since he was not to leave for the Council until 1 April 1852, he made two visitation trips up north during March to the parishes of Santa Cruz and Taos, either to kill time or for the purpose of uncovering more definite scandals by the respective pastors. Imagine his surprise when he found just the opposite. In Santa Cruz he found Padre Juan de Jesús Trujillo so much to his liking and his parish so well run that he decided to take him along to the council as his priestly aide and companion. At Taos he was so much impressed by Padre Martínez as both pastor and savant that he commissioned him to continue educating four seminarians whom Martínez had been instructing, so that he himself could ordain them in the near future, which he eventually did. He also founded his first parish at Arroyo Hondo, to which he appointed Padre Abeytia, assistant to Martínez at the time, as its first pastor. He also restored poor old Padre Leyva to his post at San Miguel, on Martínez's assurance that he was not the age-old drunkard and lecher that Machebeuf had made him out to be.[15]

Lamy left Santa Fe for Baltimore on the first day of April, taking along Padre Trujillo, although Machebeuf omitted this last fact in his later testimony.[16] What Machebeuf thought about this, and about Lamy's friendly relationships with Martínez and Abeytia at Taos, is not recorded. Ortiz might very well have derived no small consolation from these recent gestures on the bishop's part, for he was to welcome him back upon his return with the greatest marks of reverence and devotion. However, Lamy was to spend almost six months back east with sundry vicariate projects other than attending the council. During Lamy's near half year's absence Machebeuf would plunge into his first major rampage throughout the parishes, driven by an intolerant fascination for the normal male-female physical relationship. In particular, it was the "sinful" aspects of sex which he was bent on discovering and punishing among the native clergy.

---

[14] Lamy file, 15 August 1851, no. 12, *AASF*.

[15] A. Chávez, *But Time and Chance*, 99-100.

[16] Horgan Collection, Machebeuf letters, 31 May 1852, *AASF*. Pérez recalled that, besides Padre Trujillo, Lamy took a couple of other young fellows named Epifano Vigil and Romualdo Anaya, to learn the craft of printing in Cincinnati. This must have happened in a later trip that Lamy took back east. See Pérez, "Rasgo," 32.

Hatred and the Assumption
of Episcopal Authority

Before leaving for Baltimore, Bishop Lamy instructed Machebeuf, as his vicar in charge while also administering the new English language parish at the *Castrense*, to acquire a large house directly across from the old parish church and prepare it as a residence for the teaching sisters he hoped to bring with him. This Machebeuf did, as he wrote to his sister who was a nun in France. Pérez remembers the adobe structure which stood across the street from the old *parroquia* and which the sisters used for two years until Lamy bought them their permanent property which is today the site of the Inn of Loretto and Loretto Chapel.[1]

This done, the French vicar's nervous nature started getting ever more restless, whether out of envy because of the poor attendance of his own English language parishioners or else because he was irked by the nearby hateful presence of ex-Vicar Ortiz and his assistant Luján. It so happened that in this same April month of Lamy's departure, sickly Padre Rafael Ortiz passed away among his Indians of Santo Domingo. Presumably, ex-Vicar Ortiz went to the pueblo to bury his cousin—but forgetting to record the fact either in the Santo Domingo or Santa Fe burial books.[2] Sometime after this, Machebeuf decided to make himself the pastor of Santo Domingo but chose to reside in the nearby village of Peña Blanca.

---

[1] Horgan Collection, Machebeuf letters, 31 May 1851, *AASF*; and Pérez, "Rasgo," 32.

[2] Clergy of Vol. I, nos. 3, 5, and 8, *AASF*.

His reason for leaving Santa Fe, he wrote to his sister in May, was that he had nothing to do in town while the country people were totally "abandoned" and moreover "deprived of instruction and religious sermons." He overlooked the fact that he had thereby abandoned his English-language parishioners in Santa Fe, thus depriving them of sermons in their own tongue. Nor did he complain about any unfriendly attitude on the part of Father Ortiz and his assistant, for that would have been a ready excuse. After romantically describing to his sister the beautiful site of Peña Blanca with its verdant fields and groves by the Río Grande, he turned the other side of the coin, as he saw it, to describe what he considered the religious ignorance and loose life-style of its inhabitants. He went so far as to say that any priest determined to remain faithful to his calling had to place himself under the protection of Mary, "Queen of the Clergy," and in the prayers of holy souls like his sister and her convent companions.[3]

Having always led the sheltered life of the Clermont seminary, he evidently had no inkling of the loose morals current in his native France, which at this time were being immortalized by Honoré de Balzac, whose realistic fiction deliberately exposed the debauchery of French bourgeoisie. It was then that Machebeuf's frenetic preoccupation with sexual matters waxed ever stronger, so much so that in his sermons he began revealing things that he heard in the confessional. This was to eventually bring on a period of personal anguish close to panic, which, in its turn, would make him lie most shamelessly about the native priests in order to shift away attention from his own most serious infractions. This would also force his bishop and friend, despite his innate fairness, to obfuscate the issue by lying on his friend's behalf. All of these details will be brought out in their own time and sequence.

For Machebeuf at this point, what he felt about the lay people was not enough. In his mind, it was the lewd clergy who had to be investigated. His fascination with local scandal, as he saw it, began to expand toward darker action, even if he had to abandon his latest parish and leave it without sermons. Boasting the full episcopal authority which he incorrectly thought he had while his bishop was away, he traveled as far north as Taos on what he later liked to call his retreats or mission-preaching tours. He evidently expected to uncover lurid scandals there in the conduct of those priests Martínez and Abeytia whom Lamy had recently and so readily befriended. No scandals were discovered. Nevertheless, his sermons in Taos, like those in Peña

---

[3] See footnotes numbers 1 and 2, *supra*.

Blanca, would bring forth the same accusations of his violating the sacrosanct seal of the confessional.

From Taos he crossed over the Sangre de Cristo mountain range to the valley of Lo de Mora, and here he found what he was looking for but not in connection with a Mexican priest. The scandal involved the Polish priest Grzelachowski whom Bishop Lamy, after restoring Father Leyva to his San Miguel parish, had made the first pastor of Las Vegas with Mora as its chief mission annex. Evidently Padre Polaco, as the people called him, had a small house where he stayed for days at a time while visiting Mora, and someone told Machebeuf that there he had a woman of ill-repute for a housekeeper. Without further ado, Machebeuf suspended the unsuspecting Pole, replacing him as pastor of Las Vegas with a recently arrived French priest named François Pinard.[4]

But it was Mexican clerical scalps that Machebeuf was really after, and soon, on another preaching tour from Peña Blanca, he summarily suspended the pastor of Santa Clara, Ramón Salazar, on rumors that he had heard about his incontinent life. In doing so, he also appropriated the parish funds.[5] Salazar, by the way, had also been caring for a part of the Santa Cruz parish during Father Trujillo's absence as Lamy's companion.

During these and other excursions, Machebeuf left his Santo Domingo parish "without sermons," except on one occasion when he had his new foppish friend, Nicolás Valencia, take his place. Also during these summer months of 1852 he toured the Río Abajo parishes to the south, and it was in Albuquerque that he must have heard juicier rumors about its lively pastor, José Manuel Gallegos. Here he had so much fallen in love with the town, and especially Gallegos' well-appointed house, that he began coveting this parish as the one best suited for such an exalted person as a vicar general, meaning himself.[6]

Word of Bishop Lamy's impending return to Santa Fe, after his travel party had crossed the Great Plains, reached Machebeuf in mid-September. He promptly rushed as far as the Red River to meet his long-absent friend. Machebeuf, no doubt, was eager to tell the bishop about all the clerical suspensions and other reforms effected since April. This was to be expected, and there is an hint that this happened from the fact that Padre Trujillo, who

---

[4] Here Pérez was correct in his recollections, when he casually mentioned that Pinard had replaced Grzelachowski, who was suspended while pastor of Las Vegas. But he gave no reason for the latter's suspension. Pérez, "Rasgo," 74.

[5] A. Chávez, *But Time and Chance*, 102.

[6] Ibid., 102-3.

had been quite ill during the trip back across the plains, hurried posthaste to his parish, part of which had been abandoned with Salazar's suspension. Trujillo returned to Santa Cruz well before Lamy reached Santa Fe.[7]

Lamy was happy to return back home, as he always was after similar lengthy journeys. But a special kind of joy for him was bringing back a small bevy of Sisters of Loretto from Kentucky to start a school in the house which Machebeuf had prepared for them.[8] He also brought along a French fellow named Carlos Brun, who was ready for ordination. Yet, worn-out as he must have been, Lamy was just in the right mood to listen to Machebeuf about another rumored scandal, just as he had done in January after his long trip to Durango. Now he commissioned his vicar to undertake one more adventure of suspensions and parish-grabbing in Albuquerque.[9]

The bishop and his party finally arrived in Santa Fe on 26 September 1852, to be greeted on the town's outskirts by a great welcoming procession of all the faithful, which their pastor Juan Felipe Ortiz arranged. Ortiz then received his prelate at his *parroquia's* entrance with bells ringing and the same solemn liturgical rites that he provided when Lamy first arrived in Santa Fe a full year and two months before. Some native priests escorted the newly arrived nuns to their seats, presumably including Ortiz's assistant.[10]

Here, again, the Lamy biographers bland assertion that Ortiz and Lamy had become enemies from the very beginning do not ring true. Moreover, when Christmas came around with Lamy ordaining the French seminarian Brun, Ortiz accepted the latter as his new assistant at the *parroquia*.[11] Pérez wrongly recalled that "Le Brun" had been made the "second assistant" in the Santa Fe parish.[12] All of this gives rise to the question of why the former assistant, Padre Luján, was replaced by Brun, which brings up the story of Machebeuf's adventure down river in Albuquerque during the previous October, 1851, following Lamy's return in late September.

---

[7] Lamy file, 6 August 1852, no. 7; B-Santa Cruz, *AASF*; and "Practice Spanish Letterbook of Mother Magdalen Hayden," trans. By Sr. Felicitas Quinlevan as published in Mary J. Straw, *Loretto; The Sisters and Their Santa Fe Chapel* (Santa Fe: Loretto Chapel, 1984), 24-25.

[8] Horgan, *Lamy*, 164-65.

[9] A. Chávez, *But Time and Chance*, 103; and *Très Macho*, 43.

[10] See footnote 6 above; and Straw, *The Sisters*, 26.

[11] Some archive notations, as well as previous writers, place Burn's ordination on Ember Days of December 1853, but this is nullified by his own signed ministrations in Santa Fe which begin on 24 December 1852. Incidentally, he signed his surname as "Brum" until March, after which he continued with "Brun.")

[12] Clergy of the Archdiocese, Vol. I, nos. 2 and 4, *AASF*; and Pérez, "Rasgo," 74.

At the very time that Lamy and Machebeuf reached Santa Fe from Red River, Padre Gallegos had written the bishop a note in which he explained that he planned a trip to Durango, although he could not see him personally because the escort train was about to depart. In the meantime he had gotten Padre Luján, with or without ex-Vicar Ortiz's permission, to take his place in Albuquerque during his absence. And it does look as though Machebeuf had even given Gallegos oral permission to make the trip and for Luján to take his place, no matter how much this was denied later. Machebeuf then waited two full weeks, making sure that Gallegos was well on his way to Durango before traveling down to Albuquerque to dismiss Luján and take over the parish under the pretense of merely filling in for Gallegos during his absence.[13] It is after this episode that Luján had been removed from Santa Fe, and once again there was no protest from ex-Vicar Ortiz on this score. On the contrary, Ortiz accepted the newly ordained Carlos Brun as his new assistant toward the year's end.

The Albuquerque Gallegos story has always been a favorite one with the purveyors of the Lamy-Machebeuf myth, woven almost in its entirety from the boastful false accounts which Machebeuf wrote to his sister in France, along with the vicious lying he did in Rome later on. Ex-Vicar Ortiz was not yet involved in the affair, since Machebeuf's tactics lay beneath the general flow of events. However, some side notes become necessary here.

Just as he had previously done at Peña Blanca, Machebeuf began absenting himself so often from Albuquerque that he found himself obliged to obtain faculties from Bishop Lamy for publicly suspending Gallegos *in absentia*, excoriating him besides for his alleged immoral life. This was in December 1852, almost three months after Gallegos had left – not, as he always boasted, immediately after Gallegos' departure. Nor had Gallegos been thus far a travelling merchant who constantly left his parish unattended, as Machebeuf lied time and again, much less had his housekeeper been the wanton whore whom Machebeuf made her out to be. What is of utmost importance here is that ex-Vicar Ortiz in Santa Fe did not rise up to interfere on behalf of a maligned young padre whom he had once defended against Governor Manuel Armijo's false charges more than a decade before. He was not the vicar now. For the sake of peace, it was better to keep one's own counsel.[14]

---

[13] A. Chávez, *Time and Chance*, 102-03; and *Très Macho*, 44-45.

[14] In 1844 Padre Martínez wrote to Bishop Zubiría charging Gallegos with living in open concubinage and that Ortiz was doing nothing about it. The charge apparently came to nothing as Gallegos ended up being assigned the cura propio

However, the peace of the Christmastide of 1852, as far as Bishop Lamy was personally concerned, would soon usher in the new year of 1853 with what he had least expected. Under date of the Lord's Nativity he issued his first Pastoral Letter, with instructions for it to be read in all the parish churches on the Sunday following. It was a most sensible message to his flock, except for one point. It outlined a not too radical reduction of the former parish fees, also counseling all the faithful toward a good Christian life by avoiding such sinful occasions as dances, divorces, and gambling. The only objectionable point he made was in declaring that those who failed to pay their tithes would no longer be treated as members of the Catholic Church!

What is of supreme importance is that this very "Christmas Pastoral," as bandied about for years to come, made not the least reference to any of the native priests, much less to any immoral or greedy conduct on their part.[15] On the same score, neither ex-Vicar Ortiz nor any of the other padres, even when some of the latter began protesting against Machebeuf's abuses, made any reference to this pastoral – not even to that entirely uncatholic and unchristian point just cited.

But subsequent biographers took up the myth of this Christmas Pastoral as having been the immediate cause for the native priests' rebellion against Bishop Lamy himself, and what is worse, for its having touched upon their monetary greed and sexual immorality. Here ex-Vicar Ortiz himself was supposed to be just as guilty as all the rest. Even as late as in a 1997 biography of Machebeuf, the author writes that "Lamy directed strong words to the clergy" and follows with "the first fuse to blow was that of Vicar Ortiz." The source of this statement is Paul Horgan![16] Still, all of those mistaken writers are not entirely to blame in this regard because Machebeuf, and Bishop Lamy

---

of Albuquerque. See Thomas J. Steele, S. J., *Folk and Church in New Mexico* (Colorado Springs, CO: The Hulbert Center for Southwest Studies/The Colorado College, 1993), 61-63, 70 n 5.

[15] The "Christmas Pastoral" is thoroughly analyzed in A. Chávez, *Time and Chance*, 103-05; and the text is available in *Gaceta Seminaria de Santa Fe* (Christmas Pastoral), January 1, 1853.

[16] Bridges, *Death's Deceiver*, 102-03. Historian Thomas Steele, in his seminal book, *Archbishop Lamy: In His Own Words*, makes no such mistake and, in reference to Lamy's threats of defacto excommunication and triple fees for sacraments for not paying Church "tithes," writes that the Bishop "uncharacteristically...went well beyond approved authorized procedures." Steele, *Archbishop Lamy: In His Own Words*, 68-69.

himself, sad to say, initiated and kept this lie going in order to draw attention away from Machebeuf's most grievous canonical crime, his violations of the confessional seal for which Rome might have shown no pity.

CARTA PASTORAL.

JUAN, por la gracia de Dios y la autoridad de la Santa Sede, Vic.º Apᶜᵒ. de Nuevo Mejico, al clero y a los fieles de nuestro vicariato, salud y bendicion en nuestro SEÑOR JESU CRISTO.

Hermanos mios muy amados, hace poco tiempo que fué mandada la carta pastoral del Concilio Nacional de Baltimore, sin embargo teniendo necesidad de hablarles sobre unos puntos particulares, lo harémos de la manera la mas breve que se puede.

Probablemente los feligrezes de este Vicᵗᵒ. Apᶜᵒ. habràn tenido la noticia de que hemos establecido en la Capital, un convento de religiosas, para la educacion de las niñas; desde el año pasado tenemos una escuela para los muchachos, y nos da gusto de poder decir que está prosperando. Estos dos establecimientos, particularmente el para las niñas, nos han ocasionado gastos muy grandes, añadidos a otros que hemos tenido para componer la capilla de nuestra Sra. de la Luz, vulgarmente dicha la *castrense*. Pero todo lo hemos emprendido para el bien espiritual y temporal de los fieles de este Territorio, y para la decencia del culto divino. Ponemos nuestra confianza en Dios, que conoce la pureza de nuestra intencion, sin cuyo auxilio nada puede prosperar; al mismo tiempo esperamos que los fieles se aprovecharàn de la oportunidad que les es dada para procurar a sus hijos una educacion decente y religiosa, porque la mejor herencia que los parientes pueden dejar a sus hijos es una buena educacion que vale mucho mas que la fortuna la mas brillante, pues riquezas sin educacion son mas dañosas que provechosas.

En muchas ocasiones habiamos anunciado que se bajarian los derechos parroquiales, y aunque el arancel hubiera sido estable-

The Christmas Pastoral, source of much misinformation. Christmas 1852.
Courtesy of the Archives of the Archdiocese of Santa Fe.

cido por algun tiempo, hemos jusgado conveniente de establecer las reglas siguientes, que tendrán fuerza desde el primero de Enero le 1852.

Regla 1ª. Para un casamiento - - - - 8 ps.
        "   " entierro   - - - - 6
. Entierro de niño bajo de 7 años   - - - - 2
        Para un bautismo   - - - - 1

Regla 2ª. Los acomodados y los que tienen proporciones cortas daran la mitad de los derechos que quiere decir:

Para casamiento   - - - - 4 ps.
    " entierro   - - - - 3
Entierro de niño bajo de 7 años - - - - 1
    Para bautismo   - - - - 4 rls.

Regla 3ª. Las personas que piden servicio ó ceremonias de pompa se convendrán son su parroco que les llevará según su prudencia y juicio. Respecto a las funciones y misas cantadas se aguarda la misma costumbre que antes, sólamente los Srs. Curas no recibirán la limosna hasta el dia que prestan su servicio. Lo mismo se observará para todos los derechos.

Regla 4ª. Los Srs. Curas ofrecerán el Santo sacrificio de la misa ca la mes un dia de la semana, según su conveniencia, en las capillas que distan mas de una legua de la parroquia principal, y que tienen en su vecindario arriba de treinta familias.

Regla 5ª. Habiendo bajado los derechos parroquiales concedimos a los Srs. Curas una cuarta parte de los diezmos que se juntaran en su parroquia, para que tengan una subsistencia decente y digna de su Santo ministerio.

Regla 6ª. Conociendo la pobreza de los templos, concedimos tambien otra cuarta parte de los diezmos para componerlos y habilitarlos de las cosas necesarias que la decencia del culto divino requiere. Pero estos fundos se gastarán bajo nuestra direccion.

Siendo la cera muy cara y muy escasa en este Territorio, dispensamos de este punto de la disciplina eclesiastica, los lugares y personas pobres que podran entonces usar belas que se llaman de esperma.

Esperamos que los fieles testigos del uso que se hace de los diezmos para nuestro mantenimiento, el de los Srs. Curas, la decencia del culto divino, y los establecimientos de las escuelas no tendrán pretesto ninguno para dispensarse de dar religiosamente los diezmos según la disciplina establecida en los países católicos. Es verdad, no hay ley civil que les obligue delaute de los hombres; pero los católicos instruidos en las obligaciones de su santa religion saben que hay una ley de la Iglesia que les manda de cumplir en conciencia con este deber segun la proporcion que les toca de los bienes que han recibido de la providencia de Dios; y todos tienen la misma obligacion de obedecer la Iglesia en este punto como en otros. Hemos tenido mucho consuelo de ver que este ultimo año la mayor parte de los fieles han cumplido con este deber, y tenemos la confianza que los pocos que se habian rehusado de entregar esta deuda sagrada no nos obligarán de usar de la severidad que ellos merecen por su desobediencia; pero si despreciando la ley de la Iglesia, no quisieren sujetarse a la autoridad eclesiastica, tendriamos, aunque con mucho sentimiento y pesar, que negarles los sacramentos, y considerarles como no pertenecientes a la Iglesia Católica.

Hermanos mios muy amados, teniendo que dar cuenta a Dios por vuestras almas, faltariamos a nuestro deber si no les avizariamos con toda caridad de evitar unos escandalos que son muy comunes en este Territorio. Quieremos hablar de los divorcios, los bailes, y los juegos. Esperamos que no tomaran en mala parte las admoniciones que les hacemos con la libertad que nos da el evangelio. No importa lo que permiten las leyes humanas, la ley divina nos enseña tocante al matrimonio, que "lo que Dios juntó, el hombre no le separe."—Mateo xix, 6. Y los que no aguardan la fidelidad conjugal que tan solamente prometieron en la faz del cielo y de la tierra no pueden esperar una vida feliz, mas bien la maldicion de Dios. Respecto a los bailes les diré, segun las palabras de San Francisco de sales que aunque "las danzas y bailes sean cosas indiferentes por su naturaleza, segun el modo ordinario con que se ejecutan, estan inclinadas al mal, y por lo consiguiente, llenas de riesgo y peligro. Todos en el baile ostentan a competencia vanidad y como esta es la disposicion mas oportuna para aficiones malas, y amores reprehensibles y peligrosos, se engendra todo eso en los bailes."

Si, segun la opinion de San Francisco de Sales, un baile ordinario que se hace segun las reglas de la decencia es una disposicion a las aficiones malas y amores reprehensibles que serán los bailes que se ejecutan con tantos escesos y desordenes que les hacen mas semejantes a una diversion de paganos que de cristianos. Por eso se pueden con razon considerar como una escuela de inmoralidad y vicio. Cuantas personas por haber frecuentado estas recreaciones profanas han perdido el temor de Dios, su inocencia, y su honor! Tocante a los juegos segun se prácticcan aqui, no solamente son recreaciones peligrosas, indignas de un

cristiano, pero son absoluta y escencialmente malas y reprehensibles. Por eso las prohiben las leyes tanto civiles como eccle-
siasticas. Por eso la Santa Mujer Sara alegando en la presen-
cia de Dios su inocencia, decia: "Vos sabeis, Senor, que jamas
hé conversado con los jugadores."—Tobias iii. 17.

Hermanos mios muy amados, concluirèmos con el Apostol,—
Eph. iv. 27, "no deis lugar al diablo, el que hurtaba ya no hurte,
antes bien trabaja obrando con sus manos, lo que es bueno. * *
Ninguna palabra mala salga de vuestra boca sino la que sea
buena para la edificacion de la fé. Toda amargura, y enojo, y
indignacion, y griteria, y blasfemia, con toda malicia, sea des-
terrada de entre vosotros." Y en otro lugar, 1ª Cor. vi. 9, "no
os engañeis, pues ni los fornicarios, ni los adulteros, ni los la-
drones, ni los dados a la embriaguez, ni los maldicientes, ni los
robadores, poseerán el reino de Dios. * * * Mas bien glo-
rificad a Dios y llevadle en vuestro cuerpo."

Ordenamos que esta carta pastoral sea leida publicamente en
todas las parroquias el Domingo despues de su recepcion.

Dada en Santa Fé, fiesta de la natividad, 1852.

† JUAN,

VICARIO APOSTOLICO DE NUEVO MEJICO.

This great lie of the Christmas Pastoral, followed by its long drawn out
regulations, came easy for the greatly worried bishop and his understandably more panicky friend. For right after this pastoral had been published,
Bishop Lamy received the very first criticism of his policies in a letter of 5
January 1853, composed in Taos by Padre Martínez and undersigned by
some northern pastors. Hence it came in most handy for the two Frenchmen
to adopt that hoary but most effective false argument which went: *post hoc,
propter hoc* (after this, therefore because of this). Actually, Martínez's letter,
and others on the same subject which followed throughout January and
February, did not mention the Christmas Pastoral or its contents at all – nor
did Lamy's or Machebeuf's answers during this entire phase of their serious
correspondence. Neither did Martínez and his men assail the bishop's person or his legitimate authority. Rather, both men were addressed or referred
to in the most reverent terms. The sole theme of the complaints was what
they termed Machebeuf's unlawful assumption of episcopal authority, his
misappropriation of parish funds, and the hate and scorn that he had for the
native clergy.[17]

---

[17] A. Chávez, *Time and Chance*, 105-07.

All three of these, they contended, lay behind his unlawful suspensions of Padre Ramón Salazar of Santa Clara, then Padre Antonio de Jesús Salazar of Abiquiú, and lastly the absent Padre José Manuel Gallegos of Albuquerque who had not returned from Durango as yet. The Polish priest at Mora was not brought in, but Padre Martínez did have a separate civil investigation made of the matter in his prosecution of Machebeuf. To his January 5th complaint Martínez appended what was a much more serious charge – that Machebeuf had broken the seal of confession in one of his Taos villages, "at least in genre," something which was most heinous, to say the least. This of course, is what really stung Bishop Lamy, who in turn demanded proof, while Machebeuf started to become more apprehensive, so much so that he wrote Martínez a conciliatory letter protesting his innocence in this regard. A placated Martínez then absolved him of having ever breached the sacred confessional trust in his parish. Three years later, Machebeuf would still be clutching this letter to his heart during his defense in Rome.[18]

Padre Martínez, somewhat a local hero in Taos, who all his life had indulged in his vaunted expertise in canon law, was not defending the suspended priests as his clients but rather using them as cases in point for the purpose of prosecuting Machebeuf for his canonical crimes. He conceded that a couple of the suspended padres were not perfect, and that, if Lamy himself had ordered the suspension of one of them, there was nothing left to say about the matter. What he actually sought was a Church trial of Machebeuf for his own abuses, especially his misappropriation of parish funds. The bishop could be the impartial judge whether Martínez acted the part of a prosecuting attorney or friend of the court. As their mutual correspondence also shows, they even conferred personally on the matter. Lamy evidently tried to placate the Taos savant in this manner but with no intention at all of bringing his dear friend to trial.[19]

Ex-Vicar Ortiz is never mentioned in the heated controversy, and, when one looks at the entire picture and its attendant circumstances, one can safely say that he was avoiding the entire affair, even in connection with similar accusations against Machebeuf, which came from Peña Blanca. Ever since the middle of January, this town's prefect, a crafty barrister and politician named Francisco Tomás Cabeza de Baca, who was Ortiz's brother-in-law, had been pelting Bishop Lamy with other such charges against Machebeuf. In the more acrimonious and often sarcastic correspondence which he and the

[18] Ibid., 110-14.
[19] Ibid., 113.

bishop exchanged, Tomás, as he was more commonly known, brought up three specific instances to prove that Machebeuf had violated the confessional secret, and this had vastly increased Lamy's worries about his vicar and close friend. By now, in all his letters abroad to places like Ohio, Baltimore, St. Louis, France, and the Vatican, he kept repeating that the bad native priests of New Mexico had rebelled against his very own person and his authority as bishop. This attack was a direct result of the regulations contained in his Christmas Pastoral! Nothing is mentioned about Machebeuf as being the sole target.[20]

As for ex-Vicar Ortiz in this connection, Machebeuf years later accused him of having instigated Don Tomás C. de Baca. While it is entirely possible that C. de Baca had apprised his brother-in-law at Santa Fe about his purposes and that Ortiz had derived some secret satisfaction therefrom, the well-educated and sharp lawyer needed no help from Ortiz. What really must have driven him to attack Machebeuf was the fact that his younger brother, Padre José de Jesús C. de Baca, was the pastor of Tomé who had previously been driven out by the Valencia-Cárdenas schismatic combine – and now Machebeuf had placed that same Valencia in charge of the Santo Domingo parish during his absences! The priest at Santo Domingo also ministered nearby Peña Blanca. It was adding insult to injury, since Peña Blanca was both the birthplace and, at this time, the almost exclusive bailiwick of the proud Cabeza de Baca clan.[21]

However, the crushing wheel of such precipitating events was not to spare Don Juan Felipe Ortiz in what he might have deemed the safe seclusion of his *parroquia*. By the end of February, 1853, Padre Gallegos had returned to Albuquerque from Durango, and promptly, through the local probate judge named Don Ambrosio Armijo, opened another heavy barrage in Bishop Lamy's direction. Like those complaints coming from Taos and Peña Blanca, the barrage was not directed at Lamy's person or his episcopal authority, but solely at Machebeuf's abuses of power, his money madness in appropriating the parish funds, his frequent and prolong absences, and, once again, his violations of the confessional seal during his sermons. This second attack from another presumptuous layman brought Bishop Lamy's worries and anger to a high pitch, so much so that he threatened Armijo and the

[20] Ibid., 111-13, 115-16.

[21] Ibid., 116; and A. Chávez, *Origins of New Mexico Families*, 152-54. For a more current view of the Vicar Ortiz conspiracy regarding Machebeuf's violation of the confessional seal see Bridges, *Death Deceiver*, 119.

nine hundred fifty parishioners who had signed his first missive with direct consequences for having attacked not Machebeuf but his own person and authority![22] Had the bishop already come to believe the false premise which he still kept writing abroad?

Then, toward the middle of March, while this acrid correspondence with Armijo was going on, Bishop Lamy did a very strange thing – strange because, as one should think, it would certainly add to his current troubles. For at this very time, he decided to divide ex-Vicar Ortiz's beloved *parroquia* in Santa Fe. Sad to relate, it caused the aging Ortiz's very first personal disappointment and sense of loss during his long and fruitful career. Lamy's action was a shock, which may have planted the seeds of mental disturbance. Whether this had been in the offing or not in Ortiz's case, it would steadily accelerate the onslaught of what appears to be a sort of advanced senile deterioration.

---

[22] A. Chávez, *But Time and Chance*, 114-15; and *Très Macho*, 53-56.

Whose Parroquia?

The last ministerial entry by ex-Vicar Ortiz in his parish records occurs on 18 March 1853. Hence it must have been right after this date that Bishop Lamy told him that he was dividing his old parish of San Francisco into two territorial parts. One part would continue under Ortiz's charge and the other to be annexed to the *Castrense*, which would be the Bishop's "cathedral" with Father Brun as its actual rector or administrator.[1] Evidently, when Machebeuf abandoned the *Castrense* the previous year to go to Peña Blanca and then Albuquerque, Santa Fe's English-language parish was left bereft of any priest who knew English. The parish must have dwindled to nothing as far as attendance and support were concerned. Thus came about Lamy's decision to divide the old Spanish-language *parroquia* and make the *Castrense* a mixed parish of Hispanic natives and whatever English-speaking parishioners had survived. But this did not sit well with old Ortiz, who, whether he first argued about it with the bishop or not, resigned his pastorship in a huff. He did not object earlier when the English-language parish was formed; it really had not been a breaking up of his old parish but a necessary formation within it for a most laudable purpose that did not effect the entity of his Spanish-language domain. But this bold division was different. It struck at the very heart of his *parroquia* which, as the *cura propio* or irremovable pastor that he was, could neither be taken away or be divided at will. To the delight of the subsequent Lamy biographers, and careless as they were about the fact that this was the very first break between Ortiz and Lamy after a year and eight months of peaceful co-existence and cooperation, the former

---

[1] M-Santa Fe; Lamy file, *AASF*.

vicar now stood out as a stubborn, unreasonable, fat, and lazy old coot. While Bishop Salpointe wrote in his 1898 book that Vicar Ortiz and his priests "very naturally...refused to acknowledge" Lamy's authority and that this was certainly a disappointment for Lamy, it was not as serious a difficulty as has been represented.[2]

One of those representations came from Willa Cather who set an early premise about the New Mexican priests in her novel about Lamy when she wrote that New Mexico was "evangelized in fifteen hundred (sic)" and "has been allowed to drift for three hundred years." Yet, New Mexico just before Lamy's arrival, "still pitifully calls itself a Catholic country." "The few priests," she continues "are without guidance or discipline. They are lax in religious observance, and some of them live in open concubinage."[3] And Paul Horgan in his award winning 1975 biography of Lamy added that "Ortiz had shown no zeal for his duties, and under his regime his clergy had lost theirs. But in the matter of a change of bishops, he was suddenly zealous, legalistic and rudely stubborn." But Horgan understood that Ortiz had a legal basis for maintaining his whole parish, for he writes that Ortiz went to Lamy and told him "that he was the *parrochus proprius,* the established life pastor of the whole parish...."[4]

All this was simply due to Horgan's and Cather's ignorance of universal Church law and practice, ignorance which they shared with Lamy well before them. They judged past events or a person's motives at the time, by the strictly American Catholic Church practices of their own times. In the ecclesiastical ambience in which Don Juan Felipe Ortiz had been reared and educated, the status of *cura propio* was the highest post to which a secular pastor could aspire, short of being made a cathedral canon or a bishop, or at least a local vicar as he had been for so long under Bishop Zubiría. Moreover, one could not be made a *cura propio* until he had passed the stiffest examination at Durango, in this case, on canon and civil law, and on sacred scripture along with scholastic philosophy and theology. Only then was he eligible for the final approval of the bishop and his cathedral chapter of canons. Ortiz had fulfilled all of these requirements long before Lamy arrived in New Mexico.[5]

---

[2] Salpointe, *Soldiers*, 196.

[3] Willa Cather, *Death Comes for the Archbishop* (New York: Vintage Books, 1990 [originally in 1927]), 6.

[4] Horgan, *Lamy*, 113-14, 173-74.

[5] Historian and priest Thomas J. Steele notes that Ortiz's position was correct but that the Catholic Church in the United States did not recognize irremovable

Santa Fe, New Mexico, showing La Parroquia, circa 1860s. Photo courtesy Museum of New Mexico, Neg. No. 15171.

Now, while a plain vicarship could be lost at the bishop's will, or by a change in administration as happened to Ortiz when Lamy took over, his status as the irremovable pastor of a certain parish, and the parish itself, were inviolable. Only because of the gravest scandal or serious malfeasance in office could this official standing be lost, and then only after a due trial by the bishop and his cathedral chapter. The same held for the division of his parish if this were deemed necessary by those same authorities.

Bishop Lamy knew precious little about this, either because he had paid scant attention to the subject during his seminary courses or because his whole priestly life had been spent in the United States where, through strange Vatican default, these and some other universal laws had been exempted by custom. At the time the United States was considered "mission territory" by the Vatican, which meant that the Church was under the jurisdiction of *Propaganda Fide*, the Vatican congregation having to do with spreading the Gospel to places where it was unknown or where the Church was not firmly installed. This system sometimes gave local bishops increased powers to get

pastors. Lamy suspended Ortiz when the latter appealed to Rome. Steele, *Archbishop Lamy: In His Own Words*, 70. Bridges acknowledges Ortiz as "parochus proprius" but echoes Horgan, whom she footnotes. Bridges, *Death's Deceiver*, 103.

the job done. Hence, the American bishops, without the restraints of cathedral chapters, had practically become absolute monarchs of all they surveyed. Five years later, in January of 1858 – the very same month and year when Ortiz died – the Archbishop of St. Louis petitioned for a cathedral chapter for Santa Fe in Lamy's name. He was afraid that if Lamy died, the clergy would pay no attention to Machebeuf. In its reply, the *Propaganda Fide* explained that conditions of the church in the United States could be compared to those in England and other mission countries where cathedral chapters were exempted.[6]

For his part, ex-Vicar Ortiz knew nothing about this American hierarchical set-up, perhaps also harboring the suspicion, as he had done previously with regard to serious matrimonial dispensations, that a mere "vicar apostolic" did not have full powers of an "ordinary," a bishop of a full-fledged diocese. Ortiz was not acting like the stubborn old fool that Lamy and subsequent writers made him out to be, but he was sincerely standing up for the inalienable rights that were his. According to Machebeuf three years later, Ortiz also drove Bishop Lamy out of his house. This was true, as will be explained elsewhere. Apparently, the bishop, by his arbitrary action, had now shown himself most ungrateful for Ortiz's own past generosity in having refurbished and relinquished his home as Lamy's episcopal residence.

Ortiz's resignation freed Bishop Lamy to make young Father Brun his administrator of the old Santa Fe *parroquia,* which he now began considering as his cathedral proper. What cannot help but raise an eyebrow at this point is the fact that Ortiz's ancient parish of St. Francis was not divided after all. Had its proposed division been a preconceived ploy hatched by Lamy and Brun to ease old Ortiz out of the premises – a trick that had worked admirably? It does look that way. Moreover, the former English-language parish at the military chapel ceased to exist soon after this. The last known date of its still being used is a statement by Lamy in May 1853. Decades later, Don Demetrio Pérez wrote that *La Castrense* chapel had been closed: "I think it was 1856," because the services held in it were always being disturbed by the raucous goings-on at the plaza, along with jeers of the impi-

---

[6] Printed decree, 26 January 1858, no. 1, Prop. Fide, AASF. The Church's "mission status" in the United States did not change until the 29th of June 1908 when Pope Pius X issued the apostolic constitution *Sapienti consilio,* which among other things declared that tthe Church in the United States had been removed from the jurisdiction of *Propaganda Fide.*

ous.[7] All facts considered, this looks like one more hazy recollection of an old man, who possibly attributed the real reason for the chapel's closing to what could have well been actual noisy disturbances on the plaza that fronted the church.

Lamy already was planning on making some money on the property. Three years later in 1856 Lamy sought and received permission from the Holy See to sell the church. At the same time he sold all the church property right up to the walls of the Castrense's east side. The land was sold to Santa Fe merchant Levi Speigelberg who already was running a commercial concern on the south side of the plaza.[8] In 1859 Simón Delgado bought the church from the Archbishop for $2,000. Delgado demolished the main part of the church and built a store over the site. He converted what was left of the transept into his residence.[9]

It is also during these closing days of March, 1853, as may be gathered from other indications, that Ortiz composed a formal protest to the Holy See which he called his *"Apologia"* and which was evidently signed by some of his leading parishioners. Meanwhile, Padre Martínez in Taos had been apprised of the touchy situation, and his penchant for litigation, which had stood idle for some weeks, flared up anew. This time, deigning to descend from his juridical aerie in Taos, he called a meeting of a handful of padres in Santa Fe, ex-Vicar Ortiz included, of course, to discuss this recent development along with the previous one concerning Gallegos in Albuquerque. The meeting took place on April 2 during Easter week, presumably in Ortiz's residence. A solemn written protest was then drawn up and signed by some of the padres present in this order: Juan Felipe Ortiz, Antonio José Martínez,

---

[7] Pérez, "Rasga," 74-75.

[8] Deed of Sale, 22 November 1856, Catron Collection, FAC Library, Palace of the Governors. The deed is signed by Lamy and witnessed by Joab Houghton.

[9] Book C, Deeds, 105, Santa Fe County Records; Ellis, *Lamy's Cathedral*, 129 and 190; and John L. Kessell, *The Missions of New Mexico Since 1776* (Albuquerque: The University of New Mexico Press, 1980), 47. Although the Castrense or military chapel sounds like a small structure, it was not that much smaller than the Parroquia. The chapel was not as long and a little narrower than the Parroquia. However, the sanctuary was larger. This became especially evident when Lamy tried to fit the Castrense's stone carved reredos, or altar screen, in the Parroquia. That altar screen is now permanently installed in Santa Fe's Cristo Rey Church. For sizes and the reredos see Eleonor Adams and Fray Angélico Chávez, *The Missions of New Mexico, 1776* (Albuquerque: The University of New Mexico Press, 1956), 12 and 34; and Ellis, *Lamy's Cathedral*, 129-30.

José de Jesús Luján, and Rafael Chaves.[10] On the surface it looks as though Martínez's main purpose was to come to the aid of Ortiz and Gallegos, but actually it was only one more opportunity for him to exercise his expertise in jurisprudence while still angling for a church "court-martial" of Machebeuf. The latter was again the main target, with a repetition of all the charges previously made against him – and with a veiled reference to the confessional violations as still "suspected."

Finally, Martínez left off barking at Machebeuf to bring up Ortiz's own cause along with those of two others, Luján and Gallegos. He wrote in a rambling legalese, which can best be translated as follows;

> However, on seeing that your Reverence has not wished to institute a trial [of Machebeuf] according to the norms provided by law but rather has taken steps of such a nature that they look like excesses – for example, your having divided the Santa Fe parish without observing the canonical dispositions, furthermore, having appropriated said parish to be administered by yourself one of your household whom you have as an assistant [Brun], and who was, ordained a priest in this present year [actually, December, 1852] – also in keeping under suspension the lawful pastor of Albuquerque, Don José Manuel Gallegos, without having observed the law, with other like misconduct which one fears will bring harm to the spiritual ministry....[11]

This was but a sop, which Martínez tossed to three of the padres present: First to Ortiz, whom he had always envied because he was a better student and had been named Vicar, but whom he graciously allowed to sign first; then to Gallegos, who must have declined to sign since he was under Lamy's suspension, and because this was his way of doing things, as shall be seen further on; thirdly to Luján, if anonymously, who had been replaced by Brun. Moreover, it must have been at this time that Ortiz, in his guilelessness and against his better judgment, entrusted a copy of his *Apologia* to Martínez, who within a few months would be sending an extract of it to Lamy, following the elevation of the vicariate to a full-fledged diocese. Martínez wanted to ingratiate himself with the bishop and his vicar.[12] This letter of 2 April, while still professing the respect due to Lamy's episcopal

---

[10] Lamy file, Horgan Collection, Prop. Fide, 2 April 1853, no. 10, *AASF*.

[11] Ibid.

[12] A. Chávez, *But Time and Chance*, 120-21.

office, did end with some vague threats that seemed to be directed at Lamy himself. For example, it stated that such future actions on his part (as in the Santa Fe and Albuquerque cases) would be considered null and void. Furthermore, it added, an appeal would be made to higher authority (the Holy See), and this was evidently with reference to the *Apologia,* which Ortiz had prepared.

For Bishop Lamy, however, the 2 April letter was a direct assault upon his person and authority. Since early January he had been protecting his *chèr* Machebeuf by deliberately deflecting all those arrows from Taos, Peña Blanca, and Albuquerque with his own shield, as if he were the target. This recent April burst of accusations in Santa Fe had now indeed aimed a shaft or two in his direction, and he avidly took this up to further convince himself that his friend was not the target but rather himself. It was also useful to clinch his previous false contentions that it was his Christmas Pastoral that had brought on the native priests' rebellion. A week later, on 10 April 1853, he wrote to Bishop Purcell of Cincinnati:

> But now that I have commenced to reform some abuses, and to lay down rules for the clergymen, I have met with a great deal of opposition, having been obliged to suspend four Mexican priests [Leyva, the two Salazars, and Gallegos] for the most notorious faults. They have submitted [not Gallegos], but have said that I did not observe the rules prescribed by canon law...Five or six Mexican clergymen had a meeting to oppose my authority [not Machebeuf's abuses!], and they were determined to bring their claims to higher authority...the old vicario of Santa Fe is very much put out because I divided the parish, leaving him one good half, and offering him in the immediate neighborhood of the town more than I can keep, but he would not accept, and refuses to give his services.[13]

Lamy, in dividing the parish, had taken part of Santa Fe including the old *parrochia* as his cathedral's preserve, while leaving the an undefined generous "half" in his letter to Ortiz. For the latter, over and above the rape of his indivisible parish, the act added insult to injury. After his general

---

[13] Lamy file, 10 April 1853, no. 69, *AASF.* Was Lamy offering "the old vicario" territory outside the town, presumably places like Tesuque Indian Pueblo and other outlying villages, which Ortiz obviously would not accept. Or, was he offering closer places area like Agua Fria.

criticism of the native clergy, Lamy had to bring up his friend Machebeuf, and this was only because of Ortiz's *Apologia* and a similar complaint that Gallegos was said to be preparing for Rome that contained all those charges so frequently made heretofore with regard to the seal of confession. Gallegos eventually did send such charges to Rome, but it is highly unlikely that any such accusations were contained in Ortiz's *Apologia*. All Ortiz cared about, whether out of selfishness or because he thought it right not to interfere in other matters, was his indivisible *parroquia*.

Those rebellious Mexican padres, Lamy further told Purcell, envied good Father Machebeuf for his great zeal and fine personal qualities, having gone so far as to accuse him falsely of having violated the seal of confession. Here Lamy betrayed his basic apprehension by going on to say that these "unfortunate priests" might appeal to Rome. In this case, said he, Purcell should write to his friends at the Vatican as he himself had already done – that is, about the padres' rebellion against his own authority because of the Christmas Pastoral.[14]

Five days later, on 15 April, Lamy tried to close another conduit by writing to Bishop Zubiría in Durango. Here he repeated the same things, but without reference to Machebeuf:

> I think it is my duty to inform your Illustrious Lordship concerning the opposition which certain clergymen have raised against me. My having reduced the list of fees in my last pastoral letter, and my having suspended different priests for scandalous and public faults, after many private admonitions, have been the occasion for their disobedience. To this can also be added the division of the Santa Fe parish. Having the strongest reasons for dividing said parish, I offered the Sr. Vicario D. Juan Felipe Ortiz more than I was taking away from him in the vicinity of Santa Fe, but he chose rather to submit his resignation. Six or seven of the clergymen held a meeting in this city [on 2 April], making fun of my authority, and writing me a letter that they are going to take their complaints to higher authority, and that they consider as null whichever dispositions [are] made by my administration...
>
> I much regret that these clerics have not wished to subject themselves under my jurisdiction. To date I have treated

[14] Ibid.

them more as equals than as inferiors, but I can no longer
stand their foolishness. Should their complaints get to Rome,
the Holy See will have been informed within three months
about all the circumstances of this affair, and the information I sent concerning it will be backed up by some Bishops, three Archbishops, and one of the most famous Jesuits
of our century, Father DeSmet, who this year finds himself
in the Holy City.[15]

Here Lamy added that three or four priests were soon leaving for
Durango, one of them being Padre Gallegos who did indeed leave soon thereafter. Another one had to be Ortiz, as shall be seen. Two others, Otero of
Socorro and C. de Baca of Tomé, had already left together toward the end of
March for specific reasons of their own (and not the Christmas Pastoral)
which will be explained later. But what Bishop Lamy actually intended by
this letter to Durango was to warn his Mexican predecessor Zubiría to keep
hands off the whole affair, since he now had a goodly number of more influential church officials on his side. Power and influence, not right and wrong,
would be the determinate. Therefore, he should not let Ortiz's *Apologia,* or
any other complaints like those of Gallegos and others – each one presumably indicting Machebeuf on the confessional violations – get to Rome
through his own chancery office. However, while Lamy was right in sus-
pecting that Gallegos' complaints did carry those most incriminating charges
against Machebeuf, he need not have worried about Ortiz's *Apologia.* Ortiz
only cared for his own violated status of *cura propio* in connection with his
parroquia and the real estate adjoined to it.

On 31 May, when writing to the prelate of New Orleans on his not being
able to accompany him to Europe because of his troubles at home, Lamy
once again dragged forth his favorite herring. "Ever since I established some
rules to reduce the much too high fees which existed before, I encountered
much opposition on the part of the Mexican padres." Two of them, he said,
had left the territory to take their case to Rome (Gallegos and Ortiz), two had
resigned (Otero and C. De Baca), and some were left to cause trouble.[16] From
this we learn that Don Juan Felipe had left to Durango before this date, and

---

[15] Lamy file, 15 April 1853, no. 76, *AASF.* Note that in his letter to Purcell, Lamy
    wrote that a different number of priests met. Also, when referring to his treat-
    ment of priests as equals, he conveniently avoided Machebeuf's treatment of
    those same priests.

[16] Ibid., 31 May 1853, no. 9, *AASF.*

with the avowed purpose of forwarding his *Apologia* to the Vatican via the Durango chancery and the apostolic delegation in Mexico City. There was a communication from a Durango chancery official, Luis Rubio, to a counterpart named Marino Marini at the Mexican Apostolic Delegation, dated 21 July. Rubio stated that he had bothered him twice with regard to what he believed was a parcel of complaints against Lamy, which Ortiz had forwarded to Rome. Further he hoped that these would not stray in transit, since Ortiz wanted to avail himself of its safe conduct through the apostolic delegate, Monsignor Clementi.[17]

But the *Apologia* must have been shelved then and there, since it never reached the Vatican. Nor does it follow that Bishop Zubiría himself had anything to do with this, for there are no letters of his in the Vatican archives in defense of the New Mexican padres, only on the jurisdictional problems of the Mesilla-Doña Ana districts. If Lamy had somehow learned about this, he did not blame Zubiría personally in a frantic fib-fraught letter he wrote to the Cardinal Prefect of the Propaganda Fide on 31 July. The letter started with, "The opposition which I have found on the part of the Mexican See [this would have to be Durango] has placed me in certain difficulties which henceforth oblige me to address your Eminence."[18]

In short, Lamy strongly suspected that someone in the Durango chancery was taking up the cause of Ortiz and other complaints, and it appears that this letter, filled with inaccuracies, was written out of desperation, both from its tone and from what followed the introduction just cited.

> On my arrival in New Mexico, I found fearful disasters among the clergy. I dissimulated for some months and I give one instance. After my return from the Council of Baltimore, I published a pastoral letter [December 1852] in which I gave the rules to the pastors...[19]

Here he detailed the letter's contents about masses in all churches and chapels at stated times, as well as his reduction of what he called the enormous parish fees which had caused the local clergy to rebel against his own person. Nevertheless, nowhere in that lengthy Martínez and C. de Baca correspondence from January to April had these matters been mentioned. For

---

[17] Ibid., 21 July 1853, no. 3, *AASF*.

[18] Ibid., Horgan Collection, Prop. Fide, 31 July 1853, *AASF*.

[19] Ibid. A good portion of Lamy's delay involved his trip to Durango. Also, he delayed writing his pastoral letter more than a year after his return from Baltimore.

the most part, only Machebeuf's flagrant abuses had been noted. Nor had the reduction of the parish fees been that radical, as mentioned earlier. In fact, Lamy specified that the extra high fees for "ceremonies with pomp" were to continue as before. These high fees would be worked out between the pastor and those who requested them. Why not? Lamy personally availed himself of the exorbitant fees he received from the Barceló funeral and fully knew the benefits. Incidentally, his French clergy would soon be following the same practice.

Lamy then went on to write that all this had touched the clergy "in a sensitive spot" and that "they could not contain themselves for a very long time!" The majority of priests had then "openly declared themselves against me" – not against Machebeuf. Actually, only six or seven out of seventeen had complained. They also reproached him, he continued, for his having been too severe in the censures that he had imposed on certain clerics without observing the due course of Church laws. On the contrary, he exaggerated, in one case he had given the three previous admonitions (?), but the scandal involved had been so great that it had demanded a prompt and stern remedy. Finally, he arrived at his letter's main subject of criticism:

> It is above all the pastor of Santa Fe, Juan Felipe Ortiz, who brought up the most blatant pretext for complaint. He had been vicar general of the territory for several years. He has since left for Durango after I had divided the parish of Santa Fe. He claimed that, for his being a parrochus proprius, I had no right to make any change with regard to his parish. It is well to observe that he never wished to submit himself to the new rules which it was my duty to establish. Moreover, Santa Fe and the entire vicinity are much too extensive For one old fellow to administer..."[20]

This letter's bias is evident in a number of places, thus demonstrating Lamy's lack of sincerity, if not knowledge. Ortiz was a plain vicar, a *vicario furane* or rural dean of a portion of a diocese, not a "general" vicar and served as such for over twenty years. He also served Santa Fe with an assistant, which Lamy did not mention. The statement that Ortiz "never wished to submit himself" should be an obvious untruth to the reader by now.

Lamy went on to write that the circumstances had forced him to make the above changes, and that it was his right as Vicar Apostolic of New Mexico to take over the capital's parish. This cannot be denied, but only if he kept

---

[20] Ibid.

the irremovable pastor and left the parish intact. As for his designating it a cathedral at this time, that is another question. Here he told His Eminence the Cardinal that he had nevertheless offered Ortiz a more than fair trade, something he had not told Purcell or Zubiría in the preceding letters:

> Yet I offered him another parish, a good half of the capital since he had property there [sentence not clear]. I likewise granted him a pension, even though my means are very limited and my expenses enormous, whereas he is rich, and in passing I will say rich with the properties which he and his relatives have misappropriated. I offered him more than enough compensation for the improvement they have made on the parish properties, but he is demanding of me an exorbitant sum; thus I shall find myself obliged to go to court to make him restore the goods of the church.[21]

The question of church properties, a prolonged bone of contention between Lamy and Ortiz, and likewise between Machebeuf and Gallegos in Albuquerque, is something which neither Lamy nor his biographers ever understood. The latter have made much of the property question to make Ortiz and Gallegos look like unabashed thieves of sacred real estate. The fact is that in the new American Catholic system, which Lamy was following, every church or chapel not belonging to a religious order or congregation was automatically considered diocesan property. But in New Mexico, under the universal Church practice previously observed under Spain and then briefly under Mexico, only the parish churches and lands proper to them were considered diocesan property. In those times the country chapels erected by an individual or by the villagers as a whole belonged to the respective builders, making it necessary to apply periodically for "licenses" from the Durango bishop so that mass could be celebrated in them.

More specific examples in Santa Fe were, first, the ancient chapel of San Miguel, originally built under Franciscan supervision around 1625 by the original Tlascaltec servants of the Spanish, and who were augmented or finally supplanted by other servants of mixed castes. Partially destroyed in the 1680 Pueblo Revolt,[22] the church was restored in 1712 by a Confraternity of St. Michael, a Church lay organization, not necessarily run by the

---

[21] Ibid.

[22] Tlascaltec is an encompassing term used for the Indians from the central valley of Mexico. The Tlascalans from Tlascala had allied with Hernán Cortes in defeating the Aztecs.

Church. It was finally taken over by a new class of servants, the *genízaros*, during the rest of the 18th century. Then around the year 1800, the very old chapel with its lands came into the possession, whether by town grant or purchase, of Don José Antonio Ortiz, the man who added the apse and towers in 1806. How this could have come about will soon be explained.

A second example is the Rosario Chapel of La Conquistadora on the outskirts of town which the same Ortiz built in 1807 and which he donated to the confraternity of this name. Like the San Miguel chapel, it did not belong to the Santa Fe parish or to the diocese of Durango.

Then there is the famous *La Castrense*, or military chapel built on the plaza by Governor Francisco Marín del Valle in 1760. It belonged neither to the parish nor the diocese but to Spain's military ordinariate or separate diocese under its own bishop. Following Mexican Independence in 1821, it and its lands automatically were passed on to the new government, even if the latter no longer acknowledged any military ordinariate as such. When the United States took over in 1846, it came to be the American army's property, although the latter did not know by what right. Bishop Lamy had no strict right to it as he thought. He was lucky to acquire it and some good farming lands belonging to it, as shown, simply because the American authorities were unaware of their basic right even as they deemed with laudable Protestant reverence that a former house of worship should no longer suffer secular profanation.

Lastly, there was the Guadalupe chapel at the western edge of town, erected shortly after 1800 by the first group of local devotees of the Mexican Virgin of Tepeyac. It likewise belonged to its builders. Bishop Lamy would eventually take hold of it as diocesan property, but not until after a bitter court struggle and his threatened "excommunication" of one individual involved, the later famed Colonel Manuel Antonio Chaves who contested the action.[23]

All of this brings us to the buildings and lands connected in Lamy's time with the parishes of Santa Fe and Albuquerque. While these parish churches and their actual sites had belonged to the diocese of Durango since 1730 when this diocese took charge of the New Mexico missions, the old Franciscan *conventos* (friaries) adjoining them had not, nor whatever lands

---

[23] Culled from the Amado Chaves Archive, NMSCRA. Regarding Guadalupe chapel, see *The Santa Fe Gazette*, 7 and 14 February and 7 August 1858. Also see Marc Simmons, *Little Lion of the Southwest; A Life of Colonel Manuel A. Chaves* (Chicago: Swallow Press, 1973), 115-20.

the friars had cultivated. Even as far back as 1797-1799, after Bishop Olivares of Durango had secularized the Santa Fe parish by replacing the Franciscans with his own secular clergy, the bishop had been forced to concede that the adjoining friary and its lands still belonged to the recently displaced Franciscans and not to his diocese.[24] Thereafter, with the gradual disappearance of the Franciscan padres and the final demise of their historic custody, nobody seemed to know exactly to whom such properties belonged. Technically, they came directly under the Holy See, and were managed in its name by lay *síndicos*, church-run lay organizations, on the principle that Franciscan poverty forbade the friars to own property. But, following the civil and religious upheavals in Mexico, neither the Durango bishops nor the local New Mexico civil government seemed to know to whom such properties belonged after the Franciscans were long gone.

Ever since then, such properties had become a sort of no man's land which some pastors or even laymen gradually came to acquire either by civil grant or purchase – and with no clear transactions either clerical or otherwise. Of these, there are a couple of specific instances. In 1830, the civil governor approved as legal a previous sale of the Albuquerque *convento* land which Padre Leyva, the pastor at that time, had made to some laymen. A similar sale had been made as late as 1847 by Padre Gallegos, and with the civil government's approval.[25]

Returning at last to ex-Vicar Ortiz and to what Bishop Lamy was writing to Rome on this score, the evidence is clearly on the New Mexican's side. He and his relatives had not in conscience misappropriated any church real estate in Santa Fe. At this time, the chapel of San Miguel and its lands were the rightful property of Doña Gertrudis Pino (the ex-vicar's second stepmother) who had inherited them either from her late Ortiz husband or else had purchased them from her husband's Ortiz first cousins. As for Don Juan Felipe himself, his ownership of the old Franciscan *convento* structure and its lands adjoining his *parroquia* were just as legally his. He had possessed them in good faith for decades, either by those civil grants or sales just mentioned, or else, as Lamy and Machebeuf stated elsewhere, with an official act long ago of some official of the Durango chancery shortly before or after Bishop Zubiría's accession.[26] Incidentally, while Machebeuf was fighting for the Gallegos property in Albuquerque, he claimed that Bishop Lamy

[24] Loose Docs., 1799, no. 10, *AASF*.

[25] Loose Docs., 1830, no. 7; 1846, no. 2, *AASF*.

[26] Lamy file, 5 June 1854, no. 3, *AASF*.

had shared with him that Bishop Zubiría had told Lamy that he (Zubiría) had sold the Santa Fe *convento* property to Ortiz, but not the Albuquerque *convento* to Gallegos![27] Lamy and Machebeuf would later ask and then demand that Gallegos to leave the property. Machebeuf filed suit for trespass and ejectment on behalf of the Lamy and the Church. He twice wrote Zubiría to confirm what Lamy had told him about the property, which the Mexican Bishop did, perhaps, because he never had the authority to sell it. Gallegos had secured the property through civil means. After a few years of legal maneuvering the trial ended in a hung jury and Gallegos remained in possession of the rectory. Of note here is that Gallegos probably could have defended his right to the actual church but did not do so. Machebeuf then paid $1,501 for the rectory as well as all court costs.[28]

Bishop Lamy, completely ignorant of all that pre-American real estate confusion, was bent on acquiring the Ortiz property in Santa Fe according to the practice of the new American diocesan set-up, even to the point of taking the matter to court as he had previously planned to do with regard to the military chapel on the plaza. At this point in his letter to the cardinal he suddenly dropped the Ortiz case because something other than real estate began bothering him, something infinitely more pressing. Should the Ortiz and Gallegos complaints reach Rome, his dear friend Machebeuf had to be defended and his confessional missteps played down at all costs. For he felt sure that this one accusation by the rebellious padres would stand out among the lesser ones and that his myth of the Christmas Pastoral would not prove to be enough distraction. And so he suddenly plunged into the subject about Ortiz and real estate to the native priests in general:

> They also accuse my vicar general of having revealed the
> secret of confession, but these are no more than accusa-
> tions without foundation which malice and jealousy have
> invented. My vicar general is very active and very zealous.
> He preaches almost every day, is continually on tour, gives
> occasional retreats; and, since the priests here generally do
> not preach or hardly ever give instructions, they say that
> my vicar general is too vehement; and although he preaches
> only against vices, and never against persons [!], they claim
> that on certain occasions he has spoken too explicitly; they
> wanted me to get rid of him, knowing full well that they

---

[27] Lamy file, Machebeuf letters, 1854, nos. 4-5, *AASF*.

[28] Steele, *Folk and Church*, 64-67.

would have the game on their side. They have threatened me with bringing their complaints to Monsignor the Bishop of Durango to which New Mexico belonged before it was created a Vicariate Apostolic, and likewise taking their complaints as far as Rome. Some of them have already left for Durango – will they send some kind of representation before the Holy See? Should they find supporters in the Republic of Mexico, they will not fail to write to Rome and dress up their alleged rights with a real florid style.[29]

Incidentally, in his arguments with Tómas C. de Baca of Peña Blanca concerning Machebeuf's breaches of the confessional seal, Lamy had chided C. de Baca for using such a style to confuse the issue.[30] Lamy continued:

This is why I have believed it prudent to inform your Eminence of all the facts, so that if their complaints ever get as far as the Holy See, you shall have been informed of the entire matter from a good source as to how things have come to pass, and that the critical circumstances in which I find myself, the enormous abuses to which I am witness, have obliged me to be severe and to interpret ecclesiastical law in favor of order and religion. God is my witness as to how I myself have experienced a great anguish, but my duty and my conscience have forced me to take the measures. Meanwhile, I hope that your Eminence will do me the honor of examining my motives, and if it is necessary for me to avail myself of your protection, it is the favor that I beg.[31]

One may ask how his Eminence could in justice examine and then weigh Lamy's true motives, what with the inaccuracies surrounding the Ortiz case, and more so the clouding of the real Machebeuf issue by means of the false Christmas Pastoral ploy. This is why practically the entire letter has been quoted. The letter exposes the underlying false premises along with the frantic anxiety with which it was penned. To put it all in perspective, poor Don Juan Felipe Ortiz, puffing as much from the weight of his sorrow as from his

---

[29] See note 15 *supra*. Here Lamy correctly stated that Machebeuf was the target. Ortiz and Gallegos had sent complaints to Durango. Those two, plus Otero and C. de Baca, had left New Mexico for Durango. Obviously, Lamy's primary concern was to defend Machebeuf.

[30] Lamy file, Horgan Collection, Prop. Fide, 22 February 1853, no. 2, *AASF*.

[31] See note 15, *supra*.

obesity as he labored through his daily duties in faraway Durango, knew nothing about Lamy's tactics. While vainly awaiting whatever impact his *Apologia* was making at the Vatican, and not knowing that it had never gotten there, he little realized that he had continued being more of a thorn in Lamy's side than he had been before he left Santa Fe.

The Diocese of Santa Fe

At the time he was writing his frantic July 31st letter to the Roman cardinal, Bishop Lamy had not the least idea that his provisional New Mexico vicariate had been raised to the rank of a full diocese entitled the Diocese of Santa Fe, with himself as its full-fledged "ordinary." The decision made by Vatican officialdom on 20 June 1853 was issued on 18 July, and the diocese was formally erected with Lamy as its prelate ordinary on the 29th.[1] The eastern American hierarchy had been proposing it, apparently, as a result of Lamy's letters against the local padres who had rebelled against himself because of the Christmas Pastoral. Hence, this was not a promotion because of his personal merits, as all the biographers have loved to tell.

As Archbishop Kenrick wrote to Rome on 5 August 1853, just as ignorant as Lamy of the diocese's erection, he was urging that this course be taken because of what Lamy had written him about the gravest annoyances which five or six of the native priests had been causing him. They not only had ignored his pleas toward an honest behavior, he wrote, but launched the most atrocious calumnies against his vicar general, who happened to be "a most praiseworthy man." Therefore, he suggested, the creation of a full-fledged diocese would invest Lamy with the full powers and authority he needed to apply "the ecclesiastical rod" to those wicked padres.[2] This implies, as pointed out all along, that his authority as a mere vicar apostolic had been limited to a certain extent.

---

[1] Lamy file, Horgan Collection, Prop. Fide, nos. 11 and 12, *AASF*.
[2] Ibid., 5 August 1853, no. 14, *AASF*.

The exact date for the arrival in Santa Fe of the two parchment "bulls" with their leaden seals, one erecting the diocese and the other appointing Lamy as bishop, is unknown.[3] Most likely Bishop Lamy had received them well before 23 September, when someone in St. Louis wrote to him that he was now the "titular bishop of Santa Fe." Of course, he was its full bishop and not a titular one, an administrator who is not in charge of a diocese. The writer made another such error by calling ex-Vicar Ortiz his "Vicar General" when he said that the *Catholic Herald* had blundered by announcing this same Ortiz as the new Bishop of Santa Fe, "mistaking your Vicar General, Mr. Ortiz, for the Vicar Apostolic" who would be Lamy. However, he ended by saying, "the Baltimore *Catholic Mirror* carried the correct information."[4] Whatever Bishop Lamy thought of the preceding typical newspaper erratum at the time is unknown. But even if he had deemed it of little consequence, it came forth once again to haunt and vex him when the same error about Ortiz, after it appeared in the *Cincinnati Catholic Telegraph* and was picked up by the local *Santa Fe Gazette* in its 26 November issue.

What a stir it must have caused in Santa Fe, especially at the cathedral (now a true one), and at the bishop's residence where Don Juan Felipe's name and person were more than anathema! This can be assumed from the corrections which both the *Gazette* and the *New Mexican* had to make, by distinguishing precisely the vast difference that existed between a vicar apostolic, Lamy's former title, and a mere vicar "forane," as Ortiz had been under the diocese of Durango. Such precise information could only have come directly from Bishop Lamy himself, or else through Father Brun.[5]

Had Ortiz in Durango learned about the big blunder in the *New Mexican*, he might have believed it at first as a direct result of his *Apologia*'s effect in Rome – still unaware that it had not gotten past the Delegation in Mexico City. But then he also would have known about the correction made. If he had any sense of humor left, the whole thing could have given him some wry pleasure. He knew nothing, of course, and the months stretched into another year while he kept waiting in vain for some developments, meanwhile reiterating his troubles to anyone patient enough to listen, like that Durango priest whom he mentioned as Don Luisillo in a subsequent letter to Bishop Zubiría. This kindly bishop himself, as a patient listener, could also

---

[3] Bullae, 29 July 1853, *AASF*.

[4] Ibid., 23 September 1853, no. 15, *AASF*.

[5] *The Santa Fe Gazette*, 26 November, 3 December 1853; and *The Santa Fe New Mexican*, 3 December 1853.

have told him more than once that it was not for him to interfere in the affairs of another diocese, and one in a different country at that.

Speaking of that same *Apologia,* neither did ex-Vicar Ortiz know what Padre Martínez had done in this regard. Upon learning that Santa Fe had been promoted to diocesan status, Martínez wrote Lamy a most fawning letter praising him and Machebeuf. To ingratiate himself further, he betrayed Ortiz's trust by sending an extract he made of the *Apologia.*[6]

Thus the year of 1853 ended, and in January of 1854 Bishop Lamy undertook a voyage to France for the purpose of recruiting more workers for New Mexico. He, then, went all the way to Rome to carry on, among other particulars, his feud with Ortiz with regard to the Santa Fe church property.[7]

According to a letter written in Paris on 16 April, he said that he had brought along as his secretary that young half-brother of the ex-Vicar, Padre José Eulogio Ortiz, whom he had just ordained on 5 January 1854. Ortiz would remain ever faithful to the Bishop despite a hint by Horgan to the contrary.[8] Before leaving, Lamy also issued on 14 January, a brief letter to the clergy outlining the same points of the Christmas Pastoral, but here tripling the fees for the households of those who failed to pay their full tithes.[9] Again, there was no criticism of the clergy for any faults. Nevertheless, the Pastoral would soon become attacked.

According to his letter of 6 April 1854, Lamy also took along a couple of New Mexican native lads to begin their studies at the seminary of Clermont, but they apparently never continued their pursuit of a clerical career. Years later Defouri identified them as Jesús M. Ortiz and Florencio Gonzalez.[10] Don Demetrio Pérez recalled that one of these two students of 1854 was that same Jesús María Ortiz of Santa Fe who was already dead. The other student was a Severino Trujillo of Mora.[11]

---

[6] Martínez file, 22 December 1853, *AASF.*

[7] Lamy file, 16 April 1854, no. 4, *AASF.*

[8] Clergy of the Archdiocese, Vol. I, nos. 2 and 4, *AASF*; and Horgan, *Lamy,* 196. Horgan claimed that there was a vast conspiracy of all the New Mexican clergy, including Lamy's young traveling secretary.

[9] Lamy file, Pastorals, 1854, *AASF.*

[10] Defouri, *Historical Sketch,* 45-46.

[11] Pérez, "Rasga," 75. Young Trujillo had to be Zeferino Trujillo, who had studied in France and then came to be the first teacher of the authors' respective father and grandfather in Wagon Mound around 1890. Fray Angélico remembers, when a youth, Don Zeferino Trujillo as a man of about sixty.

But when Bishop Lamy finally reached Rome that June, one of the main problems he brought up, and at great length, was that of Juan Felipe Ortiz and his Santa Fe property. This can be gathered from the statement that he made before the Propaganda Fide on 5 June 1854:

> As Monsignor Lamy, Bishop of Santa Fe, N. M., now finds himself in Rome, he avails himself of the occasion to humbly beg the Congregation of the Propaganda if he can reclaim a Santa Fe church property that had been sold by Monsignor of Durango, Don Antonio Zubiría, current Bishop of Durango in the Republic of Mexico. This property consists of considerable land attached to the church of St. Francis, the sale of which, from the information I have gathered, was done without any legal formality and was signed by a [Durango chancery] ecclesiastic who is said to have been authorized by Monsignor the Bishop of Durango, this either in 1831 or 1833. This property was sold to the pastor of Santa Fe, Don Juan Felipe Ortiz, for three hundred lambs which he is to donate after his death or upon resignation. This parish has lost the only property or fund which it possessed, so that now hardly any piece of land remains to the church whereby the priest who administers Santa Fe can build a rectory. All the inhabitants of Santa Fe are witnesses to the fact that the fund and property had belonged to the church of St. Francis since the founding of the missions and they are all astonished by this alienation...[12]

Most of the correct details of New Mexico's colonial history as presently known are the result of extensive research done in the current century. Earlier people cannot be blamed for their ignorance of their past – and more particularly of the Franciscan mission program. For one example, Don Demetrio Pérez, when referring to the *Castrense* chapel built in 1760, said it

---

[12] Lamy file, Horgan Collection, Prop. Fide, 5 June 1854, no. 3, *AASF*. By Lamy's statement the sale was authorized either before Zubiría was bishop, or in his 1833 visitation. The founding of missions in Santa Fe would have dated from as early as 1607. This letter is a good example of what has been said about Lamy's hazy knowledge of the former Franciscan property. See Juan Martínez de Montoya Petition, 10 August 1608, Juan Martínez de Montoya Papers, Fray Angélico Chávez History Library, Palace of the Governors.

had been founded during Santa Fe's first years by the conquistadors![13] He was only off by 162 years.

Lamy continued:

> After my arrival in Santa Fe, the pastor Juan Felipe Ortiz resigned. I have been offered the three hundred lambs which was the arranged price for the church's land; but I refused to accept them in the past and up to the present; I do not consider the sale of said property legitimate and canonical.
>
> Another piece of real estate pertaining to the chapel of St. Michael in the same villa of Santa Fe has been alienated in the same manner; and it is the mother of the pastor Don Juan Felipe Ortiz who is in possession. The whole world considers the alienation of these properties a mystery.
>
> As for me, I think that Monsignor of Durango might have been ill-informed, and thus by a misunderstanding the church of Santa Fe might have lost them.
>
> I had wanted to have explanations on this subject with the pastor of Santa Fe, Don Juan Felipe Ortiz, for the purpose of settling things amicably; I had made him the most advantageous offers, by giving him the value of his property, leaving him half of the land during his life and one of the residences which he had built on the church's land, but he had not wished to make any such arrangement, and has demanded thirteen thousand hard silver dollars...[14]

Thirteen thousand American silver dollars was indeed a most exorbitant sum for those times, whether for acres or for sheep, and this statement is therefore subject to serious doubt. Even three thousand dollars as the equivalent of three hundred sheep or lambs, while still much too steep, sounds more reasonable, and this could have been a slip of Lamy's pen (thirteen or three or intending to write *trois-cent* instead of *treize-millex*) if not a deliberate fabrication. Or else Ortiz had actually stipulated that exorbitant sum of

---

[13] Pérez, "Rasgo," 74-75.

[14] Lamy file, Horgan Collection, Prop. Fide, 5 June 1854, no. 3, *AASF*. Note a misimpression and an error in the letter. First, Ortiz did not resign until a year and a half after Lamy's arrival. Second, Ortiz's stepmother Gertrudis Pino, not his departed mother, was in possession of St. Michael Chapel.

thirteen thousand by way of telling Lamy that the property was not for sale.[15]

Now Lamy told the cardinal prefect that he had just acquired a house for the religious community (of Loretto Sisters) and that, because of this heavy debt, he could not afford to pay even half of what he had offered for the church property.[16] Under the date of 17 June, the curial secretary's blotter briefly sums up the contents of a letter from the Propaganda officer to Bishop Zubiría in Durango, in which the properties of the church of St. Francis and the chapel of San Miguel are brought up as having been alienated by the priest "Phillipus" Ortiz and his mother to the grave detriment of the Church. Exactly what Zubiría was to do about the matter is not at all clear from the secretary's much abbreviated Latin notations, most probably suggesting that he should assist the bishop of Santa Fe in settling the problem.[17]

Actually, Lamy was way off base in his complaints and exaggerations about Ortiz. As has been demonstrated, Lamy had no comprehension, or, at best, a convenient understanding of Church law regarding land ownership and the rights of a *cura propia*. Lamy initially seems to have accepted Ortiz's ownership for he referred to Ortiz's house as "his own" in 1851. Later, the Bishop openly assumed that Zubiría in Durango had let Ortiz take advantage. In the end, the old axiom that actions are louder than words proved true. Lamy treated the whole affair like a straight business transaction, thus confirming Ortiz's claim.

On 31 August 1855, Lamy bought from Ortiz a section of land "behind the *parroquia*" which was bounded on the west by "the house of the seller" or the convent. The deed gave the selling price as three hundred sheep and the sum of one hundred pesos![18]

The sale for three hundred sheep points to another source of confusion in Lamy's letters. Ortiz states in the deed that he had held the sheep as "*pie de alter* by decision of His Holiness José Antonio Laureano de Zubiría" who had assigned the church emolument, a sort of ongoing endowment, "exclusively to the curate of this parish or to his successors." *Pie de alter* is an emolument given to a churchman in addition to his regular stipend or benefit in payment for his performed duties.

---

[15] Santa Fe County Deed Record B, p. 382, in *New Mexico Register*, 27 July 1956.

[16] Lamy file, Horgan Collection, Prop. Fide, 5 June 1854, no. 3, *AASF*. The story of the Sisters of Loretto, their school, and the Loretto Chapel is a credit to Lamy. See Mary J. Straw, *Loretto*.

[17] Ibid., 17 June 1854, no. 5.

[18] Book C, Deeds, 16, Santa Fe County Clerk's Office, Santa Fe.

In effect, then, when Ortiz was relieved of his curacy, however illegal, in 1853, the three hundred sheep passed to whoever was the new curate of the Santa Fe parish: Lamy himself. Ortiz's subsequent willingness to sell Lamy the much-needed lot provided an opportunity for the old ex-vicar to be satisfied on two scores, for Lamy paid him back by returning all rights to the flock of sheep plus one hundred pesos. Lamy, likewise recognized the reality of Ortiz's ownership when he purchased the convent and its immediate grounds from Ortiz's executor after the old vicar's death.[19]

Lamy's criticism of Ortiz's wealth was wholly unnecessary. One can only imagine the disappointment and hurt Ortiz would have felt if he had learned of such words from his church superiors. Ortiz had spent years drawing on his own and his family's resources to improve the *parroquia* and adjoining convent, as well as other churches in and around town. For the more than twenty-year duration of his vicarship, Ortiz took on the *parroquia*'s maintenance almost as a personal matter. He had inherited a run down 135-year-old building. The Vicar, whose tastes and needs were far from Spartan, immediately began remodeling. He separated the convent from the church by demolishing the convent's entire north section, including the *Parroquia*'s Third Order Chapel. By thus separating the buildings, Ortiz began work on refurbishing the convent. By 1846 he had a whitewashed residence with a porch and enclosed patio that was described by one observer as "one of the best dwelling houses in the city."[20] This is the same edifice that Ortiz graciously gave up to his new church leader only a few years later. He was rewarded by Lamy's and, subsequently Machebeuf's, prejudiced criticisms. No wonder Ortiz's initial cordiality vanished, eventually, to the point where he would tell Lamy to get out of the building.[21] Despite his displeasure with Lamy, the latter's eviction did not include the newly begun boys' school housed in the same building. The old priest would not let his personal hurt interfere with his mission in life.

Ortiz did not limit his remodeling program to the convent. The *parroquia*'s north chapel, or Conquistadora Chapel, was restored to an approximation of its original shape with a trapezoidal sanctuary that was illuminated by a clerestory window placed in the ceiling. He also deepened the main sanctu-

---

[19] Ellis, *Lamy's Cathedral*, 85, 87-88.

[20] Abert, in Emory, *Notes*, 39.

[21] Ellis, *Lamy's Cathedral*, 86, 88-89.

ary and installed new diagonal walls to create another trapezoidal rear section.[22]

Ortiz no doubt worked on the buildings in full knowledge that the most extensive previous care for them had been undertaken by his great-uncle Antonio José Ortiz.[23] As *cura propio,* and with his family's long standing support for the *parroquia,* Don Juan Felipe Ortiz must have been surprised by the critical words of Lamy and Machebeuf. They interpreted his concern as what they considered typical native greed and arrogance.

Bishop Lamy was back in Santa Fe by November 1854, preening with the assurance that the several new feathers in his cap now gave him. First of all, there was that central plume of full episcopal authority that had come to him with the erection of his Diocese of Santa Fe the year before and now sanctified. But no less a cause for legalistic joy and satisfaction, as he wrote on 29 July 1854, was the sizable crew of mostly young French clerics whom he was bringing back from his beloved France.[24] Thus far, as has been seen, the original so-called Mexican clergy had been in the majority, despite the death of one and the departure of four others. This left a dozen of the original seventeen.

One of the four departed was Padre Gallegos, who returned from Durango to run successfully for United States Congress. Lamy was indirectly involved in opposition to Gallegos during the latter's campaigns.[25]

The only non-Mexican priests whom Lamy had thus far was an odd collection of five: first, Machebeuf and Grzelachowski of 1851. Then Jean François Pinard and Carlos Brun who, Demetrio Pérez recalled, had arrived in January of 1852.[26] Machebeuf had previously met Brun in New York, misnaming him "Le Brun" as did Pérez.[27]

Finally, there was an Italian Franciscan named Fray Donato Rogieri, who had previously been stationed in the Holy Land. He had wandered into Santa Fe one day toward the end of 1853. While in Rome, Lamy had asked the

---

[22] The best description of the parroquia's physical evolution is Ellis, *Lamy's Cathedral,* 98-100, 109.

[23] Ibid., 98-99; and A. Chávez, *New Mexico Families,* 329-30.

[24] Lamy file, Horgan Collection, 29 July 1854, no. 7, *AASF.*

[25] The struggle for the Albuquerque church property was left in Machebeuf's hands. The entire long and complicated story is told in A. Chávez, *Très Macho,* 71-74, and updated in Steele, *Folk and Church,* 64-67.

[26] Peñasco I, no. 2, *AASF;* Howlett, *Life of Machebeuf,* 159; Salpointe, *Soldiers,* 218-22; and Pérez, "Rasgo," 74.

[27] Lamy file, Horgan Collection, Machebeuf letters, 16 July 1858, *AASF.*

Holy See and the Franciscan Minister General for a continuance of the Order's services through Rogieri.[28] In all, this mere handful made up a motley crew at best, his favored French vicar excepted. Naturally, what Bishop Lamy had dreamt about since the beginning was this new complement composed of young and zealous Gallican *compatriotes* who would begin replacing the naughty and lazy native clergy he felt he had found in New Mexico. Eventually, he would succeed in replacing the locals.

The second feather, or bunch of them, rather, merits passing description of the individuals concerned because of the decisive change their arrival would be starting in New Mexico – the beginnings of an all-French clerical dynasty. Some reference needs to be made to ex-Vicar Ortiz in conncection with one or the other fellow.

In his letter just cited, Lamy first mentioned young Padre José Eulogio Ortiz as returning with him and another "Spaniard" named Dámaso Taladrid. This Ortiz, as said before, always remained faithful to this bishop, even acting as a reluctant cat's paw in a small but telling incident involving his much older half-brother following the latter's return from Durango a year later.

Parenthetically, during the young padre's return voyage from Europe, his dear mother, Doña Gertrudis Pino, had died on 25 August 1854, during a cholera epidemic in Santa Fe. Her funeral had been conducted after a solemn mass in *La Castrense* – the parish church of St. Francis being closed for repairs at the time – and by none other than Machebeuf himself, who honored her with a full hour's eulogy in Spanish and English. The repair work on the old *parroquia* was delayed long enough to allow her burial inside.[29] Either she had already turned over her San Miguel chapel property to him, or else, like the rich Barceló woman, she had stipulated generous sums for the extra funeral pomp which was commensurate with her own social and financial status.

As for the other padre named Taladrid, who later became Padre Martínez's tricky nemesis in Taos, he was a priest from Spain (probably a Carlist revolutionary ex-chaplain) whom Lamy found in Rome. While at Taos, Taladrid would advise Bishop Lamy to refuse permission for ex-Vicar Ortiz to go to Durango again.[30]

---

[28] Lamy file, Horgan Collection, Prop. Fide, 5 June 1854, no. 4, *AASF*.

[29] Loretto Annals, cited in *The Santa Fe Register*, 6 May 1955.

[30] Lamy file, Horgan Collection, 30 June 1859, no. 9, *AASF*; and A. Chávez, *Time and Chance*, 122 and 130.

Now to the prize assortment of young clerics who traveled directly from France to New Mexico. These were proudly heralded by Lamy as being Frenchmen all from the diocese of Clermont Ferrand. They were Jean (François) Martin, Pierre Eguillon, Antoine (Etienne) Avel, and N. (Antoine) Juillard, all four already ordained priests in Clermont Ferrand. Then, Jean Guerin, a deacon; Eugene Antoine Paulet and Sebastien Vaur (both subdeacons), all three of whom Lamy intended to ordain priests as soon as possible. As shown in parenthesis, Lamy miswrote the first names of François Martin and Etienne Avel, and could not recall Juillard's given name.[31]

Subdeacon Sebastien Vaur unfortunately died on the day of his arrival, 18 November, from cholera he had contracted while crossing the plains,[32] the same plague that had killed Doña Gertrudis Pino in August and suggesting a continental-wide epidemic that year. Machebeuf immediately placed the first priest, named Martin at Isleta Pueblo as its first French pastor. Here he began causing the very type of priestly scandals that Machebeuf had been attributing to the New Mexico padres, and as a result, he soon disappeared from the diocese.[33]

Father Eguillon would turn out to be an excellent priest and for many years the most able administrator of Don Juan Felipe's dear *parroquia*, now a true cathedral, and no less a fine successor to Machebeuf as Lamy's second vicar general, as all the extant records and other sources show.

Father Juillard would serve less than four years in various parishes before returning to France, sick and disheartened, in 1858.[34] Father Guerin would labor for decades in Mora and Las Vegas, and likewise Father Paulet at Belén, according to parish registers. Lastly, Father Avel would be the priest in charge of the cathedral at the time of old Don Juan Felipe Ortiz's death, when he buried him in his *parroquia* with all the Church rites as will be seen anon.

One additional aside of purely local genealogical interest is furnished by two French lay youths mentioned as having come with the young cleric also just mentioned, and who are simply referred to by their surnames Vaur and Rimbert. The first was a brother of the subdeacon who had died on arrival and the second a cousin of theirs. Whether they had come as pro-

---

[31] Lamy file, Horgan Collection, 29 July 1854, no. 7, *AASF*.

[32] Ibid., Machebeuf letters, 30 November 1854, no. 7, *AASF*; Salpointe, *Soldiers*, 207; and Howlett, *Life of Machebeuf*, 199.

[33] A. Chávez, *Time and Chance*, 123.

[34] Lamy file, Horgan Collection, Machebeuf letters, 18 July 1858, *AASF*; and Salpointe, *Soldiers*, 207.

spective seminarians or not, these two fellows eventually found wives. Vaur founded a family of this name in Las Vegas, and Rimbert – who was known as old Don Juan "Rambe"[35] – started his own Rimbert family in Mora. Later, Father Guerin would bring a brother of his own from France who in turn would found the Guerin family of Las Vegas. Similar cases followed. While the clergy in New Mexico steadily became more and more French, the number of Gallic-named families also increased. These families filled the growing settlements east of the Sangre de Cristo mountain range.

However, when all is said and done, what Bishop Lamy prized the most by far at this time was the third and grandest plume in his bonnet. While in Rome he had discovered to his utmost relief and joy that no parcels of complaints from ex-Vicar Ortiz and Padre Gallegos had reached the Vatican! He and his dear friend Machebeuf no longer had to worry about any drastic prosecution from home on those old charges about the seal of confession – or so they thought.

---

[35] As a youth, Fray Angélico Chávez, the principal author of this tome, personally knew old Juan "Rambe."

Return from Durango

After a two-year's absence in Durango, Ortiz returned to Santa Fe prior to 23 June 1855. During all that time he had not heard whether his *Apologia* had reached the Vatican or not, while his friends in Durango must have gotten tired of listening to his sad story. Besides, he must have become very homesick for his native town and his widespread clan, not counting his real estate holdings. Saddest of all, he thought that Lamy would restore him to his *parroquia* which had not be divided at after all. A July 24th letter to Bishop Zubiría is presented in its entirety for revealing Ortiz's physical and mental condition in regard to some incidents and related problems as he himself saw them:

> No sooner did I separate myself from the amiable company of your Most Illustrious Lordship than God our Lord sent me a fever accompanied by a really grave dysentery. I was relieved of the first one, but I continued with the second until I arrived here, where my health which I [now] enjoy returned, thanks be to His Divine Majesty.

> Already at San Pedro Celestino, your Most Illustrious Lordship, I learned that Señor Lamy was on Visitation throughout the Río Abajo and as far as Zuñi. Upon his arrival in this city I went to present myself to him. It seemed to me that he did not receive me badly. This happened when I was convalescing, which was around the Vespers of St. John, at which time Padre Ortiz [Eulogio, his half-brother] had to leave on urgent matters of his parish [San Juan] and en-

trusted me with the patronal fiesta of St. John, where I arrived on the eve for that purpose; and after I had chanted the Vespers that evening, I received from said Lord Bishop a letter suspending me for the reason mentioned. If your Most Illustrious Lordship pleases, you may see it in copy form with others which I send to Padre Don Luisito. My last letter [of explanation to Lamy] was not answered, but about twelve or fourteen days later, he sent word through Padre Ortiz that he deemed it very reasonable for me to remain suspended, that I should write him a couple of lines or go to his house to be rehabilitated. I went, he received me with a show of fondness, I explained my reason of going [to San Juan], and he told me with frankness, and telling me that he would let me have the parish of Peña Blanca as far as Algodones. I, too, would speak to him with frankness that I could not go to minister there or in any other part of the Territory, unless it was Santa Fe. With this he remained silent and I absented myself. Most Illustrious Lordship. I have almost decided to leave this Territory once more, but if your most Illustrious Lordship does me the Favor of giving me a place where I can end my days in this Bishopric, the one of El Carrisal excepted, where I see myself going, God willing, to live and die tranquilly, as I beg of God. You Most Illustrious Lordship will do whatever is his pleasure.[1]

This first part of the letter shows that Juan Felipe Ortiz, now approaching his fifty-seventh birthday was deteriorating physically, maybe as a result of the long arduous journey which had been made doubly so by just as long a siege of diarrhea. Nevertheless, his optimism remained intact. He still expected to get his beloved parish back, whereas anyone in his right mind would have recognized it as a lost cause. The same may be seen in his continuous recourse to his former bishop and friend in Mexico, who no longer was able to help him in these and other matters.

---

[1] Juan Felipe Ortiz file, 24 July 1855, no. 4, *AASF*. San Pedro Celestino is in the Socorro parish. Vespers of St. John is on 23 June. Padre Ortiz, as mentioned, is Eulogio, ex Vicar Ortiz's half brother whose parish was San Juan. Don Luisito could be the Luis Rubio of that Delegation correspondence.

As for Bishop Lamy's hasty suspension of the sickly, aging man simply for his having helped his young priestly half-brother at San Juan, it was, obviously, a most petty gesture on his part. What comes to mind as a possible cause for such an action is that erroneous newspaper notice of two years previously announcing Ortiz as the bishop of the new Diocese of Santa Fe. This could have been sticking in his craw, as sometimes happens with executives when their high positions have been mocked in some way or another. He kept playing like a cat with a bewildered mouse after it had pawed it a bit, first with his condescending ways, and then by offering Ortiz a new parish at Peña Blanca (still with headquarters at Santo Domingo), which would be doubled in size by the addition of the one at San Felipe where Algodones was located. Recall how Lamy wrote to the Roman cardinal about the division of the Santa Fe parish saying that its territorial extent was too much for an old fellow like Ortiz. Evidently he knew beforehand that Ortiz would refuse the offer – Ortiz himself foolishly believing that he could still have his old parish back. Lamy remained silent after this, but inwardly no doubt satisfied that he now had a sufficient excuse to keep the elderly man under suspension.

Now to continue Ortiz's letter to Zubiría, in which Ortiz throws considerable light on certain charges which were going on from the old Spanish days to the new French modes of liturgy and administration, not to mention some fiscal shenanigans:

> I have not decided, Most Illustrious Lordship, to surrender to Señor Lamy the candle wax and sacred vessels from the Oratory of the late Don Antonio Ortiz because I have learned with heartbreak, and there is no doubting it, that nothing else of silverplate remains at the Parroquia than the monstrance of the the the Castrense, the chalice for which I paid the Parroquia, the one of Our Lady of the Rosary, a censer and a host-box; the rest, which your Most Illustrious Lordship knows to be plenty, is either stored away or it certainly might be that [Lamy] took a case of silverware to Europe; I know none of this for sure, and lest the former [silverplate mentioned] does not suffer the same fate, I have held up its surrender. Once again I wait for Your Illustrious Lordship to tell me what to do in this regard.
>
> Moreover, I know for certain, Most Illustrious Lordship, that the greater part if not all of the vestments, dalmatics,

171

etc., which were in abundance in this Parroquia, is evidently reduced to ashes, and among them forty dresses of gold or silver lace and other precious fabrics of Our Lady of the Rosary.

Lastly, Most Illustrious Lordship, I will let you know that the grand excuse for the division of my Curacy was the erection of a Parish at the Castrense and its sufficient number of people [the mixed parish of 1853]; but it has come to an end, for it has neither pastor nor is there any Sacrament administered there as from a Curacy, nor are its bells heard to ring, and, no doubt, [soon] after the division was made, few being the faithful in all the Curacy, it was joined to the one of Pecos.

Your Most Illustrious Lordship will forgive this importunate and tiresome story, but I have hoped that it might be of some use in some of its details, and this is what has made me communicate it to your Most Illustrious Lordship; and, besides that, you charged me to write to you.[2]

This letter is in a neat script, the signature with its rubric large and firm.

As for Bishop Lamy's actions at this time, one can see that he had been claiming Church properties which, according to the new system, he had a right to do for his diocese. But, in addition, he was unjustifiably demanding the silverplate belonging to a strictly private home chapel. This chapel of the Holy Trinity was part of the residence of old Don José Antonio Ortiz which had been inherited by his eldest son Antonio, now long deceased, and which at this time was apparently either owned or cared for by Don Juan Felipe. The latter's suspicion about the sacred silverware being surreptitiously taken to France was not so far-fetched, for such accusations were not unusual.[3]

Chihuahua silver coins and bullion, besides vessels and other articles of solid silver, had been a common and not too expensive commodity among merchants around 1800, when the original Ortiz patron had endowed the churches and chapels with them. Two decades later, after the start of the Missouri-Chihuahua trading route, the price and importance of silver had

---

[2] Ibid. Don Antonio Ortiz, the son of Antonio José Ortiz, was the patron of the 1806 church and father of Padre Ramón Ortiz.

[3] See A. Chávez, *Time and Chance*, 136-37.

increased – so much so that the state of Missouri was able to pay its debts with Chihuahua silver. Like many Europeans in America, the land of promise at this time, Lamy and Machebeuf avidly eyed the precious white metal, even if their sale of it abroad was meant to help them in solving their financial problems. For New Mexico it meant the loss of a precious part of its heritage.

What further clinches this supposition, over and above what ex-Vicar Ortiz and some other priests claimed, is the very fact that none of those many sacred vessels of solid silver have survived in all of New Mexico. They have been replaced with early brass or gilt bronze ones of French manufacture. Over forty years ago, two such silver chalices were found in the church of Santo Domingo, probably the property of Padre Rafael Ortiz who had died there, and which had escaped Machebeuf's eye – or else the Indians had prevented anyone from taking them. Both chalices were of solid silver with tulip-shaped cups gold-plated inside. The much taller one, about eleven inches high, and with a very wide base on which the Chihuahua silversmith's trade mark was stamped, even had a thick, and long inner bolt with a fancy-shaped nut of solid silver, as later tested, holding the different sections together. The Santo Domingo Indians graciously let Fray Angélico Chávez remove them to Peña Blanca where he himself used them at mass for several years. Very much later they disappeared, presumably having been sent with other old mission articles to Franciscan headquarters in Cincinnati.[4]

With regard to the old narrow Spanish-style chasubles, they were soon replaced with the ungainly French "fiddle-back" ones that were long in vogue all over this country until recent times. As Ortiz observed, the ones in Santa Fe had been burned. As to the forty precious dresses of Our Lady of the Rosary, La Conquistadora, only one of them was found several years later when Fray Angélico Chávez was restoring the famous little image and its north chapel at the cathedral, after having researched their respective histories.[5] This age-worn mantle was of light red Chinese flowered brocade trimmed with silver lace, one of the many described in the pre-1680 records of the Confraternity of La Conquistadora, the statue of Mary brought to New Mexico in 1625 and kept in the *Parroquia* and, subsequently the Ca-

---

[4] Personal experience of Fray Angélico Chávez.

[5] A. Chávez, *Our Lady of the Conquest* (Santa Fe: Historical Society of New Mexico, 1948) and *La Conquistadora; The Autobiography of an Ancient Statue* (Patterson, New Jersey: The St. Anthony Guild Press, 1954). A chausable of the old type that was used in New Mexico is in the collections of the Palace of the Governors in Santa Fe.

thedral. Moreover, the popular devotion toward this historic "Queen of the Kingdom of New Mexico and its Villa of Santa Fe" had been played down by the first French clergy through their chauvinistic promotion of their Lady of Lourdes, even to relegating the ancient little image of La Conquistadora to a dark corner of her chapel. But all this failed to dampen the people's devotion, who faithfully kept up the annual novena and processions of La Conquistadora, which they still do and which had been observed since the Vargas 1693 resettlement of New Mexico after the Pueblo Indian rebellion in 1680. Later Frenchmen, to be fair, did come to appreciate the historic value of these processions as witnessed by Salpointe and Defouri.[6]

Don Juan Felipe Ortiz ended his letter to Zubiría by referring to the division of his beloved *parroquia* of St. Francis in 1853. Here he supports a previous conclusion, made from different data, that the parish was not divided after the ex-vicar left for Durango, while at the same time the proposed mixed parish at the *Castrense* had ended for good. His closing phrase about its having been joined to that of Pecos looks baffling at first. What it means is that, for the very short time, the military chapel had remained in use. Father Brun's new cathedral assistant, Father Avel, was put in charge of the military chapel along with the outlying towns of Pecos and Galisteo.

The gravely distraught and sickly Don Juan Felipe could do little else than mope in one of his houses while nursing his ailments and wounded feelings – his *sentimiento*, or heartbreak, as he put it in his letter to Zubiría. On occasion he would rally enough to needle Lamy about his real estate and other possessions, even to the point of taking him to court, as shall be seen. But what hurt him most, the nub of his deteriorating condition, was what he considered the unjust and illegal deprivation of his old parish, something that by now had become a real *idée fixé*. Besides, he had no friends left among his old clerical subjects to offer words of consolation, since they kept away from Santa Fe. The more influential Padre Martínez up in Taos was no friend, and Ortiz should have realized this many years before. His own half-brother at San Juan, young Padre José Eulogio, had not stuck by him after that initial tiff with the bishop concerning the fiesta of San Juan. Poor simple Padre Luján, so much indebted to him as his longtime former assistant, seemed to be doing well, but as pastor of a faraway San Miguel del Vado. The more jaunty Padre Gallegos, likewise indebted to him for many favors in the past, was now out of the ministry and living in a much more distant Washington, D. C., where he was serving New Mexico as its congressional delegate. In

---

[6] Salpointe, *Soldiers of the Cross*, 163; and Defouri, *Historical Sketch*, 114-15.

this particular connection, we shall see how an unwitting Don Juan Felipe would again turn out to be a burr under Bishop Lamy's episcopal saddle, not unlike the one caused by that news error in the Santa Fe papers two years before.

What is known about the poor fellow, during this sad period until his death some three years later comes from what his French antagonists wrote, and with their usual carelessness and total disregard for the proper sequence of events. On 30 December 1855, Lamy wrote Purcell that, if he over there in Ohio had his election troubles with the Know Nothings, a political party that was openly anti-Catholic, his own situation in New Mexico was no bed of roses either.

> The party of Padre Gallegos succeeded again [in this fall's elections] and sent him to Congress. They are trying all they can to embarrass us. Besides, the old ex-Vicario Ortiz has returned from Durango, and we receive from him new vexations every day. I will be obliged to withdraw the license I gave him to say Mass. Some of our Mexican padres are more troublesome to us than the Know Nothings with you.[7]

Lamy, while not lifting Ortiz's suspension entirely, had been kind enough to let him celebrate mass privately. But then something most unusual and unexpected happened right after Lamy wrote his December 30 letter. Both Lamy and Ortiz were involved in it: Lamy as the main target of a most imposing attack; Ortiz as an innocent butt in the melee.

The thing in question is a very formal letter, dated on New Year's Day, 1856, that both houses of New Mexico's Legislature addressed to the Pope condemning Bishop Lamy. As shall be seen, however, it had been drafted and composed weeks before. The document is in the diocesen archives, a big broadside in large and fine secretarial script, and signed by thirty-three Hispanic members of both chambers, plus three other officials. Below these, as the official witness, is the signature of W. H. H. Davis, the bigoted author, who was the Territorial Secretary at the time.

Briefly, the letter starts out with a string of accusations against Lamy

[7] Lamy file, Horgan Collection, 30 December 1855, no. 14, *AASF*. Ortiz had returned from Durango six months prior to this letter. The Know Nothings were a consortium of nativist organizations that sprang up in the 1840s when Irish and German Catholic immigrants began to arrive in the United States in large numbers. Because members were sworn to secrecy, their formal name, "The Order of the Star Spangled Banner," and, then, "The American Party," was replaced with the popular "Know Nothings."

during the time he was Vicar Apostolic of New Mexico, some having to do with illegal matrimonial dispensations that he had granted. It even includes such outlandish charges as his having favored Protestants over the native Catholics. These, and the manner in which they were worded, preclude any participation by Padre Martínez or ex-Vicar Ortiz, either of whom would have outlined the complaints in much better form. Nor, what is of utmost importance to note, was there the least mention of the division of Ortiz's Santa Fe parish. In short, the whole document looks more like the work of the laymen who signed it, except for ex-Padre José Manual Gallegos who at least could have drafted it during his latest political campaign before traveling to Washington.[8]

Of more particular interest is the fact that among those signing this legislature's letter to the Pope, there are some identifiable relatives of Don Juan Felipe, besides other friends and possible kin: Francisco Tomás C. De Baca, Machebeuf's confessional gadfly and still Prefect of Santa Ana County, and whose wife was the ex-Vicar's half-sister; a brother of his, Jesús María Baca; Fecundo Pino, president of the council and half-brother of the ex-Vicar's stepmother, Gertrudis Pino; Manuel Doroteo Pino, married to a sister of Padre Ramón Ortiz of El Paso del Norte; Cándido Ortiz, a cousin whose untimely funeral will be brought up later; Antonio José Ortiz, brother of the twin padres Rafael and Fernando Ortiz; and Miguel E. Pino, Prefect of Santa Fe County who was married to another half-sister of ex-Vicar Ortiz. It is no wonder that both Lamy and Machebeuf later accused Don Juan Felipe of having so many political kin on his side, while unjustly denigrating them as poor Catholics and persons of immoral life.

Bishop Lamy soon learned about the letter and its contents, as we learn from the February letter of his quoted below. But how did he learn about it, since it was supposed to be a big secret? Secretary Davis was probably the one who told him. Davis was the only "Anglo" acquainted with the document and was the author of the prejudiced book *El Gringo: or, New Mexico and her People,* which tells about his friendly relations with Bishop Lamy at the time.[9] This imposing assault upon Lamy should not have worried the good bishop too much, especially considering the faulty and inept charges which it contained. However, as they stated in their letter, the legislators were appending all of the correspondence from January through March 1853 with Martínez of Taos, C. de Baca of Peña Blanca, and Armijo of Albuquer-

---

[8] A. Chávez, *Trés Macho,* 77.

[9] Davis, *El Gringo,* 228, 267-70; and *The Santa Fe Gazette,* 21 January 1854.

que, all attacking his dear friend Machebeuf and once again bringing up that matter of the seal of the confessional. Lamy must have been thinking that what ex-Vicar Ortiz had been unable to do with his *Apologia* to Rome or Padre Gallegos in his role as priest, Gallegos as a politician was now able to accomplish by reopening a canonical can of worms. And so he wrote to the head of the Propaganda Fide in Rome on 1 February, first about the Mesilla-Doña Ana jurisdictional problem and then about his petty troubles with Ortiz, but reserving his chief concern for the end:

> I will also submit to your knowledge some facts that have taken place these days in Santa Fe. The old priest of Santa Fe (Padre Ortiz), who has returned from Durango (since last June) after an absence of two years, has demanded his parish of me, saying that he had been cura propio. It is a notorious fact that he had been away for three years already out of spite, and had never wished to submit himself to the rules that I have established in my diocese. I offered him another parish in order to give him proof that I had forgotten what was past; but out of spite he demanded of me a bell that is not his property and taking advantage of the situation by having on the civil side his brother-in-law (Miguel E. Pino), the Prefect of Santa Fe (county), he has managed to acquire the bell in court. I was then obliged to suspend him; he also has in his power several sacred vessels and church vestments that belong to the parish. But since the civil authorities are on his side for their being his relatives, and I must tell you, Catholics of a scandalous life, we have to suffer their avarice. I expose the facts to you so that if some documents get to you in Rome on the matter, you shall have been informed of everything that has happened.[10]

This long paragraph needs no further comment when compared with what Ortiz wrote to Bishop Zubiría, except for that one item about a bell.

---

[10] Lamy file, Horgan Collection, 1 February 1856, no. 9, *AASF*. Lamy obviously is being less than truthful by claiming that Ortiz had been away for three years while referring to his rules or his Christmas Pastoral. Nor did Lamy care to understand that the "sacred vessels and vestments" belonged to the private Ortiz oratory. Lamy's statement that all of Ortiz's friends are scandalous shows an obvious prejudice.

The parish church's two belfries had a number of bells, large and small, but why did both Lamy and Ortiz place so much value on this particular one? Even if Machebeuf later said that it had been removed as though from a tower, one is tempted to guess that it actually was a large altar hand-bell made of solid silver and that Ortiz had fought for it in court – even if it was not his own – to prevent it from going to France and ending up as silver ingots. This is but a guess, but a reasoned one under the circumstances. For Bishop Lamy, however, all this badinage about Ortiz was but a build-up for what he saved for the last in his letter to the Roman Prefect, part of which is smeared and illegible.

> ...hence the legislators of New Mexico who, though Catho-
> lics in name have [failed?] to honor religion by their moral
> behavior, will perhaps send you a representation against
> me and a few rules which I have established...[11]

True, this "representation" was aimed directly at Lamy's person, and there was, for the very first time, a protest against the regulations in Lamy's brief circular to the clergy of 14 January 1854, a copy of which Gallegos was including with other incriminating papers. But what Lamy really feared now was all this enclosed correspondence disclosing Machebeuf's breaches of the confessional seal, and which the legislature's letter described as submitted under seven headings or "papers." The first five comprised the Martínez-C. de Baca-Armijo correspondence; the sixth was Lamy's 1854 circular to the clergy. The wily ex-Padre Gallegos collected the papers for his purposes of personal revenge, chiefly against Machebeuf who had been his particular nemesis in Albuquerque but also against Lamy for his having backed up his vicar in effecting his own suspension and ejection from his parish. The seventh "paper" was described as a "Petition from the faithful of the Santa Fe parish," evidently ex-Vicar Ortiz's *Apologia* undersigned by some of his relatives and leading parishioners. Although all of the first six papers have turned up in the Vatican Archives, this seventh one is not among them.[12] Had Gallegos failed to get the *Apologia* from Don Juan Felipe as he had planned because the latter had no copy of it on hand or because he had declined to cooperate? Who knows?

With particular regard to ex-Vicar Ortiz's own person, the legislators made a strange petition to the Holy Father toward the end of their missive, when they urged him to remove Lamy from office and name Don Juan Felipe

---

[11] Ibid.

[12] Ibid.; A. Chávez, *Time and Chance*, 125-26; and *Très Macho*, 78.

José M. Gallegos. Photo by Frederick Gutekunst, courtesy Museum of New Mexico, Neg. No. 9882.

to succeed him as Bishop of Santa Fe! This, understandably, must have made Lamy's anger erupt more than it had three years before when that newspaper blunder came out. Perhaps he blamed Ortiz for that other one, too, as he now fumed at him for such effrontery.

Now, it is altogether likely that the ex-vicar did have at least some general knowledge about the proposed action of the Legislature, whether from visits which Gallegos had made to him during his fall campaign or from any of his kin who were among the signers of the complaint to the Pope. But it is difficult to believe that he had anything to do with its composition, otherwise certain chronological errors and others regarding strictly chancery matters would not have been made. Gallegos, on the other hand, who had never exercised the duties of a vicar, was capable of such mistakes, as were the laymen involved. Moreover, knowing about Don Felipe's sole fixation about having his old parish back, it is just as unlikely that he allowed his name to be used as an episcopal candidate. Even Gallegos, who knew about the man's advanced age and ill state of health, would not have made such an outlandish proposition. Hence it had to be some of his less sophisticated relatives in the legislature.

Lamy's reaction to the legislature is evident in a letter that he wrote to Bishop Purcell on 30 April – and this was weeks after he had sent Machebeuf to Rome in order to counter the charges brought up in the legislature's letter.

> Though the time rolls on, the strong opposition raised altogether by few of our old padres does not seem to stop. The old Padre Ortiz, ex-vicario, is suspended; he induced the members of the Legislative Assembly of N. M. to make a petition to the court of Rome against me, and the most remarkable is that he had the humility to propose himself as the Bishop of the Diocese of Santa Fe and to have us suspended or at least removed. This very week he wrote us an insolent letter, asking me to show him a document of the sovereign pontiff by which I could prove that I was authorized to take his parish.[13]

Here, without realizing it, Lamy was canceling out his first statement, about Ortiz's ambition to be the new bishop. Had this been so, the old fellow would not have kept insisting upon something much less ambitious, the same

---

[13] Lamy file, 30 April 1856, no. 13, *AASF*. Ortiz was in no way involved with the legislative action. Lamy's attempt to tie Ortiz to the legislature is a complete fabrication.

old piteous song about gaining his parroquia. This was all he wanted, his fixation precluding any other aspirations of whatever nature.

Oh, What a Tangled Web

For Don Juan Felipe Ortiz, the year of 1856 continued to be a singular one, although he was totally unaware of it all. The year started in Santa Fe with his name being proposed as an episcopal candidate in the legislature's letter dated 1 January. Then, in late June, his name would be repeated time and time again, but this time with repetitious jabs at his own person and character as Vicar Machebeuf regarded them, while defending Bishop Lamy and more particularly himself against the charges brought up by the legislature's letter. Machebeuf was very concerned about the much more serious accusations brought against him in that old correspondence enclosed with the same letter.

All this brings us to a panic-stricken Vicar Machebeuf after he reached Rome that June. As Bishop Lamy wrote, Machebeuf had left Santa Fe in March as his agent or representative on various diocesan matters in France, but ultimately in Rome also. Yet when one considers those incriminating enclosures with the legislature's letter and the manner in which Machebeuf responded to them in Rome, it is altogether likely that he had insisted on making the European trip himself instead of the bishop. He had his own reasons. And for reasons of their own, Congressman and ex-Padre Gallegos in Washington had waited until April before forwarding the legislative parcel of papers to the Vatican, but it got there in plenty of time to await Machebeuf's arrival in June. He happened to be visiting the tomb of St. Peter on his feast-day, says a Vatican document, when he was "summoned" before the tribunal of the Propaganda Fide.[1]

---

[1] See A. Chávez, *Time and Chance*, 126-27; and *Très Macho*, 81.

Upon being presented with all the New Mexico "evidence" that Gallegos had forwarded, Machebeuf began filling copious large folio sheets with a hurried and almost illegible French scribbling – more dashes than regular punctuation – that betrayed the ill temper and panic animating him as he continuously lied about his own experiences with the native people of New Mexico and their padres in particular. One section, which he entitled *Remarques,* dwelt on the legislature's letter itself and those who sent it. Another, which he called *Defense,* centered on his own activities which had brought on the padres' protests against his many abuses, including the confessional charges. And here he inserted that letter of Padre Martínez, who had absolved him of all guilt in this matter, but only where his parish of Taos was concerned. A third section, *Notice sur José Manuel Gallegos,* had to do with his many battles with the Albuquerque pastor. But in all three sections he continually took pot-shots at the native padres whose names happened to appear in all the correspondence; about some he made simple false statements, while others he truly blackened with the most lurid tales.[2] Ex-Vicar Ortiz, of course, was recipient of a major share of those poisonous barbs, and this requires a detailed treatment of what Machebeuf wrote about him.

In his *Remarques,* Machebeuf began by belittling New Mexico's Hispanic population as a totally depraved and vicious people, hence deserving of their legislative representatives who were even worse.

In contradiction, many of these legislators were no less educated than Machebeuf himself. What exists of their writings shows a Spanish syntax superior to Lamy's or Machebeuf's French, not to mention their penmanship which, most unlike the two Frenchmen's, look as though they had mastered a then non-existent Palmer method. As for their morals, they must have been neither better nor worse than those of their Catholic brethren anywhere. Machebeuf gauged them by his own strict, pietistic, and quite possibly Jansenistic post-Reformation upbringing, which used as standards such things as faithful attendance at Sunday Mass and so forth. These had not been part of the Hispanic upbringing. Machebeuf was also scandalized by their frequent cases of close intermarriage, which had been a hedge against diluting of their blood heritage as well as for keeping land inheritance intact. In these *Remarques* Machebeuf had this to say in passing:

---

[2] Lamy file, Horgan Collection, Prop. Fide, June 1856, nos. 12a, 17, and 18, *AASF.*

> ...it is therefore necessary to picture a legislature composed
> of *ignorant* men, the greater part *vicious*, of bad faith, all
> under the influence of an old priest who was suspended [in
> margin: <u>Mr. J. F. Ortiz</u>]...before whom many of them
> trembled...[3]

All underlines here and those to follow are Machebeuf's, while much
necessary punctuation is ours. Here the big lie is that Ortiz not only influ-
enced his political countrymen in their decisions, evil ones naturally, but
that they actually feared him. This might apply to that stern and belligerent
Padre Martínez of Taos, a habitual politician who brooked opposition from
no one. But Don Juan Felipe, as has been demonstrated all along, was just
the opposite. Then there is Machebeuf's own personal defense where, more
than any other padre except Gallegos, and for whom a special section was
reserved, old Don Felipe gets a long and thorough drubbing:

> Juan Phillips Ortiz is a Mexican priest more than 60 years
> old — he had been in charge for over 20 years as vicar gen-
> eral of the ecclesiastical administration of the territory of
> New Mexico which Mgr. D. Zubiría, Bishop of Durango,
> had visited 3 times during those 20 years. Since Mr. J. P.
> Ortiz has not lived in New Mexico except for a short time
> after the nomination [arrival] of Mgr. Lamy to the See of
> Santa Fe, no proof has been brought forth against him with
> regard to certain accusations about his private life.[4]

This was the unkindest cut of all. It means that Machebeuf really believed that Ortiz had to be as debauched as all of the native padres were in
his estimation. However, even if nothing positive had come out of the old
gossip, he had to insinuate its possibility to the Roman Curia! From what has
been seen, while the jolly and fat former vicar had in years past enjoyed his

---

[3] Lamy file, Horgan Collection, Prop. Fide, Machebeuf Remarques, June 1856, no.
12a, *AASF*. Jansenism, named for Cornelius Jansen (d. 1638) who wrote a book
attacking the theology of the Jesuits and created a movement in France that
promoted predestination and was rigorist and very moralizing. The Catholic
Church did not accept the book as well as the movement. Nonetheless, the
philosophy lingered in the hearts of the French laity and, in turn, the clergy.
See Richard McBrien, *Catholicism* (Winston Press, 1980) 638-39.

[4] Ibid., Machebeuf Defence (vs Ortiz), June 1856, no. 12a, *AASF*. Machebeuf, like
Lamy, did not understand what kind of Vicar Ortiz was. His reference to Zubiría's
three visitations is a misleading criticism of the Bishop's zeal. Also, like Lamy,
Machebeuf exaggerated Ortiz's absence from New Mexico.

liquor in good company, attended balls and parties among his peers, and occasionally placed his bets at the Barceló salon, there is no evidence whatsoever that he was a womanizer. Not only did his high position force him to be most discreet, while also being shielded by the genuine love and admiration of all his many relatives and friends, but he seems to have been of that type of obese priest common in picaresque Spanish and French literature – and this is said without being flippant – who had sublimated whatever lustful appetites he had from the bed to the table. Machebeuf went on:

> At the first news of Mgr. Lamy's arrival through Texas, El Paso, Mr. Ortiz wrote a Circular commending all priests and lay folk to receive him with all the honor which his dignity deserved; he offered him his own residence wherein to reside for an *indefinite time*, and he went to live in another – he offered to accompany him as far as Durango in order to have a correct understanding with Mgr. De Zubiría concerning his jurisdiction – but as soon as Mgr. Lamy had published his first pastoral letter first by reducing the fees in vogue to a third of what they had been – second, by obliging the Pastors to visit and say Holy Mass at least once a month in every village farther than a league from the principal church, and having at least 30 families — third, by reiterating the obligation to preach every week and on feast days, and other rules of discipline dictated as much out of prudence as out of charity, and *necessity* ...[5]

It is surprising that Machebeuf started out by praising Ortiz, but this was evidently meant as a sharper contrast to what would follow. Also, since no copy of the 1852 Christmas Pastoral had been included with the legislature's letter, Machebeuf found himself free to lie about its actual contents. Moreover, since he and Lamy had first practiced to deceive everyone with that same Christmas Pastoral as the one cause of the padres' rebellion, Machebeuf now wove in these "rules of discipline" as if to imply that the pastoral had outlined rules of moral conduct for those naughty priests. In another part of this Defense, he deliberately falsified the entire contents of the Christmas Pastoral.[6] Machebeuf continued:

> Mr. Ortiz, the first one of all the other priests who rose up en masse to complain and protest against the pastoral letter

---

[5] Ibid.
[6] Ibid., A. Chávez, *Très Macho*, 81-84.

> [in margin: See adjoined an extract of the pastoral letter],
> provided the faithful with the bad example of insubordi-
> nation...[7]

Ortiz was most certainly not the first to rebel with the others, much less
against the Christmas Pastoral. He had remained aloof from the whole written controversy concerning Machebeuf's abuses between Lamy and the critics at Taos, Peña Blanca, and Albuquerque. It was not until his parish was
divided that he signed his very first protest months later in that letter on 2
April 1853. Machebeuf continued:

> Immediately after the return of Mgr. [from Baltimore in Sep-
> tember 1852], Mr. Ortiz obliged Mgr. Lamy to get out of his
> house [March 1853], but where else could he find lodging?
> ...he did not have a piece of land belonging to the Church
> on which to reside – the ancient rectory was being claimed
> by Mr. Ortiz under the pretext that he had acquired it from
> Mgr. of Durango. Mgr. Lamy demanded of him to produce
> the books, and he showed him a very small leaf of paper on
> which were writings, some lines supposedly of Mgr. of
> Durango...[8]

Here Machebeuf went into an involved discussion as to how the Bishop
of Durango could have alienated so much Church property into private hands
as he had done with Ortiz. As explained earlier, Franciscan property had
never belonged to the diocese of Durango. How it came into Ortiz's possession is a problem in itself. It could have been acquired by casual permit,
with the string of those 300 sheep attached as a *pie de alter*, from a Durango
chancery official as far back in 1831. The latter very likely was the "very
small leaf" that Machebeuf mentions. Or he acquired it later in 1833 by
some oral confirmation by Bishop Zubiría when he became bishop and chose
Ortiz as his vicar. Or else the Bishop transferred the property to Ortiz during his first visitation in 1833. Now, said Machebeuf, Bishop Lamy had pru-
dently decided not to bring a court suit against Ortiz, but was waiting for
the Holy See to resolve the question. As shown earlier, Lamy had presented
this very subject in Rome during his *ad limina* visit in 1854 but apparently
had not been given any satisfaction. Now Lamy, Machebeuf went on, after
having been chased out by Ortiz, had found another mansion. He also had

---

[7] Ibid., The marginal note refers to a false letter that Machebeuf had penned!
[8] Ibid.

found another church edifice in Santa Fe (the *Castrense*), which he restored
at great personal sacrifice. As Machebeuf put it:

> As soon as it was restored for worship [this had been done
> by Machebeuf back in the fall of 1851 when Lamy and Ortiz
> were Durango!], Mgr. Lamy divided the Villa of Santa Fe
> into two parishes [in March 1853], equal insofar as the lo-
> cale allowed him, left to Mr. Ortiz his own parish with the
> residence, gardens, and all the upper part of the Villa, and
> reserved for himself the restored church as temporary ca-
> thedral, as also the lower part of town so as to have the
> means for procuring the resources necessary for livelihood.[9]

What is shown in these direct quotations is a very tangled web that
Machebeuf kept weaving, and no less tangled by his hurried and largely
unpunctuated scribbling with frequent underlines of key words meant to
catch the eye of the curial official who was to pass judgment. "The division
of the Santa Fe parish," he continued at this point, "was the signal for the
revolt on the part of Mr. Ortiz." This was in March of 1853, and he had
forgotten his earlier statement about Ortiz as having been the very "first" to
rebel with the other padres long before. Then Ortiz, he said, had assembled
a mob of his friends and cronies, *"for the most part vicious men of every
stripe,"* who came yelling and howling to Lamy's house, and *"threatening to
chase him out of the Villa."* What stopped them from doing it, he said, was
the fear they had of the American civil authorities, whereas he claimed elsewhere that it was Ortiz's political relatives who ran the entire town and
country.

All of this is obviously a lie, since Don Juan Felipe was not the type of
man who would resort to violence. What Machebeuf did here was to insert
one such event which had taken place during ex-Padre Gallegos' first campaign for Congress in the fall of 1853, when the *Santa Fe Gazette* and its
partisans brought the name of Bishop Lamy into the fray. They made it look
as though the bishop was on their own side against Gallegos, and consequently some of the latter's men went to threaten Lamy just as Machebeuf
now described the event. This particular lie appears to have been deliberate,
since Machebeuf kept tying Ortiz to Gallegos as his fellow-conspirator in
past political battles.[10] Clearly Machebeuf was desperate for examples of
Ortiz's infractions and he resorted to the same old tired tales time and again.

---

[9] Ibid.

[10] A. Chávez, *Trés Macho*, 82.

Next, Machebeuf had to bring in Ortiz's avarice. He possessed "great goods, thousands of sheep, several houses...*amid a deplorable poverty.*" This was true to a certain extent, heir that he was to the wealth of the long and well-established Ortiz clan. He did have a lifelong interest in real estate. But all this was most certainly not contrary to his status as a secular priest – there were many such rich *cures* in France – nor were there any canonical prohibitions against it. During his absence, Machebeuf went on to say, Bishop Lamy had repaired the big parish church, but now Ortiz on his return had refused to surrender the sacred vessels and vestments. This was embroidering the truth, as Ortiz had found that most of the silverplate was already missing, presumably sent to France, while the old Spanish chasubles and dalmatics had been reduced to ashes. What Ortiz had refused to surrender were those previous articles pertaining to an Ortiz private chapel to which Lamy had no right.

Here Machebeuf brought in the bell which Ortiz, as seen earlier, had refused to turn in. It had been donated, said he, by one of Ortiz's own "relatives" as shown by this donor's "testament," and later Ortiz's henchmen had used violence to take it down. If what Machebeuf said is true about one of Ortiz's relatives being the bell's donor by means of a testament, one cannot help but think of Doña Gertrudis Pino, Ortiz's second stepmother and the mother of Padre José Eulogio, who had died while Lamy and her priest-son were on their way from back Europe. Evidently she had willed her San Miguel chapel holdings to the Church on her deathbed; this serves to explain that elaborate funeral that Machebeuf gave her with an hour-long eulogy in both Spanish and English.

Once again Machebeuf unjustly connected Ortiz with Gallegos and whatever "act of violence" the latter's political followers may have committed. The best proof, he said, was the fact that, "Mr. Gallegos and Co. had proposed him to his Holiness for the See of Santa Fe...a beautiful recommendation; it is a long time since he [Gallegos] has been suspended from all his faculties."

All of his sarcasm aside, this clearly shows that Machebeuf as well as Lamy had learned that Gallegos had been the prime mover behind the legislature's letter to the Pope. Here Machebeuf added what he called a "Supplement" or postscript to his long tirade against Don Juan Felipe, again falsely associating him with Gallegos and those legislators who had not only composed that letter but who continued to attack Bishop Lamy and the French clergy who had arrived since.

The postscript ended with: "*One word* concerning the administration of Mr. J. P. Ortiz before the arrival of Mgr. Lamy." The reason for his great popularity, Machebeuf said, was the "*silence*" that Ortiz had observed under all kinds of circumstances when he was vicar. No words of catechetical instruction, no sermons except on a feast-day or Holy Week; worst of all, no correction by him of "the greater part of the priests [who] lived in the *most revolting disorders.*" As on example, he now brought up a Juan de Jesús Luján, Ortiz's former assistant, who had led "the most scandalous life" without Ortiz ever raising a finger.[11]

This mention of Padre Luján calls for a postscript on what Machebeuf wrote about Luján in connection with ex-Vicar Ortiz. This incident was mentioned long before, but it bears repeating. While Luján was pastor of Belén, Machebeuf began by saying that Bishop Zubiría on his last visitation of New Mexico (in 1850) had ordered Luján to go to Santa Fe and brush up on "spiritual matters," thus implying some serious moral lapse on Luján's part; but Luján had not even opened a book, and all of this had been due to Vicar Ortiz's "guilty indulgence" or neglect of duty.[12] As explained long before, this incident had occurred further back in 1846 after Luján was no longer pastor of Belén. While at Tomé between appointments, Luján had heard the confessions of some women, something he could not do according to the canonical regulations of the times that required that he abstain from such activities. Deeply worried about this mistake, Luján had related his woes to the pastor of Tomé and then Bishop Zubiría learned about the transgression. According to an Ortiz letter of February, 1846, this bishop ordered Luján to Santa Fe to review his canon law – not any spiritual works – and there he did at least open the canon law book before undergoing an examination by Padres Gallegos and C. de Baca. Subsequently, Vicar Ortiz gave him permission to say mass, all that he was empowered to do, while reserving the granting of further faculties to the bishop himself.[13] But here Machebeuf not only made it a question of personal morals, but blamed Ortiz for his "guilty indulgence" in the matter. Paul Horgan later extended this phrase to mean that Ortiz was also guilty of sexual immorality in his private life.[14]

[11] Ibid.

[12] Lamy file, Horgan Collection, Prop. Fide. Machebeuf Defense IV, (vs Luján), June 1856, *AASF.*

[13] Ibid.

[14] Horgan, *Lamy*, 128; also see "scandalous behavior of Ortiz" in the index, 518.

Another of Machebeuf's accusations against Luján was that he had more than one paramour, one of whom was a scandalous woman at whose funeral procession he had been most conspicuous, walking at its tail-end without wearing his surplice and shedding copious tears – all of which shocked the Protestant bystanders who told Machebeuf about it. Besides, Luján had invited all the civil and military officials to attend.[15] This was none other than that funeral of Doña Gertrudes Barceló that Bishop Lamy had conducted in January of 1852 since Ortiz was still in Durango at the time. Now, both Ortiz and Luján had been Doña Tules' dearest friends, the first from her widowed mother's marriage into the Pino family, the second from his long acquaintance with the Barceló family since it had come from Mexico to settle in the Tomé parish many years before. And popular lady that Doña Tules had been among rich and poor alike, there had been no need for anyone to invite the whole town to her funeral. Thus Padre Luján had good reason to weep and, if he did not wear a surplice over his cassock, it was because Lamy had not recognized his priestly presence at the ceremony. Nor did Machebeuf mention the fact that the bishop had thereby cheated Luján, as pastor in charge, of that large sum of money provided for in Dona Tules' will to pay for the extra funeral services.[16] Old Don Juan Felipe, had he been present and in charge of the funeral instead of Lamy, would have played a role in this canard of Machebeuf's as well.

---

[15] See Chapter II, Part II, supra.

[16] Lamy file, Horgan Collection, Prop. Fide, Machebeuf Defense IV, (vs Luján), June 1856, *AASF*.

Elegy for a Fat Vicar:
Death of a Mexican Church

The saying goes that truth will win out, but it failed miserably that fateful year of 1856 when Machebeuf's great tangled web in Rome effectively promoted what he and Bishop Lamy had first practiced to deceive through the Christmas Pastoral and kindred prevarications. The curial official who wrote the final verdict, in neat minuscule Italian, must have labored hard deciphering Machebeuf's atrocious French script, or else he was satisfied by a mere scanning of it while guided by the heavily underlined words and phrases. He concluded that Machebeuf had satisfactorily answered all the charges against himself and Bishop Lamy. First, he wrote, the evil priests of New Mexico, a province formerly belonging to Spain, had rebelled against Lamy because of his first pastoral of 1852 that attempted a reform of their lives. Second, an ignorant and vicious people backed up these bad priests. Third, the chief promoter was an Albuquerque priest named Gallegos who was living with a woman of ill repute. Lastly, another priest named Martínez, who was no friend of the bishop, had cleared Machebeuf of all guilt in connection with the seal of confessional![1]

As mentioned earlier, neither Don Juan Felipe Ortiz nor Congressman Gallegos for that matter ever learned about the commotion that the legislature's letter to the Pope and its enclosures had caused in Rome that June. They knew even less about Machebeuf's most scurrilous assaults on their own persons and those of some other native priests. These had gotten

---

[1] See A. Chávez, *But Time and Chance*, 128; and *Très Macho*, 85-86.

Machebeuf off the fisherman's hook.[2]

This mention of Gallegos at this point brings up another incident, which took place in a different capital, in Washington, in the following month of July, although here ex-Vicar Ortiz is only indirectly involved. Gallegos was enjoying his second political victory, won in the 1855 fall campaign against a young man named Miguel Antonio Otero, when the latter appeared before Congress to challenge his seat. In a long speech before the United States House of Representatives, Otero revived and reviewed all of the printed falsehoods and verbal gossip against New Mexico's native padres that this book has been treating all along, while defending Bishop Lamy as a much maligned and persecuted heroic figure.

During the years since the United States occupation of New Mexico, animosity had been growing. The old local rule Álvarez faction, or State-hood Party, that primarily consisted of New Mexico's native population, still championed the traditions and attitudes of the territory's Spanish-speaking New Mexicans. In opposition, the Territorial Party, mostly made up of newly arrived Americans beholden to federal patronage and tied to the military, tried to undermine Hispanic influence. Even though the statehood cause was lost with the establishment of the Territory of New Mexico in 1850, the Álvarez faction continued to win a majority of elective posts.[3]

The old military group, that is to say the party made up of many Americans who came to the territory in or with the military during the Mexican War, tried to win the native vote but failed miserably, perhaps because of their insincerity. Then, to prove Hispanic distrust, they began looking for scapegoats, and the Catholic Church – apart from the recently arrived Frenchmen – fit nicely. The anti-Hispanic politicians accused the native priests of actively interfering in politics. Prominent among these frustrated would-be leaders was W. G. Kephart, a Presbyterian minister and agent of the American and Foreign Anti-Slavery Society who became editor of the *Santa Fe Gazette* with Territorialists Joab Houghton and Thomas S. J. Johnson. Kephart,

---

[2] A current interpretation glosses over the Rome Defense as Machebeuf merely defending Lamy and himself against the rebelling Mexican clergy. The violation of the confessional seal is not considered in detail and is written off as the now age old conspiracy. See Bridges, *Death Deceiver*, 110-11, 119. Another recent but more detailed publication notes that this episode and Lamy's defense of Machebeuf was at a time when the Archbishop's friendship and loyalty to Machebeuf "overcame his normal recourse to unemotional, impersonal, principled reasoning." See Steele, *Archbishop Lamy: In His Own Words*, 71.

[3] T. Chávez, *Alvarez*, 146-53.

who was called "Padre" Kephart by the opposition, regarded the Catholic Church as his prime adversary.[4]

The local rule people also understood the value of the press. In 1850, Manuel Álvarez raised $1,500 from his like-minded friends to purchase a printing press. Richard Weightman, a political ally, located one in Washington, D. C. for $500 but speculated that shipping would take at least six months. Both Gallegos and Ortiz contributed $100 for the purchase, thus indicating their sentiments even before the arrival of Lamy in New Mexico. Obviously, Lamy's biographers failed to see that the subsequent problems were rooted in a more complex context than distaste for Lamy and his vicar.[5]

Lamy and, especially, Machebeuf apparently shared Kephart's attitude toward the native clergy. Thus, as has been noted, the *Gazette* was fed information to discredit local rule candidate Gallegos. The *Gazette*'s brand of journalism was condescending to all native clergy. Nor did the bigoted tirade stop with the prejudiced press. Kephart's two partners were among eight Americans who sent a memorial to President Millard Fillmore on 5 April 1851, in which they stated, in part, that

> "There is no hope for the improvement of our Territory unless Americans rule it, and that the spirit of Mexican rule must be corrupt, ignorant and disgraceful in a Territory of the United States...."[6]

Within this context the young St. Louis-educated Otero, an aristocratic New Mexican who would marry a southern belle from Charleston, South Carolina, became involved. He became a member of the Territorial party and with the backing of Lamy and Machebeuf challenged Gallegos for his seat. Otero's action was a calculated move by his party. From the point of view of most Congressmen, a non-English speaking ex-priest had no chance against a sympathetic English-speaking Hispanic, and the Territorialists were sure of it.

---

[4] Larson, *New Mexico's Quest for Statehood*, 62-63.

[5] Oliver Lafarge, *Santa Fe: The Autobiography of A Southwestern Town* (Norman: The University of Oklahoma Press, 1959), 7-8; Draft, 16 July 1850, no. 28, and Richard Weightman to Manuel Álvarez, 12 October 1852, Business Papers, *Manuel Álvarez Papers*, NMSRC.

[6] Memorial, 5 April 1851 as quoted in Larson, *New Mexico's Quest for Statehood*, 73. Richard Weightman, a local rule leader, along with other members of his party, used the memorial to their advantage.

Congress was also suffering through some of the most disruptive years in United States' history. Congressmen faced all the problems brought on by slavery and state's rights issues that threatened civil war. The very survival of the Union was at stake. Congress would give little or no thought to a New Mexican problem.

Nevertheless, Otero rose before the House of Representatives and proceeded to mouth his sentiments, using Gallegos and the native clergy as prime examples of his subjective opinion. The opposition party "calling itself the Mexican party" has been "indulging in great hostility against the institutions of these states," Otero claimed.

With the aid of "corrupt priests" and their "hypocritical" Padre Ortiz at San Juan (Eulogio), who is a zealous partisan of Gallegos, Otero continued, a fraudulent majority secured the election.

Those same bad padres, Otero contended, had worked against him during the campaign. He, then, gave one instance. There was the priest, Ortiz, at San Juan, he said, who had meddled at the polls, and he himself had delivered to said Ortiz a letter that Bishop Lamy wrote him about desisting from such activities. Now, whether this was true or not, the priest at San Juan happened to be Padre José Eulogio Ortiz, the bishop's faithful friend and servant. Paul Horgan, writing almost a century and a half later misidentified him as the "ex-dean," meaning ex-Vicar Ortiz![7] *Sic historia crescit eundo,* "Wrong history rises again." Otero then went on in a vindictive tirade while defending Lamy:

> [Lamy] found the church sunk into the most deplorable condition of immorality. The priests themselves were notoriously addicted to the grossest vices. They were, in many instances, the disgrace of every gambling house and drinking saloon, and the open frequenters of brothels. In a word, they personified vice in all its hideous and revolting aspects.

He then concluded by parroting Machebeuf's letters and his political party's bitter rationale for not garnering the Hispanic vote:

> It is not surprising that the corrupt and degraded priests, who were formally the worst enemies of the people, imposing upon their credulity and cultivating their wicked as-

---

[7] Horgan, *Lamy*, 234-36; A. Chávez, *Time and Chance*, 140 and *Très Macho*, 90.

cendancy, should find fault with the measures of reform adopted by the new dignity.[8]

Ortiz had given his answer to Otero's charges of church meddling prior to Otero's address. He merely reiterated what Richard Weightman had started. The only participation by the priests had been to defend their faith against the untrue assaults of a few ambitious men. Weightman asked the Congress to imagine if they would be surprised to see any religious denomination in the United States defend itself if any one of them had been assailed as the Catholics had been in New Mexico. Weightman was praised for his defense by a Baltimore Catholic newspaper. The paper agreed with Weightman's position that the "Catholic people be undisturbed in the exercise of their religion."[9]

Gallegos did not fare so well, for Congress gave his seat to Otero. In New Mexico, Padre Ortiz was silent, possibly unwittingly receiving the indignity of Otero's false and self-serving comments about himself and his fellow priests.

Incidentally, the ever so neutral Bishop Lamy, when writing to Rome, lavishly praised the young Otero, who had unseated Gallegos by his lying tirade, for having brought out the truth before Congress in favor of order and religion. "Providence," Lamy wrote, "had sent Otero to come to the defense of church discipline" and point out "the scandals of which he himself is witness."[10]

Poor and once so affable Juan Felipe Ortiz, before whom no one had ever trembled – except Machebeuf while frantically defending himself in Rome – evidently had signified his intention of leaving New Mexico sometime during this summer of 1856. For on June 1, Father Taladrid, that Spaniard whom Lamy had sent up to Taos to harass a much-disturbed Padre Martínez, cautioned Lamy about giving Ortiz permission to leave. Perhaps Lamy did gladly allow him to depart, now that worse problems were beginning to face him as the result of the injudicious double trick he had played on Martínez. All this has been brought out in fullest detail in a biography of the latter.[11]

---

[8] *Congressional Globe*, 34th Congress, 1st session (House), 23 July 1856. Horgan used this same speech to vindicate Lamy, ignoring the political context that points in a direction contrary than his analysis. Horgan, *Lamy*, 234-36.

[9] Larson, *New Mexico's Quest for Statehood*, 71-72; Weightman to Álvarez, 10 September 1852, *Alvarez Papers*, NMSRCA.

[10] Horgan Collection, Prop. Fide, 1 December 1856, nos. 14 & 17, *AASF*.

[11] A. Chávez, *Time and Chance*, 132.

Ortiz was gone for about six months, but it is unknown whether he went to faraway Durango or stayed closer to home at El Paso del Norte with his cousin, Padre Ramón Ortiz. He had returned to Santa Fe as early as February, or at least prior to 3 March 1857, when Lamy wrote to Purcell that he was still being harassed by "Gallegos, the ex-delegate, the old Ortiz, and worse than these two together, the old Padre Martínez of Taos..." Here he accused all three of trying to prevent the faithful from paying their tithes and of having enriched themselves in the past with the exorbitant demands they had made upon the people.[12] Soon upon his return to Santa Fe, Padre Ortiz must have resumed his own pathetic campaign for recovering his old parish, according to a note of 2 May 1857 that he sent to Lamy:

> Monseñor, I returned from my trip with nothing unusual occurring, thanks be to God; and I came back hoping that Monseñor on my return, moved by your pastoral zeal and by the strict justice due concerning what I have addressed you, should deign to answer the contents of my letter of February the 5th past, which reply I now respectfully request for my future guidance. I am your subject who kisses your hand. Juan F. Ortiz, cura propio, Santa Fe.[13]

The note is written in a strong and very handsome script, but the signature is just the opposite, larger but very shaky. In other words, Don Juan Felipe no longer trusted his once fine handwriting and got someone else to pen the short message. Nevertheless, the fact that he included *cura propio* shows that he was not backing off his correct position. As for Bishop Lamy, it looks as though he had decided to ignore the old man completely, meanwhile keeping him under suspension.

In this connection, the memoirs of Don Demetrio Pérez have an interesting passage. Uncertain about precise dates as usual, he recalled that ex-Vicar Ortiz had returned from Durango after an absence of about four years, incapacitated by advanced age and by infirmities resulting from the faithful exercise of his lifelong duties.[14] As for the four-year absence in Durango, Pérez was telescoping Ortiz's two trips south, in 1853 and 1856. There follow two disparate published incidents that touch Don Juan Felipe's person, if anonymously, but as falsely as anything that Machebeuf had concocted.

---

[12] Lamy file, 3 March 1857, no. 5, *AASF*.

[13] J. F. Ortiz file, 2 May 1857, no. 5, *AASF*.

[14] Pérez, "Rasga," 73.

Vicar Ortiz to Lamy, May 2, 1851. Ortiz informs Lamy of his return and asks him to reconsider his position. Courtesy of the Archives of the Archdiocese of Santa Fe.

In his bigoted book *El Gringo*, Davis criticized the Catholic clergy for their extraordinarily high burial fees. As an example, he brought up the funeral of a young Mexican in Santa Fe sometime during the spring of 1856, going so far as to itemize fourteen separate charges that amounted to $141.00.[15] While all this was true, readers of this passage have attributed it to the old so-called Mexican clergy, hence specifically to ex-Vicar Ortiz when he was the pastor of Santa Fe. However, the pastor in charge of his old *parroquia* at this particular period was the French Father Etienne Avel, not Ortiz. Besides, no such burial had taken place during the spring of 1856, but rather in April of the following year. This funeral, by odd coincidence, was that of a deceased young man, Cándido Ortiz by name, who was a relative of the ex-vicar and was buried by priests and with considerable pomp inside the Guadalupe chapel on 2 April 1857, a privilege which helped to raise the burial fees. As mentioned earlier, he was one of the signers of the legislature's letter to the Pope. Although he was thirty-four years of age, *The Santa Fe Gazette* called him a "young man" who since his earliest years had been

---

[15] Davis, *El Gringo*, 186; and Horgan, *Lamy*, 222-23.

highly educated. He spent two years at a college in Chihuahua, then three at the Seminary in Durango, and finally four years at the College of San Elizario in Mexico City. Upon his return home he served as a lieutenant in the local Indian wars as well as a popular speaker while a member of New Mexico's territorial legislature.[16]

The second incident, likewise appearing in print, is about a clock that once upon a time had been installed on the façade of the old Santa Fe *parroquia*. It tells how that old traveling merchant, Josiah Gregg, had been employed by its pastor to install the clock, which had a curious mechanism by which a Negro "figure" came out and danced whenever the clock struck the hours. The price agreed upon was $1000.00; but, because the job had been finished much sooner than the contract called for, the priest refused to pay Gregg more than $700.00. Then, when the mechanism broke down sometime later, the priest wrote Gregg to come back and fix the thing, which the merchant did after the padre promised to pay the full amount agreed upon.[17] Here the inference has been that the miserly and crooked clergyman was none other than Don Juan Felipe Ortiz.

Now there is no record of any such clock on the old *parroquia* during Ortiz's tenure prior to Bishop Lamy arrival. There are, however, old photographs showing a large clock dial above the church's main entrance at the time when Lamy's stone cathedral was beginning to rise around the old adobe church. According to newspaper accounts of October 1869 and April 1872, more than a decade after Don Juan Felipe passed away and two decades after Gregg had died, the current pastor, French Father Pierre Eguillon, purchased a big clock to install on the façade of the stone cathedral when it was finished. It cost him $700.00 (a figure mentioned in the Gregg tale), plus fifty more for its installation. Eguillon then had it placed temporarily above the main entrance of the old adobe church, as shown in those early photographs. But by April of 1872, the newspaper says, the clock had filled up with dust and was no longer serviceable.[18] And, as an aside, Lamy's finished stone cathedral was spared such a monstrosity.[19] However, poor and long-dead

---

[16] *The Santa Fe Gazette*, 4 and 11 April 1857.

[17] Editor's note in Magoffin, *Down the Santa Fe Trail*, 35-36.

[18] *The Santa Fe New Mexican*, 12 October 1869, and 12 April 1872. Josiah Gregg died in northern California on 25 February 1850.

[19] Ellis, *Lamy's Cathedral*, 149-51. Ellis gives a thorough and accurate account of the clock, which was installed by 1869. It never worked well. The sheet metal face, painted black with white Roman numerals is in the collections of the Archdiocese of Santa Fe at the Cathedral in Santa Fe.

Don Juan Felipe Ortiz was not spared, simply because a certain kind of bigotry that refused to die posthumously hung the mechanical monster around his neck.

By way of contrast, Spanish-born United States Consular Agent Manuel Álvarez wrote a memorial in 1842 to Daniel Webster, the United States' Secretary of State, in which he had many negative things to say about the Mexican government. But when it came to Vicar Ortiz, Álvarez told a story about a protest he made over exorbitant marriage fees being charged to United States citizens. While Álvarez was dissatisfied over the reply he received from Governor Manuel Armijo, Vicar Ortiz pacified him with a very rational and satisfactory answer that included a copy of the pertinent official document. Álvarez, who referred to Ortiz as a "gentleman," obviously had a deeper respect for the vicar than did Otero, Machebeuf, and their cohorts.[20]

Don Juan Felipe Ortiz passed away in one of his Santa Fe residences on 20 January 1858, at the age of sixty years and some four months, a ripe old age for those harsh times. Writing to Bishop Purcell on 1 February 1858, Lamy remarked that the old vicar, brother to the young priest José Eulogio Ortiz who had accompanied him to Rome, had "died of apoplexy after receiving the last rites."[21] Unless this is a slip on this author's part, Lamy was now telling an outright lie.

Nor do we know if Bishop Lamy was in Santa Fe at the time except that he was there over a week later when he wrote the letter just cited. In it he also mentioned that he had been making the rounds of different parishes during the closing months of 1857, including perhaps the month of January.

Three outside pastors traveled to Santa Fe upon hearing the news of the ex-vicar's death. They were Padres Juan de J. Trujillo of Santa Cruz, whom Lamy always liked; Ramón Medina, whom Lamy had ordained two years previously; and Thomas de Aquino Hayes of Chama, a native of Ireland whom Lamy had also ordained just the year before. What is of particular interest here is the fact that on 22 January, on the very morning when the funeral was to take place, Padre Trujillo deposed before Medina and Hayes that Don

---

[20] Memorial to Secretary of State Daniel Webster, U. S. Department of State, Consular Dispatches, Santa Fe, Manuel Álvarez, Washington, D. C., 1842, microfilm M-199, Roll 1, (copy in the Fray Chávez History Library, Palace of the Governors, Santa Fe). Also published in T. Chávez, *Conflict and Acculturation; Manuel Alvarez's 1842 'Memorial'* (Santa Fe: The Museum of New Mexico Press, 1989), 38.

[21] Lamy file, 1 February 1858, no. 15, *AASF*; and Horgan, *Lamy*, 256 and 480.

Juan Felipe, on his deathbed, had asked for Bishop Lamy in order to receive the last rites from him (thus implying the lifting of his suspension beforehand). This information, Trujillo said, had come from a certain David Baca.[22]

In other words, no Church burial had been contemplated even at this late hour by the pastor in charge, young Father Etienne Avel, who scarcely would dare allow a Church funeral for a priest who had died under suspension. He would certainly incur his bishop's ire by doing so. Most likely, the deceased man's close relatives had approached him on this score, his dear half-sister Ana María especially, and he had regretfully explained his own predicament. However, what looks very suspiciously to have been the actual case is that the three padres mentioned had seen the vast crowds of every status and persuasion paying their respects to the venerable corpse at the Ortiz residence by day and all during the two nights' *velorios*, or wakes, and now, with that Baca declaration in hand, persuaded a much-confused Avel to allow a Church funeral with all the rites expected for a prominent figure. Otherwise, the three must have told him the fury of the entire capital would have been brought upon them. As for Bishop Lamy himself, he would say nothing because of David Baca's testimony.

David Baca may have been a relative of Don Juan Felipe from Peña Blanca who might have been taking care of Ortiz during his final illness. If Baca's report were true, the poor man had not died that suddenly of a stroke. This also suggests that the bishop was away visiting some parish at the time. In any case, all this has a direct connection with his funeral. The entry in the Santa Fe burial register by Father Etienne Avel states that "the deceased padre Juan F. Ortiz" had died in his home in Santa Fe and that his body was interred inside the cathedral on 22 January 1858, specifically mentioning Fathers Trujillo and Medina as witnesses – but of what?[23] This obviously refers to that previous deposition that had provided Father Avel with a legitimate reason for giving the old suspended priest a "Christian burial." Here, as said before, Baca's testimony had come in handy at the very moment needed to prevent serious popular repercussions had the Church burial been denied. This can also be gathered from the whole town's response when the funeral took place.

According to the local *Gazette*, Ortiz had died suddenly on 20 January, and, in consideration of the important positions he had once held, the legislature requested the military to contribute its honors. Colonel John Garland

---

[22] Trujillo file, 22 January 1858, no. 1, *AASF*.
[23] Burial, Santa Fe, *AASF*.

complied by lowering the flag on the plaza to half-mast and a special resolution was passed by the legislature to render Ortiz special honors as a former president of the council.

A special obituary followed in the next issue of the paper,[24] one which stated that he had died at his descendant's house – which meant two Hispano-Celtic type wakes during the entire nights of 20 and 21 January, with casual but constant visits during the daylight hours. He was then buried inside the adobe cathedral on 22 January, probably in the dirt floor of the south Ortiz-built side-chapel of San José. The governor, the legislative body, Colonel Garland, and all the civil and military officials besides the ordinary citizens overflowed the church for his magnificent funeral. Good order was maintained through it all. The newspaper continued with some biographical data: The deceased had been born on 16 September (actually 12 September 1797) and ordained in 1824, right after which he had been made the pastor of San Juan (actually two years later, in 1826). In 1831 he attended a *concurso* in Durango whereby he had been made the *cura propio* of Santa Fe, and in 1832 he became the bishop's vicar for New Mexico. In 1837 he went to Mexico City as a deputy to the Mexican Congress, and much later, in 1851, he was elected president of New Mexico's Legislative Council when it received the very first laws from the American federal government. The newspaper concluded by saying that "some friends of the deceased" furnished all this information.[25]

Ortiz died at 11 o'clock in the morning and was barely able to move when he received the last rites of absolution and extreme unction. (No doubt, this last report came to the paper through the immediate female Ortiz and Pino relatives.) There was a tolling of bells at the parish church and all the other chapels in the city.

Nowhere is there any mention of Bishop Lamy being in attendance. Years later, Lamy's biographer Paul Horgan could hardly contain himself when dealt a final blow at the corpse by criticizing the funeral. Horgan could not understand why the vicar's "friends," who created the final tribute, did not mention any "intrigues and disgraces." Nor could he contain himself by describing the grand funeral with a sarcastic comment; "the 'Friends' were at pains to note that since 'the year by ecclesiastic authority he was elected Vicar of this territory,' he had given 'special satisfaction to the wise and virtuous Bishop the Right Revd. Dr. Zubiría' – quite as though Lamy had

---

[24] *The Santa Fe Gazette*, 23 January 1858.
[25] Ibid., 30 January 1858.

never been heard of."[26] The fact that Ortiz was beloved and those intrigues and disgraces did not exist in reality would never dawn on Lamy's latter-day advocate.[27]

All in all, it was Don Juan Felipe's day of belated and much deserved tribute, not Lamy's. It was homage from the faithful of his own blood and background, in unison with many sympathetic newcomers of other ancestries and religions. They remembered the affable fat gentleman of a notable family who had been their friend, as well as a good priest and pastor, long before Lamy and Machebeuf had made their appearance in New Mexico. Except for the eldest among the townsfolk, none could be expected to assess those many hard years much further back. They would not remember those years devoted to faithfully but gently carrying out his former bishop's orders and wishes – sometimes in the face of opposition from some of his own priests, and even some communities as in the Cárdenas-Valencia debacle shortly before Lamy arrived. Much less could they be expected to recall those many occasions when he left the relative comforts of his Santa Fe vicarage to attend, for weeks at a time, those several outlying places without a priest that clamored for the solaces of faith. Nor had they ever had cause to suspect any moral blemish in his conduct. That gossip impugning his character came from certain newcomers to the area, not from all, by any means,

---

[26] Horgan, *Lamy*, 256 and 480.

[27] In her biography of Machebeuf, Lynn Bridgers goes to strenuous lengths to discredit Fray Angélico Chávez's defense of the local New Mexican clergy in his two biographies of Padres Martínez and Gallegos that are cited throughout this book. In the process of her criticisms Bridgers contrasts Pulitzer Prize winners Willa Cather and Paul Horgan, who by virtue of the awards are obviously in greater command of the sources, which comprise the major part of her source material. This is faulty logic to say the least. Then she criticizes Chávez's position as symptomatic of a climate of "misunderstanding" whose vehemence demonstrates how the divisions between those of Hispanic and European descent continue to this day." Bridgers misses the point that one of the very seeds of that "misunderstanding" originated with the establishment of the U. S. Catholic Church and its haughty if not biased treatment of the local Mexican clergy and that subsequent novelists such as Cather and Horgan as well as some histories, including Horgan here as well, exacerbated the misunderstanding by never looking at the full record. So, when Chávez is driven, as Bridgers writes, "to meticulously track down any discrepancy he can possibly detect" he is doing what a good historian should do and is exactly what this book is attempting to do as well. Even in her criticism Bridgers could not demonstrate that one of Chávez's discovered "discrepancies" was in error. See Bridgers, *Death's Deceiver*, 106-08.

and fanned by a Catholic Machebeuf.

Finally, there is an indirect epitaph to Don Felipe's memory. Ten years after his death, in 1878, his half-sister Doña Ana María Ortiz donated toward the construction of Lamy's stone Franco-Romanesque cathedral, both a large sum of money and the very the silver altar vessels and precious Spanish vestments that her half-brother had refused to relinquish to the bishop.[28] Significantly, despite this posthumous donation, only French gilt chalices and related vessels made of brass survived in the cathedral sacristy.

There used to be a "museum" in the old church's apse, which stood behind the stone cathedral's sanctuary and which contained a number of Spanish style chasubles, the ones just mentioned. These disappeared when the rear part of the cathedral was ravaged some years ago in the name of spatial renovation. At the same time the bones of a once-chubby Don Juan Felipe, along with those of others buried in the earth floor of the *parroquia*, were unceremoniously mixed together in boxes and taken to the Rosario Cemetery north of town for what one hopes was a last internment. *Sic transit...*

This book concludes the epilogues of biographies of three outstanding, nineteenth century New Mexican priests. The other two biographies are about Padre Martínez of Taos (*But Time and Chance)* and Padre Gallegos of Albuquerque *("Très Macho," He Said)*. Vicar Juan Felipe Ortiz, while a much better person than the other two, lacks their color and appeal.

All three of these New Mexicans personify a New Mexico with almost two-and-a-half centuries of settlement behind it before the area and its people became a part of the United States. Then came Lamy to become the head of the Church. The careers of these three men, especially Ortiz's, are conduits to a more accurate story of a part of the history of what happened when the United States took over the old Spanish and Mexican territory. Here is evidence that the church was directly involved in the type of racial stereotyping that we still seek to overcome even today.

Lamy and his compatriot friend Machebeuf revealed their anti-Mexican biases repeatedly and openly. Significantly, their subsequent biographers as well as novelists exacerbated the errors of their subjects, perhaps, to vindicate themselves or a history that they thought lacking. None of these writers, like their French-American heroes, were New Mexicans. Nor did they use source material available in Spanish. Yet given the long historiogra-

---

[28] Defouri, *Historical Sketch*, 146.

phy glorifying the early American administration of the church as well as denigration of the New Mexican clergy, many curious observers of New Mexico have continued to wonder why Lamy is not favorably recalled within the New Mexican Hispanic community.

A study of those Mexican priests, especially like the three above, through an accurate reading of the French documents, careful checking of Lamy's and Machebeuf's facts, an understanding of Church law, and an investigation of the documents written in Spanish that still exist in the Archives of the Archdiocese of Santa Fe, begin to tell a different, more accurate view than heretofore exposed. Vicar Juan Felipe Ortiz had a far greater role in the story of New Mexico's church history than heretofore realized. His life, in many ways, illustrates the problems of acculturation in this country, much less within the Church in New Mexico. Thus his story is justly deserved and, all this considered, appropriately titled.

Bibliography

Archives and Collections:

The Archives of the Archdiocese of Santa Fe (AASF). These consist of two main
sections.

I.   MISSIONS: Loose Documents (1680-1850), Diligencias Matroniales (1678-
        1869), Patentes (copied official letters, 1697-1853), Accounts (1710-1855),
        books of Baptisms, Marriages, Burials of various missions, varying dates.
        All of these were calendered in A. Chávez, *Archives of the Archdiocese of
        Santa Fe, 1678-1900,* have been transferred to Persons and Places in second
        Diocesan Section

II.   DIOCESAN: Loose or bound records from 1851 to the present, filed
        according to Persons and Places, such as Archbishops, Clergy, Chancery,
        Parishes, etc. – A special file, *Horgan Collection,* consists of Lamy-
        Machebeuf Papers (from United States, France, Vatican Propaganda Fide)
        that Paul Horgan donated to the Archdiocese of Santa Fe.

Buxton, Margaret (Mrs. Robert J.), genealogy researches, Albuquerque.

The Huntington Library, San Marino, California
        The William G. Ritch Collection.

National Archives, Washington, D. C.
        Consular Dispatches, Santa Fe, Manuel Álvarez. Record Group 199, Vol. 1.
        Diplomatic Correspondence, Record Group 59. Microfilm copy in Fray
        Angélico Chávez History Library, Santa Fe.

New Mexico State Records Center and Archives, Santa Fe, New Mexico.
        Manuel Álvarez Collection.
        Amado Chaves Collection.
        Mexican Archives of New Mexico.
        Benjamin Read Collection.

United States Censuses, Territory of New Mexico (on microfilm).

Palace of the Governors, Fray Angélico Chávez Library, Santa Fe, New Mexico
Catron Collection.

Diary of Dr. Andrew Randall, 19 April 1849, Cincinnati, Ohio – Santa Fe,
New Mexico.

La Revista Católica. A Jesuit weekly. Las Vegas, 1875-1900.

The Santa Fe Daily New Mexican

The Santa Fe Gazette

The Santa Fe Register

Santa Fe County Records

Deed Book C.

Probate Court Records, Santa Fe.

Books and Articles:

A Biographical Congressional Directory. Washington, D. C.: U. S. Government
Printing Office, 1903.

Abert, Lt. James W. *Abert's New Mexico Report, 1846-47.* Albuquerque: Horn &
Wallace, 1962. (Also printed in Emory listed below).

_____. *Western America in 1846-1847.* San Francisco: J. Howell, 1966.

Adams, Eleanor B. *Bishop Tamarón's Visitation of New Mexico, 1760.* Albuquerque: University of New Mexico Press, 1954.

Adams, Eleanor B. and Chávez, Fray Angélico. *Missions of New Mexico, 1776.*
Albuquerque: University of New Mexico Press, 1956.

Barrerio, Antonio. *Ojeda Sobre Nuevo México….* Puebla: Mexico, 1832 in H. Bailey
Carroll and J. Villasana Haggard, trans. & editors. *Three New* Mexico
Chronicles: *The Exposición of Don Pedro Bautista Pino, 1812: The Ojeda of
Lic. Antonio Barreiro, 1832.* Albuquerque: Quivera Society Publications,
1942.

Bloom, Lansing Bartlett. "New Mexico Under Mexican Administration," *Old
Santa Fe (OSF),* Vol. I, 1913. 3-49.

Barry, Louise. *The Beginning of the West: Annals of the Kansas Gateway to the
American West, 1540-1854.* Topeka: Kansas State Historical Society, 1972.

Bratton, Sam G. *New Mexico, Mythology, Tradition, History.* United States Senate
Document 147, 71st Congress. Washington, D. C.: U. S. Government
Printing Office, 1930.

Brewerton, George Douglas. *Overland With Kit Carson: A Narrative of the Old
Spanish Trail in '48.* New York: Coward-McCann, inc. 1930.

Bridgers, Lynn. *Death's Deceiver: The Life of Joseph P. Machebeuf.* Albuquerque:
University of New Mexico Press, 1997.

Cather, Willa. *Death Comes for the Archbishop.* New York: Alfred A. Knoph, Inc.,
1927.

Chávez, Fray Angélico. *Archives of the Archdiocese of Santa Fe, 1678-1900.*
    Washington, D. C.: American Academy of Franciscan History,1957.

_____. "A Nineteenth Century New Mexico Schism," *New Mexico Historical*
    Review. Vol. I, 1983, 35-54.

_____. "Addenda to New Mexico Families," *El Palacio,* Vols. 62-64, 1955-1957.

_____. *But Time and Chance: The Story of Padre Martínez of Taos, 1867-*
    Santa Fe: The Sunstone Press, 1981.

_____. "El Vicario Don Santiago Roybal," *El Palacio,* Vol. 55, 1948,
    231-52.

_____. "Genízaros," *Handbook of North American Indians.* Vol. 9. Washington, D.
    C.: Smithsonian Institution, 1979.

_____. *La Conquistadora: The Autobiography of an Ancient Statue.* Patterson, New
    Jersey: St. Anthony Guild Press, 1954.

_____. *My Penitente Land: Reflections on Spanish New Mexico.* Albuquerque:
    University of New Mexico Press, 1974.

_____. *Origins of New Mexico Families in the Spanish Colonial Period.* Santa Fe:
    Historical Society of New Mexico, 1954.

_____. "The Inter-Relation of History and Folklore," *New Mexico Folklore*
    Record, Vol. 5, 1950-51, 1-3.

_____. *Très Macho – He Said: Padre Gallegos of Albuquerque, New Mexico's First*
    Congressman. Santa Fe: William Gannon, 1985.

Chávez, Thomas E. "Don Manuel Álvarez (de las Abelgas): Multi-Talented
    Merchant of New Mexico," *Journal of the West.* Vol. 18, 1979, 22-31.

_____. *Conflict and Acuulturation: Manuel Álvarez's 1842,"Memorial."* Santa Fe:
    Museum of New Mexico Press, 1989.

_____. *Manuel Álvarez (1794-1856): A Southwestern Biography.* Niwot: Univer-
    sity Press of Colorado, 1990.

_____. "Santa Fe's Own: A History of Fiesta," *El Palacio.* Vol. 91, 1985, 6-17.

_____. "The Trouble With Texans: Manuel Álvarez and the 1841 'Invasion,'"
    New Mexico Historical Review. Vol. 53, 1978, 133-44.

Davis, W. W. H. *El Gringo: or New Mexico and Her People.* Santa Fe: The Rydal
    Press, 1938 (originally 1857).

Defouri, James H. *Historical Sketch of the Catholic Church in New Mexico.* San
    Francisco: McCormick Brothers, Printers, 1887.

Ellis, Bruce T. *Bishop Lamy's Santa Fe's Cathedral With Records of the* Old Spanish
    Church (Parroquia) and Convent Formerly on the Site. Santa Fe: Historical
    Society of New Mexico/University of New Mexico Press, 1985.

_____. "New Notes on Bishop Lamy's First Years in New Mexico," *El Palacio.*
    Vol. 65, 1958, 26-33, 73-75.

_____ and Stanley A. Stubbs. *Archaeological Investigations at the Chapel of San*
    Miguel and the Site of La Castrense, Santa Fe, New Mexico. Santa Fe:
    Laboratory of Anthropology/Museum of New Mexico, 1955.

Emory, Lt. William H. *Notes of a Military Reconnaissance,1846-1847.* In Ross Calvin, editor, *Lieutenant Emory Reports.* Albuquerque: University of New Mexico Press, 1951.

Espinosa, Aurelio M. *The Folklore of Spain in the American Southwest.* Norman: University of Oklahoma Press, 1985.

Garrard, Lewis H. *Wah-to-yah and the Taos Trail or Prairie Travel and* Scalp Dances, With a Look at Los Rancheros from Muleback and the *Rocky Mountain Campfire.* Norman: University of Oklahoma Press, 1974.

Gibson, George Rutledge. *Journal of a Soldier Under Kearny and Donaphan, 1846-1847.* Southwest Historical Series, vol. 3. Ralph Bieber, editor. Glendale, Ca.: Arthur A. Clark, 1935.

Gregg, Josiah. *Commerce of the Prairies.* Max L. Moorhead, editor. Norman: University of Oklahoma Press, 1954 (originally 1844).

Horgan, Paul. *Josiah Gregg and His Vision of the Early West.* N. Y.: Farrar, Straus and Giroux, 1979.

_____. *Lamy of Santa Fe: His Life and Times.* N. Y.: Farrar, Straus and Giroux, 1975.

Howlett, W. J. *Life of the Right Reverend Joseph P. Machbeuf, D. D.* Pueblo, CO.: Franklin Press, 1908.

Keleher, William A. *Turmoil in New Mexico, 1846-1868.* Santa Fe: The Rydal Press, 1952.

_____. *Violence in Lincoln County, 1869-1881.* Albuquerque: University of New Mexico Press, 1957.

Kenneally, Finbar, O. F. M. *United States Documents in the Propaganda Fide Archives: A Calendar.* Vols. I & VII. Washington, D. C.: U. S. Government Printing Office, 1972.

Kessell, John L. *The Missions of New Mexico Since 1776.* Albuquerque: University of New Mexico Press, 1980.

Lafarge, Oliver. *Santa Fe: The Autobiography of A Southwestern Town.* Norman: University of Oklahoma Press, 1959.

Larson, Robert W. *New Mexico's Quest for Statehood, 1846-1912.* Albuquerque: University of New Mexico Press, 1968.

Magoffin, Susan Shelby. *Down the Santa Fe Trail and Into Mexico, 1846-1847.* Stella M. Drumm, editor. New Haven: Yale University Press, 1926.

Mares, E. A. *I Returned and Saw Under the Sun: Padre Martínez of Taos.* Albuquerque, The University of New Mexico Press, 1989.

Meriwether, David. *My Life in the Mountains and on the Plains.* Norman: University of Oklahoma Press, 1965.

Pérez, Demetrio. "Rasgo Histórico" in "New Notes on Bishop Lamy's Years." Bruce T. Ellis, editor (See Ellis listed above).

Poldervaart, Arie. "Black-Robed Justice in New Mexico, 1846-1912," *New Mexico Historical Review*, Vol. 22-23, 1947-1948.

Puckett, Fidelia Miller. "Ramón Ortiz: Priest and Patriot," *New Mexico Historical Review*. Vol. 25, 1950, 265-95.

Read, Benjamin M. *Historia Ilustrada de Nuevo México*. Santa Fe: Compania impresora del Nuevo Mexicano, 1911.

Salpointe, Jean Baptiste. *Soldiers of the Cross: Notes on the Ecclesiastical History of New Mexico, Arizona, and Colorado*. Banning, CA.: St. Boniface's Industrial School, 1898.

Segale, Sister Blandina. *At the End of the Santa Fe Trail*. Milwaukee: Bruce Publishing, 1948.

Simmons, Marc. *Little Lion of the Southwest: A Life of Colonel Manuel A. Chaves*. Chicago: The Swallow Press, 1973.

_____. "New Mexico's Quest for Diocesan Status," *Tradición Revista*, Vol 4, No. 3, Fall 1999, 34-37.

Steele, Thomas J., S. J. Editor and translator. *Archbishop Lamy: In His Own Words*. Albuquerque: LPD Press, 2000.

_____. Editor and translator. *The Complete Sermons of Jean Baptiste Lamy: Fifty Years of Sermons (1836-1886)*. Albuquerque: LPD Press, 2000.

_____. *Folk and Church in New Mexico*. Colorado Springs, CO: The Hulbert Center for Southwest Studies/The Colorado College, 1993.

Steele, Thomas J., S.J., Barbe Awalt and Paul Rhetts, Editors. *Seeds of Struggle Harvest of Faith: The Papers of the Archdiocese of Santa Fe Catholic Cuarto Centennial Conference: The History of the Catholic Church in New Mexico*. Albuquerque: LPD Press, 1998.

Straw, Mary J. *Loretto: The Sister and Their Santa Fe Chapel*. Santa Fe: Loretto Chapel, 1984.

Sunder, John W. Editor. *Matt Field on the Santa Fe Trail*. Norman: University of Oklahoma Press, 1960.

Turner, Henry Smith. *The Original Journals of Henry Smith Turner with Stephen Watts Kearny to New Mexico and California, 1846*. Dwight L. Clark, editor. Norman: University of Oklahoma Press, 1966.

Twitchell, Ralph E. *The Leading Facts of New Mexican History*. 5 vols. Cedar Rapid, IA: Torch Press, 1912.

_____. *The Military Occupation of New Mexico, 1846-1851*. Denver: Smith-Brooks, 1909.

United States 34th Congress, House, Miscellaneous Documents. Washington, D. C.: United States Government Printing Office, 1856.

Warner, Louis H. *Archbishop Lamy an Epoch Maker*. Santa Fe: Santa Fe New Mexican Publishing, 1936.

Weber, David. *The Mexican Frontier, 1821-1846: The American Southwest Under Mexico*. Albuquerque: University of New Mexico Press, 1982.

Wroth, William. *Images of Penance, Images of Mercy: Southwestern Santos in the Late Nineteenth Century*. Norman: The University of Oklahoma Press, 1991.

Index

ALSO FROM LPD PRESS

HOLY FAITH OF SANTA FE: 1863-2000
BY STANFORD LEHMBERG

NICHOLAS HERRERA: VISIONES DE MI CORAZÓN
BY BARBE AWALT & PAUL RHETTS

FACES OF FAITH/ROSTROS DE FE
PHOTOS BY BARBE AWALT; FOREWORD BY THOMAS J. STEELE, S.J.

PORTFOLIO OF SPANISH COLONIAL DESIGN IN NEW MEXICO
BY E. BOYD HALL

FRANK APPLEGATE OF SANTA FE: ARTIST & PRESERVATIONIST
BY DARIA LABINSKY AND STAN HIERONYMUS

ARCHBISHOP LAMY: IN HIS OWN WORDS
EDITED AND TRANSLATED BY THOMAS J. STEELE, S.J.

THE COMPLETE SERMONS OF JEAN BAPTISTE LAMY: FIFTY YEARS OF SERMONS (1837-1886)
EDITED AND TRANSLATED BY THOMAS J. STEELE, S.J.

SEEDS OF STRUGGLE HARVEST OF FAITH
THE PAPERS OF THE ARCHDIOCESE OF SANTA FE CATHOLIC CUATRO CENTENNIAL
CONFERENCE: THE HISTORY OF THE CATHOLIC CHURCH IN NEW MEXICO
EDITED BY THOMAS J. STEELE, S.J., BARBE AWALT, & PAUL RHETTS

OUR SAINTS AMONG US: 400 YEARS OF NEW MEXICAN DEVOTIONAL ART
BY BARBE AWALT & PAUL RHETTS

THE REGIS SANTOS: THIRTY YEARS OF COLLECTING 1966-1996
BY THOMAS J. STEELE, S.J., BARBE AWALT, & PAUL RHETTS

SANTOS: SACRED ART OF COLORADO
EDITED BY THOMAS J. STEELE, S.J., BARBE AWALT, & PAUL RHETTS

HISPANIC NEW MEXICAN POTTERY: EVIDENCE OF CRAFT SPECIALIZATION 1790-1890
BY CHARLES M. CARRILLO

CHARLIE CARRILLO: TRADITION & SOUL/TRADICIÓN Y ALMA
BY BARBE AWALT & PAUL RHETTS

TRADICIÓN REVISTA: THE JOURNAL OF TRADITIONAL & CONTEMPORARY
SPANISH COLONIAL ART & CULTURE [QUARTERLY MAGAZINE]
BARBE AWALT & PAUL RHETTS, PUBLISHERS

LPD PRESS
925 SALAMANCA NW
ALBUQUERQUE, NEW MEXICO 87107-5647
505/344-9382 FAX 505/345-5129
INFO@NMSANTOS.COM WWW.NMSANTOS.COM